THE LABOR REVOLUTION

THE LABOR
REVOLUTION

Trade Unions in a New America

GUS TYLER

New York / THE VIKING PRESS

196179

First published in 1967 by The Viking Press, Inc.
625 Madison Avenue, New York, N.Y. 10022

Published simultaneously in Canada by
The Macmillan Company of Canada Limited

Library of Congress catalog card number: 66-19166
Printed in U.S.A.

Second printing December 1967

To both Davids
father and son

CONTENTS

THE LABOR REVOLUTION

CHAPTER 1

Prophets: Left and Right

American labor is in the midst of a deep and quiet revolution. Unions are organizing new kinds of workers in new industries. In the past, most union dues payers wore blue collars and worked for wages; in the future, legions of new members wearing white collars and working for salaries will pour in. From 1935 to 1965, the labor movement grew most rapidly in the great basic industries: automobile, rubber, electronics, aircraft, transport, maritime, chemical, atomic, steel; at present, unions are growing most rapidly in the service trades, especially among employees of government at the local and state level. Until recently, professional people looked upon their "societies" as the retort to unions; today professionals are converting their guilds and associations into unions or are forming and joining unions outright. As a result of these trends, total labor-union membership is climbing rapidly toward a new plateau: the doubling of membership experienced in the 1930s and 1940s promises to be repeated.

As the size and composition of the labor movement change, the locale of action shifts. In the past, the scene was industrial and urban America. Now the industrial and political battleground moves to the suburbs. In the past, the geographic base of unionism was almost entirely in the North and West and Midwest. Now the focus shifts to the South and the Southwest.

Among the older and established unions, automation poses

3

challenges that compel fresh responses. At the bargaining table, unions seek new types of security for the mechanically dispossessed, the workers who are automated out. In the shops, unions must start almost from the beginning shaping wage policy as new production methods wipe out old job definitions and create new and hitherto unevaluated work categories. At the polls, labor voters turn out to vote for programs that will guarantee full employment and continuing income despite the threats of automation, computerization, cybernation. Consequently, even among the settled unions there is a mood of unrest that expresses itself through new contract clauses and a heightened interest in politics.

As the old order changes, so does the old guard. A generation of top leaders exits, with about one-third of the high command in the AFL-CIO Executive Council stepping out at one convention (1965); a younger generation steps in; and, in the wings, a generation still younger impatiently awaits its cue.

This new labor movement—changing in composition and in character—is coming into being in response to the personal and collective needs and attitudes of the new labor force that has been growing since mid-century. Yet, self-centered as these groups necessarily are, they find that they cannot go it alone. They seek allies out of necessity and compassion. Increasingly the labor movement seeks ententes with civil rights groups, with social planners wrestling with megalopolis, with economic programmers seeking full employment, with warriors against poverty, with internationalists crusading for a world of peace with freedom. Consequently, the massive impress of the labor movement in a great liberal coalition is changing the face of the nation.

This quiet revolution has been progressing without public notice. It has proceeded largely unnoted because, first, the process is in its early stages; second, unions are habitually neither introspective nor image-minded; third, the current change—unlike the earlier one in the mid-1930s—was not dramatically launched with a split in the ranks and the formation of a new federation; fourth, many intellectual commentators on the labor movement have either grown so far away from the unions as to have lost sensitive contact with current developments or are so immersed in recording and reinterpreting the past as to have lost interest in the future. Hence, a great phenomenon in the making may go unheralded until it overwhelms both the seers and the doers, the intellectuals and the trade unionists.

The timing of the revolution is ironic. It comes at a moment when labor's repute is at a nadir among progressive intellectuals and militant youth. From among labor's "friends" in academia pour books on the "disillusioned trade unionist" and the "decline of the labor movement" and works decrying the state of the unions and depicting the "crisis" in unionism. "For all its accomplishment," says a voice from the "new left" in 1964, "American labor is withering on the vine, isolated by its own short-sightedness and venality." The labor movement, predicts the sophisticated *Fortune*, isn't "going to make much headway talking in a dead language." Dozens of books and hundreds of short pieces record the decay and death of organized labor in America.

The forecasts of labor's doom are based on a variety of arguments: statistical, technological, political, and spiritual. Some of the seers mourn the inevitable interment of the trade unions; some relish the notion; still others simply record it with scholarly indifference. But they agree that the American labor movement is passé, with about as much a future as the dodo.

The statistical argument notes that the total number of organized workers in the United States has declined from its peak and that the percentage of trade unionists, measured against the total labor force, has declined even more drastically.

The technological argument points to the changing nature of the American economy under the impact of automation and cybernetics. The mechanized nervous system and brain tend first to make the blue-collar worker superfluous and then to make most of the total labor force obsolete. In this process, the composition of the labor force is changing, with the "whites" predominating more and more over the "blues." Since the blue-collar worker, in manufacturing, mining, construction, and transport— the traditional strongholds of trade unionism—is our latest vanishing American, the labor movement is consequently our latest vanishing American institution. Should the unions try to plant their feet on new ground among the white-collar people, organized labor would once more find itself on quicksand: first, because these new aristocrats of labor do not find unionism congenial, and, second, because ultimately they, too, will be replaced by the superaristocrat of labor: the thinking machine.

The political argument insists that labor is playing an ever less influential role in an economy that is ever more subject to governmental management. While labor continues to diddle with petty solutions in specific industries through collective bargaining, the great crises and major decisions occur in the economy as a whole, outside the grasp and ken of the conferees at the bargaining table. The economic parochialism of the trade unions blinds them to the challenges of a changing economy. This same narrowness of the unions makes them a negligible, if not a negative, factor in dealing with the vast social questions of civil rights, education, war, peace, human values, and societal survival.

The spiritual argument lugubriously claims that spiritually the trade unions are already dead. What remains is the uninspired body, the palpitating corpse of a once vibrant movement. Having lost its vision, the labor movement must perish. The days of dreams, courage, and struggle have given way to the empty nights of self-indulgence, cowardice, and inaction. In their present lethargy, the unions have no vital role to play—and perhaps our republic would be better off if this sick man of the American democracy, with his bureaucratic arthritis and his lecherous appetites, were pushed off to an early tomb.

All these arguments about the non-future of American unions contain a grain of truth. In 1965, fewer workers (as a percentage of the labor force) were organized than in 1957. Automation has come to many unions as a sudden trauma, challenging their ingenuity and even their existence. American unions are traditionally more trade-minded than politically conscious. Those unions that have come of age—big, rich, established—do not have the fire and fight of their youth and are constantly exposed to the temptations of personal profit or perennial power. In short, a surface diagnosis of American labor in the early sixties hints at numerical anemia, automational trauma, political myopia, and spiritual malaise. What is missing in the diagnosis is a consideration of the physique and the psyche of the patient: his inherent strength and his recuperative powers, which provide the basis for a positive prognosis.

The revolution in labor is a belated response to changes in the direction of the economy from production toward service, from private toward government employment, from city toward suburb, from North toward South. Behind these brief phrases are concealed the dynamics of labor's future.

In brief, the present dynamic is this: Statistically, union membership is on the rise and, in certain unions such as the American Federation of Teachers and the American Federation of State, County and Municipal Employees, the membership grows so fast that the numbers change before the ink is dry on the membership ledger. Automation is not abolishing the labor force: the number of workers is greater in 1966 than in 1956, and the percentage of the population in the labor force holds steady. Politically, the labor movement today shows greater strength and expertise than ever and remains the mass base of a liberal-labor coalition in America. Spiritually, the unions are beset by the dangers of institutionalism, but they are the beneficiaries of ideas and idealism from the newly awakened sectors of the labor force. The American labor movement has shown not only its capacity to survive adversity—the Taft-Hartley Act, the Landrum-Griffin Act, state right-to-work laws—but the further capacity for renewal and growth.

In its responses to the challenges of the second half of the twentieth century, labor is late—as it was at the turn of the century when the American Federation of Labor began to take hold and again in 1935 when the Committee for Industrial Organization was formed. Labor as of necessity always must be late, because the preconditions of unionism are, first, the existence of a sizable body of workers in given occupations; and, second, the development of group consciousness with a common purpose and a common will. The AFL was formed after many years of futile efforts by craftsmen and craft unions to form an effective federation; the CIO after almost two decades of repeated failure to organize the workers in the newly expanding and explosive mass-production industries. And the new revolution comes some ten years after the shift in our economy toward white-collar, service, professional, and governmental employment.

Just as labor has been late in recognizing and responding to this change, so too has the labor intellectual been late in recognizing and responding to the changing labor movement. The critics note the "stagnation" that set in after 1957, but they fail to note the new forces germinating. The consequence is that many of these thinkers who should have been able to foresee and to foretell continue to repeat old clichés.

This cultural lag is regrettable. Some of the best brains and most dedicated souls in the liberal community are wandering in a wasteland of worn-out words for failure to appreciate what is happening in American unions. Because their short-sightedness often passes for prophecy among young students, there is danger that a generation of creative, dedicated, and socially inspired youth will be misled by tired radicals of the "old left"—whom the youngsters denigrate but also imitate.

In the coming decade, there will be many vital social forces issuing from the civil rights movement, the new left, the war against poverty, and the search for world peace. Unless these movements are able to work out a *modus vivendi* with the existing and emerging labor movement, the young radicals of the '60s will end as frustrated and embittered cynics in the '70s and '80s.

The new era of unionism is the third great labor epoch in the twentieth century. The first was the period between 1900 and 1935 and was almost solely a movement of craft unions. The second period, 1935 to 1960, added the industrial unions to the legions of organized labor. The third period runs from the 1960s on and embraces the "new" unionists of the white-collar and service trades.

These periods are most clearly marked off by a census of trade-union membership in America. From 1904 to 1933, the unions represented between 10 and 12 per cent of the nonagricultural labor force. From 1937 to the present, they represented between 20 and 32 per cent. While in both these periods there have been fluctuations in membership, to focus on the annual ups and downs conceals rather than reveals the great truth about the American labor movement: in the years from Franklin D. Roosevelt to Lyndon B. Johnson the average percentage of unionists in the labor force has been about twice that of the preceding three decades.

This long view of the labor movement—by periods rather than by individual years—has the special value of providing foresight about the decades to come. The forecast is for a new kind of labor movement living on a new plateau.

The newest unionism will inherit many features of the old, just as the labor movement after the organization of the great industrial unions still resembled its craft-based predecessor. But the difference between new and old is a difference that will count, both qualitatively and quantitatively.

One may ask where the unions will find the kind of leadership needed to organize these new kinds of workers. The old-timers knew how to organize the workers in their trades. But do they know how to talk to the new types in the changed labor force?

The question has validity because, as a rule, the old leadership is not adept at organizing the newcomers to the labor force. The old-timers do not know the problems of the newly burgeoning occupations; they know neither the lingo nor the attitudes. The labor establishment can be helpful only with money or with organizational support, and even these items are likely to be rationed out with some skepticism as to the organizability of the hitherto unorganized. In sum, it is absolutely true that the old-timers are really not the best people to organize workers in the new trades.

Leadership for these workers will come—as leadership always has come—from the ranks of the new trades or from dedicated organizers who have identified themselves emotionally, intellectually, and occupationally with the cause of these workers. This truism should come naturally to intellectuals. Leadership is not a manufactured product turned out in a bureaucratic factory. New leadership in a movement is part of the historic process that produces new elements in a culture: it is endemic.

The opening of this new frontier of labor should long ago have been predicted by the labor intellectual. Its coming has been inevitable. Yet, perversely, a chorus of prophets has been forecasting the reverse, under a theory that the American unions had reached a saturation point. In the war of words, the "saturationists" seemed until recently to have won. They are now refuted by precisely those workers whom they considered unorganizable. The impenetrable areas have become the fertile lands of union recruitment: the fools of labor are rushing in where the intellectual angels fear to tread.

The great damage caused by the myopia of these intellectuals has not been to the unions per se, since the movement lives by a dynamic that is not derived from punditry. The real injury has been to the future of the progressive intellectuals, especially the younger ones, who have been trying to build a broadly based movement in this country without any realistic appreciation of the trade-union role. Their unwarranted assumption is that the labor movement is a has-been. Hence, they draw up designs for the future without taking into account the great and expanding power of trade unionism.

Failure to appreciate the dynamics of the labor movement is especially damaging to the young radicals who have thrown themselves with so much dedication into the struggles of the South. For it is precisely in the South that the American labor movement is likely to find its next generation of militants.

The South is undergoing a triple revolution: industrial, proletarian, and racial. The South is a twentieth-century fact, resting on a nineteenth-century economy, ruled by an eighteenth-century aristocracy. More concretely, the South is part of an industrial-metropolitan society, now emerging from an agricultural economy, governed by the sociopolitical relations of a slavocracy.

Among the various transitions occurring in the South, three developments will be of major import to the labor movement. First, industrialization will provide the traditional base for unionization. Second, the Southern Negro, responding to his new self-image, is becoming active as a unionist and as a voter. Third, these factors, plus the trend in federal law and national opinion, are liberalizing Southern politics.

Historically, the South is repeating the pattern of the Northeast and the Midwest: first industrialization, then unionization, and then a liberalization of government. The special feature of the present Southern dynamic is the closeness in time of the three developments, plus the added drive emanating from the civil rights movement. The great labor breakthrough in the South is likely to come all at once, like piled-up waters breaking a dam. This happened in the North in 1886; it happened in the Midwest in 1937; it will happen in the South as present cracks widen and traditional resistance to unionism gives way.

The young civil rights worker should be part of this movement. He can bring to it his personal involvement and social perspective; he can get from it a mass base and the feel of reality. A united front of young civil rights workers and Southern unionists, particularly in those trades where labor organization is on the move, would be mutually enriching.

Some of the young militants will not accept this. A few of them will mount the barricades only long enough to pass the ritualistic test of social involvement or to exhaust the kicks; some will insist upon a separate movement, whose purity of purpose must not be defiled by cohabitation with other and less radical organizations. Others, however, will find themselves accepting the marriage of the two movements, even while rejecting it intellectually. They will find that once Southern Negroes have won certain rights, those rights are empty without jobs. And once the jobs are available, they will learn that a job for a Negro worker in the

South can be a painful and perilous experience unless that worker—like other oppressed workers in the past—is protected by a union. The young militants, like their young predecessors of the 1930s, may have started their work with the dispossessed out of a mystique about "liberation" but, because of their involvement with the cause of these once-dispossessed, they will stay on to give leadership in the material march to the better life.

If social reconstruction is to be a life's work for some of them, they must think beyond the present dramatic defeats to the first victories, when Negroes get their first jobs and cast their first votes. When that time comes, the Negro will have not ended but just *begun* the nitty-gritty grind for the substance rather than the shadow of freedom. And in this hard upward climb, the Negro will need solid, lasting, effective organization—in short, he, along with his white workmates, will need labor unions. And if these unions are not to sink into the soggy depths of parochial self-interest (as any can and as many have), the young militant should do his part to elevate the sights of this mass movement, by finding his place within it as a pragmatic participant with a social conscience.

The entrance of the young militant into the labor movement in the '60s and '70s will again be a repetition of the experience of the '30s and '40s. When the great mass of industrial workers poured into the unions three decades ago, leaders were needed to sign up, guide, and consolidate the recruits. There was a leadership shortage. The vacuum was filled by the young radicals of the time—Socialists, Communists, reborn Wobblies, and their camp followers. Some of these were bona fide workers; many were unemployed intellectuals. These young people played a great and often heroic role in the renascence of the 1930s. They also formed a cement between the unions and the political progressives.

One of the chief reasons these young idealists were able to play this role was their positive orientation to the labor movement. They were not ideologically alienated. They came with their doctrinaire baggage—their criticisms and their panaceas—but they came. And, as a result, they became physically involved with the

labor movement. Hence, they were not organizationally alienated. At the same time, they learned from their experiences, even
while preaching their grand—sometimes only grandiloquent—
purposes. And out of the amalgam of proletarianized intellectuals
and intellectualized proletarians issued a movement that lifted
the unions from 5 million to 19 million and lifted the nation
from the poorhouse to the welfare state.

Regrettably, the young militants of today are not ideologically
prepared for the coming era of American labor. To say that this is
labor's fault is both true and untrue. The unions have done little
to try to make the intellectual community labor-minded. For better or worse, the unions do not think of themselves—except in
rare cases—as educators of the educators. Nevertheless, the modern labor movement has done far more toward reaching out for
joint purposes and common ideals with the liberal intellectuals
than did the unions of the 1920s. Yet it was in the 1920s that a
whole generation of young radicals developed a positive view of
labor's role in social progress. And these young people were
schooled by the radical intelligentsia of the day.

It is the great failure of today's progressive intellectuals—the
would-be teachers of the young—that they have taught nega-
tively. They have not prepared their students for life. Many of
these leftist critics—once involved in and now divorced from the
unions—have turned their alienation into a way of thought which
they have passed on to a younger generation that, in turn, mocks
the teacher by turning alienation into a mass movement. Many of
the teachers themselves have joined the camp—going way "out"
as a way to get "in." As a result, two generations of progressive
intellectuals, who could and should make valuable contributions
to an effective political coalition of labor and liberals, are out of
the great action.

While young and old radicals have been hitting the unions
from the left, the business community has been attacking from
the right. While the radicals charge that unions are too weak, the
businessmen cry that the unions are too strong. While the former
charge that unions are props of capitalism, the latter charge that

unions are the force behind creeping socialism. While the former insist that the unions are politically impotent, the latter suggest that labor is politically omnipotent. While the former suggest that unions are the lap dogs of management, the latter argue that unions are usurping the role of management.

Thus *The Wall Street Journal* in describing editorially the 1964 strike of the auto workers against General Motors comments that the "UAW [United Automobile Workers] wants a much larger hand in running the plants of General Motors." A strike victory, continues the editorial, would mean a "little more power and prestige for the union bosses. And there's nothing in history to suggest that union officials can do a better job of running General Motors than GM's managers do."

That unions are *too strong* is far more widely accepted than that they are too weak—judging by legislative behavior since the end of World War II. Legislation has been devised to curb unions, but none to strengthen them. The Taft-Hartley Act was passed in 1946 largely as a legislative way of protesting a coal strike that pitted the power of a union against the government. President Truman vetoed the bill, but his veto was easily overridden by a combine of Republicans and Democrats who were voicing the mood of their constituencies. When, a decade later, Congress passed the Landrum-Griffin Act, in the background were Senate hearings on the teamsters' union which convinced millions that the nation was facing a showdown: James Hoffa versus Uncle Sam.

In a score of states, laws have been passed to outlaw the "union shop"—so-called right-to-work laws. In almost every case, such laws are intended to bridle the unbridled unions. And in almost every case, such laws are passed in states where the labor movement is weak and where the right-to-work law amounts to putting a bridle on a lamb.

On the grounds that the unions are too strong, further legislative proposals are pending: to forbid industry-wide bargaining, to place the unions under the anti-trust laws, to outlaw the union shop everywhere in America, to prevent strikes of public employees, to compel arbitration in vital industries. And the reason, according to Barry Goldwater, is that "trade unions have been scoring bull's-eyes for thirty years taking away freedom."

One of the most scathing assaults on the all-too-powerful American labor movement comes from Donald Richberg, an early brain-truster in the New Deal. Says Richberg: "Today, the greatest concentrations of political and economic power are found in the under-regulated, under-criticized, under-investigated, tax-exempt and specially privileged labor organizations."

Richberg's fears were updated by Richard Batchelder, president of the anti-union National Education Association, in a speech before the 1966 convention of the Chambers of Commerce. Noting the rapid rise of the American Federation of Teachers, Batchelder warned that "organization of the nation's one-and-three-quarter million school teachers will merely be a stepping stone to organization of millions of white collar workers in government, in our new space industries and business . . . through the indoctrination of pupils and teachers to the labor movement philosophy in order to advance the interests of unionism in this country."

If labor were to see itself as others see it, the trade unions would be confronted with a double image: the impotent and the omnipotent. Which is the truth?

Neither is correct. The prophets of left and right echo their own frustration or fear.

The handful of articulate left-wing critics are disillusioned with their own illusions about the past and sometimes a little guilty about their own separateness from the trade unions. The raucous right-wing critics assume that labor is taking over all power because management has suffered some restraints on its one-time absolute power. Curiously, both left and right hanker for the good old days when bosses were bosses and labor action was one long, loud rebel yell.

Stuck in a past both imagined and real, these critics fail to understand the realities of the last thirty years and the present revolution in labor. They damn the labor movement for being everything and nothing, for being too political and too nonpolitical, for knowing too well where it is going and for not knowing where it is going, for being strike-happy and for lacking militancy.

In point of fact, the labor movement is all these contradictory things and it is none of them. Some unions are weak and others strong; some are passive and others militant; some are apolitical and others are intensely political; some are parochial and others cosmopolitan. Critics on both left and right can find cases in the labor movement to prove any point—just as the devil can quote Scripture. But the labor movement, as a whole, cannot be characterized by quotations out of context. The movement as a whole does have a larger and more balanced personality—a character that is now passing out of one stage and into another.

Within a few short years, when the contours of the revolution in labor begin to stand out more clearly, these questions will be asked: Who made this revolution? What ideology underlies it? While both questions are inevitable, they are also almost irrelevant. They will produce the wrong answers because they are the wrong questions.

The ambition of leaders and the conflict of ideas have spiced labor's life. But neither persons nor programs have been solely decisive. The great molder of labor's personality has been the American civilization—as it was and as it is becoming. The labor movement is, first of all, a *movement*—not any single leader or ideology. It is a deep-seated reaction to a social situation—not a bright idea of some imaginative men.

In its long life, the American labor movement has seen many leaders and would-be leaders: in the 1820s, the notorious Fanny Wright, champion of free labor and free love, and the carpenter-politician Ebenezer Ford, who was elected to the New York Assembly on the Workingman's ticket; in the 1830s, the radical agrarian Thomas Skidmore with his plan for a rural "communism" and the wealthy Robert Owen with his plans for cooperative utopian commonwealths and modified Rousseauian schools; in the 1840s, Sarah Bagley, worker turned teacher, with her Female Labor Reform Association, and George Henry Evans with his land reform; in the 1860s, William Sylvis, iron molder, warring against the gilded age with cooperatives, education, unions, and politics, Ira Steward with his eight-hour movement. After the Civil War came John R. Sovereign and Terence V. Powderly, with their Noble and Holy Order of the Knights of Labor; the Dutch Jew Samuel Gompers and the Irish Catholic Peter J. Maguire, the architects of the American Federation of Labor and spokesmen for pure and simple trade unionism; in the early 1900s, the Socialist Eugene Victor Debs and the syndicalist William D. Haywood. More recent are John L. Lewis of the miners and Philip Murray of the steel workers, the first two presidents of the Congress of Industrial Organizations; William Green and Matthew Woll, the latter-day interpreters of the "pure and simple" spirit; and the more modern articulators of a labor view: George Meany, now president of the AFL-CIO; Walter Reuther of the auto workers; David Dubinsky of the garment workers; Jacob Potofsky of the men's clothing workers; Al Hayes of the machinists; Joe Beirne of the communication workers; James Hoffa of the teamsters; Michael Quill of the transit workers. Each of these has left a mark on the movement, as have others. But no one of them, nor even all of them collectively, was the primary pressure in shaping the movement. The labor movement is much more than the sum of its leaders.

Many ideologies have competed for direction of the American labor movement. Free love and free land, seizure of the workplace and *coup d'état,* socialism and communism, cheap currency and cheap interest rates, Democrats and Whigs, Republicans and Progressives, Tammany Hall and the Locofocos, Trotskyists and De Leonists, Wobblies and Moral Rearmament have all, at one time or other, wooed labor. But none has ever dominated. And because no one ideology has ever taken over the labor movement, it has always been easier to talk about "the movement" than to define its philosophy.

Ironically, there are those who maintain that the American labor movement is no movement at all precisely because it does not correspond with any well-defined "ism," or because it has no one great ideologic leader, or because it is devoid of homogeneity. "Perhaps unions never were a movement," suggests one commentator, in discussing the "role of the working class." Perhaps, "they only gave the appearance of being one and a very brief appearance at that."

The argument that the unions are not a movement is in the same category as the argument that American unions have no philosophy. In one sense, both assertions are true. American labor has no written-down philosophy, with a clear end-purpose such as socialism. Hence, the acts of the trade unions look more like many motions than one movement. Yet, a second look reveals both a philosophy and a movement.

During a conversation at the University of Wisconsin in the mid-1940s with the wise Selig Perlman, some of us were complaining that American labor lacked a philosophy. The old teacher blinked his eyes, cocked his head to the clouds, and asked: "Well, now, can we say that primitive languages have no grammar either because the people who speak the language do not know the rules or, perhaps, because no one has yet written down the rules? I would think that even without a self-conscious codification of the rules a grammar does exist in these languages —as it exists in all languages. Is not the same true of American labor? Is it not a language with a grammar, a movement with a philosophy, even if the exact rules may have escaped some of us —either because *they* or *we* are too unsophisticated?"

Unfortunately, the kind of people most interested in discovering the philosophy of the movement are often those least qualified to do so. They tend to be intellectuals who search for answers in writings rather than in acts. In the absence of written proof that the movement is a movement, it is a nonmovement. The problem is doubly twisted for the intellectual with idealistic pretensions. His measure tends to be utopian: a movement qualifies as such only if it is millennial in its purposes. A movement to raise the wages of 20 million workers is not a movement, because it does not solve the problems of another 60 million unorganized workers. The difficulty is trebly twisted for the idealistic intellectual who evaluates the labor movement with a precast total program: socialism, for instance. By this approach, a labor movement is truly part of "the movement" only if it has publicly stated goals consistent with the ultimate transformation of our civilization into a socialist society.

American trade unionism fits no one of these three criteria: it does not have a clearly articulated philosophy; it does not really believe that it will create the perfect society; it is not committed to socialism. Yet organized labor in America is a movement: a vast subculture within the American culture, rooted in American traditions, drawing nourishment from its continuing contact with the American people.

The present revolution in labor is a response to a changing society. Basically, the unions are responding to a new economy that is creating a new kind of work force. But this is not the only factor underlying the change in labor's personality. The movement is responding to the increased politicalization of the American people; it is responding to the metropolitan ferment; it is responding to the awakening of the Negro and to the remaking of the South. It is responding to the challenges of the second half of the twentieth century and is doing so through the attitudes of a changing membership and leadership. The time has come for a critical evaluation of this revolution in labor: its roots, its dynamic, its future, its impact on American civilization.

CHAPTER 2

Genesis: The Past Century

The modern American labor movement is a child of the century from 1864 to 1964—in a sense, from the death of Lincoln to the death of Kennedy. The end of the Civil War was the beginning of a new industrial and urban civilization. Out of this evolving milieu developed new classes, social movements, and political programs. The most numerous of these new classes was that of the wage earner—in industry, mining, transportation, construction—whose organized expression through trade unions has been at the vital center of the economic and political transformations of modern times.

The victory of the Union armies was more than the triumph of North over South. It was a social revolution, enthroning a new class: the capitalists of the land—financial, industrial, mercantile —were in the saddle. They had won power through the Grand Army of the Republic; they intended to hold power through the Grand Old Party. And for the first three decades after Lincoln's death, the GAR and the GOP were almost one, with the veterans of the victorious army composing the machine of the victorious party.

"The Second American Revolution," wrote Charles Beard of the Civil War, "while destroying the foundation of the slave owning aristocracy, assured the triumph of business enterprise. As if to add irony to defeat, the very war which the planters precipitated in an effort to avoid their doom augmented the fortunes of the capitalist class from whose jurisdiction they had tried to escape. . . . When the long military struggle came to an end they [the capitalists] had accumulated huge masses of capital and were ready to march resolutely forward to the conquest of the continent." As a result of the Civil War, Louis Hacker summed up, "the industrial capitalists, through their political spokesmen, the Republicans, had succeeded in capturing the state and using it as an instrument to strengthen their economic position."

In the days that followed, the face of America changed. The frontier was pushed to the Pacific. The land was crisscrossed with railroads. The bowels of the earth were emptied for their riches in coal, ore, oil. Forests were turned into railroad ties, shingles, and toothpicks. Factories began to dot the land, crowd the land, and then spread their smoke across a once virgin countryside.

With the rise of the factories came the rise of the cities, drawing people from America's farmland and Europe's weary soil. By the end of the nineteenth century the United States had as many urban dwellers as rural. By the middle of the twentieth century there were more than twice as many urban. And increasingly cities and suburbs were merging into great metropolitan areas that, in turn, were merging into megalopolises.

Presiding over this emerging metropolitan civilization for well over half the century was the Republican Party—in firm possession of the White House from 1860 to 1932, except for the terms of Cleveland and Wilson. On the image of Lincoln, on the bayonets and ballots of the boys in blue, and on the finances of the new Establishment, the GOP erected the truly grand old party of the land. It laid claim to the loyalty of many. The GOP was the patriot party; it had saved the union; its election precinct captains bore battle scars; its candidates were all generals, either professional like Grant or semipro like Hayes, Harrison, and Mc-Kinley; when they ran out of political arguments, they waved the bloody shirt. The GOP claimed the loyalty of the farmer to whom it had made the land available through the Homestead

Act. It claimed the loyalty of labor whose livelihood depended on jobs in the expanding economy. It claimed the loyalty of the Negroes whom it had liberated. And it had a most well-founded claim on the loyalty of the professional politicians—those holding office under GOP hegemony—who were most deeply indebted to a party and a nation that let them handle the public trust as a private trough.

While the base of this political pyramid was broad, its apex was narrow: a select group, guiding the organization very much as a board of directors might guide a corporation and with very much the same motives.

The business mind believed that the business of politics was business. Speaking for his "corporate body," Mr. Havemeyer of the American Sugar Refining Company explained matter-of-factly that his trust had "no politics of any kind . . . Only the politics of business." In a similar vein, Frederick Townsend Martin bluntly proclaimed the politics of his economics: "We are the rich; we own America; we got it, God knows how, but we intend to keep it if we can by throwing all the tremendous weight of our support, our influence, our money, our political connections, our purchased senators, our hungry congressmen, our public-speaking demagogues into the scale against any legislature, any political platform, any presidential campaign that threatens our estate." These rich who owned America composed the inner circle of the GOP board of directors.

As practical men of affairs, however, these manipulators of money and men did not limit their influence to the GOP, especially in those states where Democrats were in control. When necessary and prudent, the nonpartisan plutocracy subordinated the politics of parties to the politics of business, with the certainty born of experience that the Democrats, too, had their purchasable senators, their hungry congressmen, and their dutiful demagogues. "The class I represent," continued Martin, "care nothing for politics. . . . When we are discussing pro and con the relative merits of candidates or the relative importance of political policies, the discussion almost invariably comes down to a question of business efficiency. . . . In a single season a plutocratic leader hurled his influence and his money into the scale to elect a Republican governor on the Pacific coast and a Democratic governor on the Atlantic coast." From Atlantic to Pacific, the new plutocrat did not care who reigned so long as he ruled.

The new plutocracy that had arisen out of the ashes of the old slavocracy was not altogether a surprise to some of the leaders of the vanquished South. In 1837, John C. Calhoun, in defending the relative stability and humanity of the chattel-slave system, stripped all social systems down to their naked ugliness to expose the shameless nature of man. "There never has yet existed a wealthy and civilized society in which one portion of the community did not, in point of fact, live on the labor of the other. . . . It would not be difficult to trace the various devices by which the wealth of all civilized communities has been so unequally divided, and to show by what means so small a share has been allotted to those by whose labor it was produced, and so large a share given to the non-producing classes. The devices are almost innumerable, from the brute force and gross superstition of ancient times, to the subtle and artful fiscal contrivances of modern."

For Calhoun the old system of chattel slavery had certain virtues: first, it was stable, with each in his place; second, it was paternalistically humane. To break this system was to unleash the terrors of instability and cruelty. There would be a war of classes, he warned, "for there is and always has been in an advanced stage of wealth and civilization a conflict between labor and capital." And should it ever come to pass that the Negro be liberated to turn against his white master, then the nation would be plagued "with disorders and dangers."

The Civil War that crowned King Capital also started two quiet revolutions: the labor movement, whose militant voice was heard almost immediately following the silence at Appomattox; and the Negro movement, whose militant voice was not heard until a century later.

The hundred years from 1864 to 1964 fall into three great eras.

The character of that century was shaped in the formative years from war's end to the 1890s. The years from 1890 to 1932 were the great divide: the watershed of industrial struggle, social ideals, political programs. The years from 1932 to 1964 brought the revolutions in economic concepts, civil rights, and political structures.

In the formative years the trade unions were beginning to think and act in national terms. Permanent national unions began to form out of the local and sporadic organizations. Two nationwide federations were set up: the Knights of Labor and the American Federation of Labor. As business enterprise stretched from coast to coast and as the American people began to develop a national consciousness, the labor movement, ever in tune with the culture, started to go national in typically federated, pluralistic, American fashion.

The great debate within labor—the rift between the Knights and the Federation—was over the question of whether labor could or should abolish the wage system or should learn to live within it. The Knights wanted to return to an earlier stage of society, where the worker owned his own tools. If the individual worker could not be self-employed, the tools would be owned cooperatively. And where this was impossible, the tools would be owned by the government. Cheap money and easy credit would be means for financing the transition to the past. The central instruments for achieving this new-old society were education—of worker and public—and political action. To the AFL, the Noble Order of the Knights of Labor was too noble, too orderly, and too much out of tune with things as they were. The budding AFL, organized some two decades after the Knights, believed in working to get something here and now, something touchable and spendable. The AFL plan for the far future was to leave it to the future. The central means for achieving the AFL goal of more, sooner, was higher wages and shorter work hours.

Collectively, the Knights and the Federation represented a democratizing counterpoint to the plutocratic theme of postwar America. The labor movement sought to democratize wealth by higher wages, to democratize leisure by a shorter work week, to democratize education by expanded schooling, and to democratize politics by participation in elections, legislation, and government. The Knights put the emphasis on the last two areas: education and politics, and most notably education for politics. The Federation put the emphasis on the first two: wages and hours.

For millions of workers, the trade unions were the training grounds of democratic behavior, where they learned to give voice and effect to their desires and demands. In the unions they learned to argue and to compromise, to debate and to decide; here they learned to chair meetings, to organize majorities, to lead their fellow members. In the unions, millions of workers in the industrial plutocracy of post-Civil War America learned the skills of freedom.

"When the full story of self-government in America is written," commented Charles Beard, "reviewing the commonplace, no less than the spectacular, pages on the cellular growth of local craft unions will be placed beside the records of town meetings."

To the rich who owned and ran America, however, the rising unions were not viewed as harbingers of a greater democracy, but as the forerunners of a new oligarchy. The five men who headed the Knights were depicted in the pages of the *New York Sun* as the new tyrants of the American republic. "Five men in this country," reported the *Sun,* "control the chief interests of five hundred thousand workingmen and can at any moment take the means of livelihood away from two and a half millions of souls. These men compose the executive board of the noble order of the Knights of Labor. The ability of the president and cabinet to turn out all the men in the civil service, and to shift from one post or ship to another the duties of the men in the army and navy, is a petty authority compared with that of these five Knights. The authority of the late cardinal was, and that of the bishops of the Methodist Church is, narrow and prescribed, so far as material affairs are concerned, in comparison with that of these five rulers."

This news item on the five rulers was, of course, somewhat exaggerated. The mighty five were not only unable to order their rank and file into the foray, they actually spent a good deal of time and energy persuading their ranks not to strike, since the Knights placed their basic faith in education and voting and not in picket lines. Neither the Knights nor the Federation nor both of them jointly ever had power beyond that of the president and cabinet, the cardinal, and the bishops of the Methodist Church. Nor has any labor organization of five or five million had such power then or since. The story of the five was far less a description of labor's strength and structure than it was a journalistic projection of plutocratic anxieties.

But the anxieties of the rich who owned America served a positive purpose. The *Sun* story was reprinted; it was retold and grew with the retelling. "The Knights of Labor," reported its leader Terence V. Powderly plaintively, "began to boom, but those who sought its shelter were led to believe that they could secure the cooperation of the 'five hundred thousand workingmen' referred to in the *Sun* article." The numbers of the Knights doubled in one year, but Powderly complained, "the majority of the newcomers was not of the quality the Order had sought for in the past." The newcomers were strike-happy; they felt that with the great power of the mighty five backed by the greater power of the almighty five-hundred thousand they could set a date for the millennium. They set May 1, 1886, for the coming of the eight-hour day.

The Knights formally dissociated the organization from the eight-hour movement. This did not immunize their membership from breaking out in a rash of strikes for the shorter work day. The newly born AFL had passed an eight-hour resolution in 1885. Again in 1886, a similar resolution was passed, with some amendments. Although these resolutions, when carefully read, leave some doubt as to whether the Federation was reaching out for an eight-hour day by contract or by law, in the minds of the workers there was little doubt: the time for the eight-hour day had come. Labor struck!

From that moment forward, the AFL grew and the K of L declined. Although the popularly assigned reason is the diverse action of the two organizations on the eight-hour movement—

and on the subsequent defense of the Haymarket martyrs—the true reasons are more complex. The basic weakness of the Knights lay in the fact that they were not primarily oriented toward doing something here and now, through immediate action for measurable gains, to improve the livelihood of the wage earner. Philosophically, structurally, tactically, the top leadership of the Knights sought to do away with, rather than live within, the wage system. The Federation, on the other hand, was superpragmatic. Its premise was the wage system and its continuance. It had no plan for the future beyond improvement of the present. The AFL that issued from the formative years was labor's response to the capitalism that issued triumphant from the Civil War.

From 1886 to the present, the philosophy, structure, and tactics of the American Federation of Labor have determined the basic character of the American labor movement. But over the years that character has matured, changed, defined, and redefined itself—always in response to a changing culture.

In the 1890s the American republic was torn by an inner conflict. Body and soul seemed to be at odds. The limbs were large, the hunger insatiable, the passions rampant, the expectations unlimited. Yet where was the soul to match the body, the food to sate the hunger, the compassion to humanize the passions, and the plans to meet the great expectations?

Quantitatively America was huge and growing more so daily; but qualitatively it was shrinking. Riches were accumulating and were being spent with less taste than ever. The nouveaux riches were multiplying their numbers and their wealth, which they were squandering on the bitch goddess Success. The new leisure class was wallowing in a trough of what Thorstein Veblen christened "conspicuous consumption" and "pecuniary emulation." One multimillionaire "kept" the opera house in New York City as a handy way to "keep" his girls. The nation was proving the mastery of matter over mind.

America was producing goods in overwhelming volume. It was, indeed, producing too much. Periodically, the glutting of the market was such that farmers could not sell their produce or workers their labor. The cornucopia of plenty was running over and drowning all kinds of little people in the deluge. Production and consumption were out of balance. The resultant depressions and crises were euphemistically called "business cycles," the normal ups and downs of the economy. The human casualties were charged off as an overhead cost of "progress."

Corruption became the slick man's lubricant for the business and political machine. Gould, Fisk, Vanderbilt, and Rockefeller came up the sly and slippery way. They fought their competitors and their workers with gangsters and company police. They bought and sold laws and lawmakers.

Into this moral and economic swamp poured the new immigrants from eastern and southern Europe. Many were imported as "contract" labor to lower wage standards and break through picket lines. They were corralled by political bosses who peddled citizenship papers and purchased votes. At the bottom of the system, the newer immigrants became its props.

The forces of contrast—democracy versus plutocracy—that had been gathering since the end of the Civil War were ready for confrontation. "The decade of the nineties," noted Commager, "is the watershed of American history. . . . In this period came at last a full-throated recognition of the crowding problems of agriculture, urban life, slums, trusts, business and political corruption, race prejudice, and the maldistribution of wealth, and with it, convulsive efforts to adapt a federal political system to a centralized economy, and a laissez-faire philosophy to a program of social democracy."

The 1890s marked the end of one century and the beginning of the next sociologically as well as chronologically. That decade was the beginning of the great divide that separated a predominantly agricultural economy from the predominantly urban one which followed. Since the end of the Civil War the center of American civilization had shifted from countryside to city.

"The city," said Plutarch, "is the teacher of man." And the modern American city is the instructor of the twentieth-century

American—the metropolitan citizen. The city teaches by a public dialogue of contrasting circumstances: Cadillacs above subways, penthouse apartments alongside slums, *haute couture* and *haute cuisine* alongside ragged children and soup kitchens. The city teaches by a rote inherent in its density, where the very proximity of man to man in massive factories, in crowded tenements, and in swarming neighborhoods makes ideas contagious and conclusions simultaneous. The city teaches Socratically by asking the right questions: what do we do about slums, poverty, crime, epidemics, air and water pollution, housing, wages, transportation, hospitals, the aging, the insane? The city teaches by encouraging a cross-pollination of ideas among its citizen-students: the agitator has an audience and the masses have a teacher; the factory gate is a point of matriculation; the street corner is a classroom; and a mimeograph machine becomes a publishing house.

Above all, however, the city gives man the faith that he is somewhat beyond the whims of nature. The farmer is much more exposed to the vagaries of wind and weather, of soil and flood, of drought and hail. He knows that he is basically at the mercy of nature. And when he moves to change his environment, it is usually directly and personally. He is the rugged individualist. To the city dweller, the civilization—those skyscrapers rising out of concrete—is man-made. The city is also more the product of the collectivity. The city man senses that his culture is the creation of his community. He is likely to agree with Henry Demarest Lloyd's view of the relationship between man and his environment that the "laws that rule men are the laws that men make." When plagued by the sorry scheme of things, the city man is inclined to start remaking it nearer to the heart's desire.

To the Establishment, the teachings of the city appeared as a threat. Workers in unions threatened the economic order; voters in urban wards threatened the political order. To keep the unions in check, the Establishment used a variety of weapons: violence, persuasion, yellow dog contracts, blacklists, spies, injunctions, contract labor. To counter labor's voting legions, the Establishment turned to the disenfranchisement of the white worker in the

North and the black worker in the South. In the North, this was accomplished by a system of legislative malapportionment and maldistricting that discounted the vote of industrial and urban areas. In the South, disenfranchisement was achieved by the practical nullification of the Fourteenth Amendment. The result in both North and South was to exaggerate the political say of conservative forces that wished to perpetuate the concepts and controls of the nineteenth century into the twentieth.

The last decade of the nineteenth century also marked the beginning of the end for the Republican monopoly of federal politics. The election of Democrat Grover Cleveland in 1884 and his re-election in 1892 broke the previously unbroken record of GOP victories from 1860. These two Democratic terms, plus the fact that in the election of 1888 Cleveland won a majority of the popular vote, gave a broad hint to the Republicans that they could no longer take the country for granted.

More significant, however, was the appearance of the Populist Party on the ballot in 1892. Fundamentally, the Populists were men of the soil, disgruntled and rebellious farmers, the junior partners in the grand alliance of the GOP, who saw no relief in either major party. In their first try for the White House, the Populists polled about 8 per cent of the vote, carried the electoral votes of several states, returned a batch of Congressmen, and took over several state legislatures. From this point on, the GOP could no longer count on the descendants of the homesteaders for votes. In good times, the farmers tended to revert to the Republicans with their nineteenth-century concepts of laissez faire and limited government; in bad times, the farmers turned to the Democrats for relief, intervention, controls, and supports.,

In subsequent years, populism reappeared in a variety of forms: as part of the Democratic vote in the 1896 campaign of the Great Commoner, William Jennings Bryan; as part of the Farmer-Labor parties in the states of the old Northwest Territory; as part of the La Follette vote in the Progressive Party campaign in 1924; as part of the New Deal coalition under Franklin D. Roosevelt; as part of the surprise victory vote for Harry S.

Truman in 1948. With the 1890s, American farmers—at least the more unhappy among them—liberated themselves from the GOP.

In the period from 1900 to 1932, American workers moved decisively away from the Republican into the Democratic camp. This transfer of loyalties was brought about, not by the work of the top trade-union leaders, who favored and fought fiercely for a policy of nonpartisanship, but by the doings of the Republican Establishment, which pushed the labor vote into the rival party.

As the twentieth century opened, American corporations decided to play a practical joke on the unions. The big companies got their able lawyers to persuade the courts that the Sherman Anti-Trust Act was meant not to bust the trusts but to make the unions illegal. Court after court interpreted the law to mean that union action constituted a conspiracy in restraint of trade and commerce.

Faced with a political challenge, the unions turned to political action at the federal level. In 1908, the AFL petitioned both national parties for relief from injunction through an amendment to the anti-trust laws that would distinguish between steel and souls, between hams and humans. The GOP turned down the request and named William Howard Taft, famous for his anti-labor injunctions, as its candidate for President. "The Republican reactionaries," Samuel Gompers reported acidly, "told Labor to go to Denver." And it was at Denver that the Democrats listened to labor, took an anti-injunction stand, and named William Jennings Bryan as their candidate for President.

Gompers campaigned for the unsuccessful Bryan in 1908 and again for the successful Wilson in 1912. Under Wilson's New Freedom, labor won new status: the Department of Labor was created and William Wilson, a practicing trade unionist, was named the first Secretary of Labor; the Clayton Anti-Trust Act was passed to proclaim that labor was "not a commodity." Labor called the new law its Magna Charta.

The labor shift to the Democrats was further consolidated in 1928 behind Alfred E. Smith, with his broad appeal to the immigrant masses of the cities, and in 1932 behind Franklin D. Roosevelt, with his similar appeal to the jobless and the near-jobless of the nation.

The candidacy of Alfred E. Smith is popularly discussed, in terms of an earlier slogan, in relation to "rum and Romanism," as a referendum on Prohibition and Catholicism. Smith was, however, also the candidate of rebellion—of the city poor who saw in him more than his religion or his stand against Prohibition. To millions of working stiffs, Al Smith, the guy with the brown derby who started in the Fulton Fish Market, was their man—a commoner combatting the gentry.

From the 1890s on, a steadily increasing proportion of the American working class was Catholic. In the thirty years after 1890, more than 16 million immigrants poured into the United States, mostly from the predominantly Catholic countries of eastern and southern Europe. They poured into the cities, into the factories, and into the unions. Labor leadership was provided largely by the Irish and South German Catholics. The rank and file were the later immigrant Catholics, Italians, Slavs, Hungarians, Rumanians. In 1890, the Catholic Church in America counted 9 million faithful; in three decades, the number doubled —one American out of six was Catholic. And among wage earners and trade unionists the percentage was much higher. The new great mass of urbanites, most of them parched, papist, proletarian, were attracted to Smith—the first Catholic candidate for president in American history: antithesis of the blue nose and the blue blood.

The drift of Negroes into the North in the 1890s meant a shift in their voting allegiances. As they moved into the industrial and urban areas, they began to imitate the electoral habits of other working people. The party of Lincoln that had liberated the Negro from chattel slavery did not seem to be doing too much about liberation from wage slavery. Slowly but perceptibly the black voter, especially the lower-income Negro, moved into the Democratic column and, in slum wards, into the city machines. The big switch of Negroes into the Democratic fold, however, did not take place until the campaigns of FDR.

While all these movements—farm revolt, labor upheaval, Catholic growth, and Negro migration to the cities—were giving the Democratic Party a mass base in the North and West, a variety of lesser movements and independent intellectuals were prodding the growing democratic coalition with ideas. Foremost of these prods was the American socialist movement whose philosophy had grown out of a critical examination of capitalism and whose program of immediate reforms and ultimate socialism proposed remedies for the ills of that selfsame capitalism.

In 1892, the candidate of the Socialist Labor Party, Simon Wing, polled 21,532 out of a total of more than 11.5 million votes in the presidential election. That was the year in which the Populists polled more than a million votes, many of them coming from the ranks of socialists. In the dozen years following the beginning of the century, the Socialist vote rose rapidly: in 1900, it stood at 94,000; in 1904, at 402,000; in 1908, at 420,000; and in 1912, at 897,000. The last was the year of maximum Socialist electoral strength in America. Yet even then it was only about 5 per cent of the total national vote.

Despite the limited voting power of the national Socialist tickets, however, the movement exercised considerable influence on the shaping of the first half of the twentieth century. Socialists carried great weight in some areas where they were an effective pressure group; they had firm roots in the labor movement; they had an extensive educational and propaganda apparatus; they had a vast intellectual following and periphery. Because of its pinpointed strength, the Socialist Party before 1916 was able to elect 56 mayors, more than 300 lesser elected city officials, several dozen state legislators, and a couple of Congressmen. By 1912, about one-third the delegates to the national convention of the American Federation of Labor counted themselves as Socialists; at one convention, they put the AFL on record as favoring nationalization of public utilities. In an alliance with the miners, the Socialists were even able to depose Samuel Gompers from the presidency of the AFL for one term. The Socialist press in 1912 consisted of 5 English and 8 foreign-language dailies, 262 English and 36 foreign-language weeklies, and 10 English and 2 foreign-language monthlies. And in intellectual circles, during this period, to be un-Socialist was to be unfashionable.

Although the Socialist Party was shattered during World War I and never recovered, the influence of the Socialist ideology has continued into the present. The Socialists argued that it was the responsibility of government to play a creative and central role in the economy. While the Socialists would have turned over all the major means of production, distribution, and exchange to the cooperative commonwealth, a much more limited use of the governmental power in the economy has become a reality of American life. The Socialists set forth detailed programs for the here and now, advocating old-age, health, and unemployment insurance, minimum-wage and maximum-hour legislation, abolition of child labor—most of which have since become law. The Socialists believed that both their immediate and ultimate goals could be obtained through use of the ballot by education of the voter. Socialists counted on the wage earner, through his union, to be the mass base of the movement toward an industrial and social democracy. Socialists insisted that a political party should have character, that it should be an expression of ideology committed to enact and enforce a platform rather than a loose collection of individual politicians and political machines. Above all else, the Socialists believed that they were moving with history, that their agitators were the chosen people, that any sacrifice of self would ultimately be rewarded in the realization of the good society. This last conviction among Socialists produced doers—dedicated, selfless, indefatigable, and self-assured—decade after decade and generation after generation. Socialist influence, which started as a separate stream of action and ideas in the last half of the nineteenth century, became a current in the political mainstream by the middle of the twentieth.

Within the Republican Party early in this century there were two major revolts, schisms of an organizational nature. In 1912, Theodore Roosevelt bolted the GOP to put his own Progressive Party ticket in the field under the banner of the Bull Moose. In

1924, another Progressive Party, headed by Senator Robert La Follette of Wisconsin, polled nearly 5 million votes.

In the period of the great divide (1890 to 1932) the forces of revolt against the old regime were gathering. The great depression united these forces to put an end to the post-Lincoln era and to introduce the Roosevelt era: the beginning of a triple bloodless revolution.

The era of the Roosevelt coalition that was to dominate the political life of America for two decades had certain parallels with the post-Lincoln era. Both came into being in a time of trauma: the Civil War; the great depression. Lincoln saved the nation from disunion; Roosevelt saved the nation from economic crisis. Lincoln put business in power; Roosevelt saved business from bankruptcy. Lincoln gave land to the farmer; Roosevelt saved that land from foreclosure. Lincoln opened the way for an industrial expansion that meant jobs to millions; Roosevelt rescued the wage earner from unemployment. Lincoln liberated the Negro; Roosevelt lifted the Negro's economic and social status. Out of these events arose broad political coalitions—the first dating from the Lincoln victory over the South and the second dating from the Roosevelt victory over the depression.

The bloodless revolution that followed FDR moved at three levels: economic reform, social revolution, and political restructuring. The economic reforms are contained in that potpourri of programs called the welfare state. The social revolution is the change in the status of the Negro. The political restructuring is the shift of decision-making from local to federal government and from rural to urban America. Any one of these revolutions might, in other countries and at other times, have meant blood. Section 7A of the National Recovery Act, encouraging workers to join unions of their own choosing, meant a rapid rise in labor organization and the admission of the common man to the governing councils of the nation. The Civil Rights Act of 1964 intends to do for the Negro what the NRA did for the wage earner. The Supreme Court decision in *Baker vs. Carr* seeks to relocate legislative power from a dominant rural minority to a hitherto submerged metropolitan majority. In a peaceful and piecemeal way in the years since 1932 the democratization of decision-making in America has brought about revolution.

Although all these revolutions can be traced back to the Constitution of the United States in a prophetic sense—"to promote the general welfare" (the welfare state); "to secure the blessings of liberty to ourselves and our posterity" (civil rights); "to form a more perfect union" (the strengthening of the central government); and "to guarantee the equal protection of the laws" (the reapportionment and redistricting of legislatures)—the last three decades have witnessed a highly dramatic application of the American dream.

From 1932 to the present, the America that was once Republican in character has become Democratic. With the exception of the Eisenhower interregnum, the White House has been the property of the Democrats. The Congress has been in the hands of Democrats for all but four years—1946–1947 and 1952–1953. A count of voters in the 1960s showed registration heading toward a two-to-one preference for the Democrats.

The transformation of America after 1932 involved more than a change of party labels. It was a change of political heart. America has espoused the welfare state—first out of love, and then out of habit. Every Democratic president tried to restate his devotion in his own words. Franklin Delano Roosevelt called it the New Deal—a cross between two earlier phrases foreshadowing the modern era, the Square Deal of Theodore Roosevelt and the New Freedom of Woodrow Wilson. Harry S. Truman called it the Fair Deal. John F. Kennedy carried the idea forward into the New Frontier. Lyndon B. Johnson has called upon America to continue to the Great Society. Even the titular Republican Dwight D. Eisenhower paid a right-handed compliment to welfarism by his dedication to "modern Republicanism."

In the presidential elections during this period, the debate has been not so much about direction as about pace, less about where we are going than how fast. In part, this was due to the repetitive last-minute victories of the "modern" wing of the GOP at national nominating conventions—victories inspired by a winning name and financed by funds of the old Establishment of the Eastern seaboard. Wendell Willkie won the nomination in 1940, backed by the internationalist wing of the party and cast in the role of the barefoot boy from Wall Street; Thomas Dewey, a successful Governor of New York, pushed the Taft forces aside in '44 and '48 with the promise of bringing to the GOP banner the massive electoral votes of the Empire State and its populous neighbors; Dwight Eisenhower overshadowed Taft with the sheer glamour of his military splendor. Even Nixon, a son of the right wing, had, by 1960, made sufficient legislative and linguistic adjustments to modern times to become the unanimous choice of his party.

During the crucial decade of transition from Roosevelt to Eisenhower (1945–1955), America demonstrated that it had reached a consensus above faction, according to Eric Goldman: "Gradually, with many a contrary movement and sidewise venture, a greater and greater percentage of the population decided that the Half-Century of Revolution in domestic affairs was here to stay and that it should be forwarded."

Following 1932, the trade unions evolved with the nation. In Roosevelt's first term, the established unions in the established trades expanded rapidly. Philosophy changed with maturity. Even the most conservative craft locals recognized that they could not pull the country out of the swamp of unemployment through collective bargaining; they needed federal legislation. Full employment—or the nearest thing to it—became the center of labor's legislative efforts. By 1936, the unions were enthusiastically for FDR and helped to supply the huge majorities by which he won re-election then and in the two subsequent campaigns.

In Roosevelt's second term, labor began to move into the once unorganized basic industries: automobiles, steel, rubber, shipping, chemicals, textiles. The newly launched Committee for Industrial Organization (CIO) * was the spearhead. In a matter of months, new millions joined CIO unions. Although the AFL

* The meaning of the initials CIO was changed to Congress of Industrial Organizations when the CIO unions were expelled from the AFL in 1937.

expelled the CIO, the former learned from the latter the value of industrial organization in mass-production industries and the AFL too continued to grow. And the newcomers—the NRA babies —sucked in politics with their organizational milk.

Through the war years of Roosevelt's third term, the unions went on growing. Labor was scarce and unions tried to make the most of the scarcity. Wage controls during the war years turned the unions to demands for "fringe" benefits: funds for health, welfare, vacations, retirement, hospitalization, death insurance. And the variety of governmental boards, regulating wages, prices, production, and strikes, reinforced the trade-union conviction that in a "politicalized" economy labor must go political.

In the first postwar election, a war-weary nation returned a Republican majority to Congress. One of its historic measures— intended to chop down both the economic and political power of unionism—was the Taft-Hartley Act, regulating, restricting, and retrenching labor action. Although President Harry S. Truman vetoed the bill, Congress overrode his veto. The result recalled 1908, when a reluctant Gompers took the stump for Bryan: the American Federation of Labor for the first time in its history organized a permanent political organization, Labor's League for Political Education. (The CIO had formed its Political Action Committee in 1943.)

The full meaning of labor's evolution from 1932 to 1948 did not become apparent until the election of Truman in the latter year. The Republican Party candidate, Dewey, looked like a certain winner: the country was ready for a change. The Communists put their shoulders behind the newly created Progressive Party whose candidate was former Vice-President Henry A. Wallace. The deep South put a ticket in the field to protest a Truman report on civil rights. The pollsters counted the straws and counted Truman out. Yet he won: he won as a result of the "green revolt," by the farmers who feared GOP tampering with their prices, and the trade-union electioneering, now goaded into a new spurt of activity.

From 1948 on, the labor movement—operating separately through the AFL's League for Political Education and the CIO's Political Action Committee—concentrated heavily on Congress. The lesson of 1946 had not been lost: the passage of the Taft-Hartley Act by a conservative Congress over the veto of a liberal President. Each year the liberal count in Congress mounted. When Eisenhower was elected in 1952, he carried a Republican majority into the Congress on his coattails, but it was a hairbreadth majority and actually rested on a minority of the popular vote. By 1954, the Democrats were back in control of Congress and stayed there through all the Eisenhower years and, subsequently, through the Kennedy administration and to the present.

In 1964, a new conservatism, gathered around the candidacy of Senator Barry Goldwater, challenged the great consensus that had developed since 1932. Its prime locus of power was in the right wing of the Republican Party. Its object was a triple counterrevolution: to undo the New Deal, to reverse the civil rights revolution, to strip from the Supreme Court its power to pass judgment on the apportionment and districting of legislatures. It sought to repeal the twentieth century.

In the election, this new conservatism suffered the greatest electoral defeat rendered to any major party in more than a hundred years. It was an ironic centennial for the Grand Old Party. Five of the six states carried by the GOP were in the deep South—Mississippi, Louisiana, Alabama, Georgia, and South Carolina; the sixth was Goldwater's home state of Arizona. The party of Lincoln closed the century by winning states in the anti-Negro South with an appeal for "states rights." History was repeating itself as tragicomedy, with the Republicans playing the role of the pre-Civil War Democrats. The party that issued from the election was defeated, dejected, and divided. The metropolitan civilization which the GOP had created seemed to have outgrown its creator.

Now there was a New Establishment—Lyndon B. Johnson, his liberal and labor colleagues, and the vast coalition that huddled around the Democratic candidate out of fear of Goldwater. Would this grand coalition be able to manage the complex colossus that was America?

To some the election of Lyndon B. Johnson in 1964 was the first move toward the Great Society—that civilization beyond the present which LBJ repeatedly depicted during the campaign. But to others, the vote for the Democratic candidate was a sign of inertia: a vote of confidence in the status quo, a reluctance to move in any direction, right or left. The age of advance of the early Roosevelt years had become an age of affluence that had, in turn, become an age of apathy. The labor movement that had played a significant role during the '30s and '40s seemed to have played itself out. Now that labor was an accepted American institution, it appeared to be behaving like an institution. Material riches were bringing spiritual ruin. Viewed in this light, the election of LBJ did not herald a new golden age. The rally around Johnson was a defensive gathering of the twentieth century against a challenge out of the past but was not an aggressive affirmation of new purpose.

A new anxiety set in, articulated primarily by social critics who felt that there was much unfinished business before the country: the old problems of poverty, unemployment, human rights, urban chaos; the new problems of caring for the growing number of aged, educating the growing number of young, and adjusting to an exploding world and an imploding universe. The metropolitan civilization had established itself, but could its special problems be handled by the new Establishment? In the century-long rise of metropolitan man, labor had fulfilled a mission. But would the same movement—now mature and itself established—be able to see and move through the miasma of affluence and apathy?

CHAPTER 3

Leviticus: The Laws of the Movement

The "roots" of the labor movement are political.

The labor movement is a political entity in four different uses of the word *political:* (1) in the Aristotelian sense of the term, whereby man is a "political animal," a citizen of his *polis*—the worker is a citizen of a "polis" delineated by his craft, trade, or workplace; (2) in the Lasswellian sense, in which politics is defined as the study of "who gets what, when and how"—workers through their organizations are involved in deciding these questions for the shop, industry, or economy; (3) in the vulgar use of the term—through the involvement of organized workers in the electoral processes of the nation; and finally (4) according to the Machiavellian definition of politics as decision-making through the manipulation of persons, words, factions.

The birth of a movement in the "polis" of the workplace is as inevitable as the appearance of man's political character in any civilized community. Its first cause is the "class struggle," the push and pull of who gets what and how much. The terms of its existence both inside and outside the workplace are conditioned by a political government within which labor must ultimately seek a voice. And in the performance of all this, the leaders of labor must master the art of politics, the manipulation of men and ideas.

Various attempts have been made to account for the labor

41

movement in terms of a single explanation. One theory holds that trade unions are basically only gatherings of men with a common background, whose economic goals and political involvements are secondary or less. Another view is that trade unions are bread-and-butter outfits concerned only with jobs and earnings. Still another is that unions are—or at least, should be—primarily instruments of political reform and revolution. The most cynical view is that unions are only the playthings of labor bosses who use wage earners as their power base.

Each of these single-track explanations of labor's origin tends to become a caricature rather than a characterization. A union is not just a fraternity, not just a collective-bargaining agency, not just a faction in a political party, and not just an arena for warring labor barons. Yet, in proper measure, unions are each and all of these—whether they wish it, know it, or admit it.

Let us consider all these definitions separately, with a view to the future of labor in the United States.

When Aristotle said that "man is by nature a political animal," he certainly did not mean that every man was an active voter in a widespread democracy. In ancient Greece, slaves were totally excluded from the political process. Those citizens who did have a voice did not always use it. And those who used it did not do so equally. Yet, with full knowledge of this, Aristotle insisted that man was "by nature" a political animal.

From what we now know of man's early origins, Aristotle was probably right. For Homo sapiens appears on the scene not as a lonely individualist but as a herd creature, moving with the mob. Society does not seem to have been started by a convention of separate souls who signed a compact to live together for mutual defense and advance. Society seems to have begun with the group, with man as an organic part of the polis. Indeed, the submergence of the individual in the group was probably so profound and instinctive that the appearance of the individual as individual, apart from the inherited culture, comes very late in man's evolution. And when such brave solo personalities arise, they seem to be men against the gods, defying mores and morality.

"During long millennia which dwarf written record," notes John Bowle, "the sparse forbears of mankind displayed an animal solidarity. . . . There was apparently little individuality or family sense, and the earliest social pattern was matriarchal and totemistic. . . . When, in the Upper Paleolithic, Homo Sapiens became the dominant human type, his societies were socially solid and mentally co-conscious; they had to be to survive. The basis of the earliest communities is primarily the pack. . . . The ancient assumption that civilization derives from a social compact, reflecting the deliberate choice of rational individuals, has long disappeared, and history is seen as a branch of a relatively new science of biology, concerned with a creature which owes much of its existence to an intense sociability. . . . The sense of common purpose implied in Aristotle's dictum thus goes back to the earliest beginnings."

In trying to tap the psychology of the mass mind, Will Durant many years ago suggested a mathematics of group behavior. In the mass, there is a multiplication of suggestibility, a division of responsibility, and an addition of power. One might add, too, that there is a subtraction of self. The sum of the equation is an individual who is, though he be as individual as Thoreau, still the child of his culture.

That man is a herd animal is generally accepted as valid in describing tribes and nations. What is equally valid is that man is also a group creature in his many subcultures: religious, geographic, linguistic, racial—and professional.

Any grouping within a society constitutes a subculture, with its own view of itself, its code, its dress, and even its own language. This is most apparent, and most easily admitted, when we examine subcultures from the top of society down, beginning with the super-subculture of the aristocracy. Men set themselves apart with a variety of pretenses. They give themselves titles, like "sir" and "lady"; they delineate the limits of their circle with an Almanach de Gotha or a "blue book"; they set up a code of behavior so refined and well-obeyed as to expose most pretenders to immediate ostracism; they have a fixed dress for tea, the races, the dance, the morning, and the evening; and their language immediately distinguishes them as patrician. This aristocracy is the union of the ruling class, with a closed shop and closed doors.

Below this group come the academicians. They set themselves up an "academy" of one sort or another and open it only to themselves and those with whom they prefer to associate, if not personally, then at least professionally. They give themselves titles like "doctor" or "master" or "bachelor" and use the titles to establish a pecking order. They use esoteric languages that have no meaning for those outside the profession. They gather in conventions and elect a hierarchy; they become involved in internal maneuverings, politicking, and back-stabbing worthy of the Borgias or Stalin. As Bowle points out about cultures in general, these subcultures are internally bound by an "intense sociability." The full-time professional military men certainly represent a subculture, where rank is reflected in uniforms and decorations. The underworld is still another subculture, with its rigid hierarchy, with an argot all its own, with an iron-clad code, with a stern morality.

The labor movement is also a subculture: the social expression of a class. And within this huge subculture of the class are the separate subcultures of the specific unions with their specific jurisdictions. They also have their own special form of address; in America it is often "sister" and "brother." They have a pecking order called "seniority." They have a notion of their role in society, expressed in programs for economic change or political reform. They have their internal politics, their hierarchy, their "ins" and "outs," their snobs and their snubbed.

This view of the labor movement does not set it up as something different. It is quite similar to other cultures within our culture.

In what environment does modern labor find this tap root? In his still exciting and invaluable little book, *A Philosophy of Labor*, Frank Tannenbaum puts it simply:

"What the workers had in common was their employer, the industry they worked in, the hours they labored, the bench or the machine they worked at, the wage rate they received, the foreman who ruled over them, the materials they worked with, the whistle that called them from their beds in the morning or brought a halt to their labors. In addition, they had each other in common. They worked together at the same bench, inside the same mill or mine, struggled with the same refractory materials, and were dependent upon one another's cooperation. Here was a new social factor. The same process that had gathered these laborers together had formed a *'society,'* in which a sense of identity became inevitable. Their personal helplessness was apparent to each. Their collective strength was yet to be revealed, but it could be discovered in the fact that they were all equally dependent upon the power that had brought them together. Their mutual association and experience, their similar skills, their relationship at the work bench, the tools they used, and the materials with which they worked *gave them a common language. They acquired the language of the craft, the job, the shop and the industry.* They shared the special points of pride and shame that can have only specific and local meaning. They could complain about light and heat, or cold and dampness. They could indulge in interminable talk about the job, infinitely interesting in its repetitious monotony because it detailed the daily round of the little things men share. It gave them a common, if local, vocabulary. The employer became the catalytic agent that crystallized them into a self-conscious group. When a conflict stirred, this provided the stimulus to bring it to the surface. . . . This functional coalescence became the firm foundation upon which the trade union movement grew, and which, in fact, made it inevitable."

Although trade unions arose almost inevitably from the culture of the workplace, the labor *movement* is a broader concept than trade unions alone. The movement includes political parties and action groups, mutual-aid societies, fraternities, unannounced strikes, spontaneous grievance committees. Jacob Viner noted this fact: "The mores and codes of trade unionism can develop without formal organization. Even in the days when trade unions were not very strong, were loosely organized, and when only minorities of the workers joined and paid dues, workers, whether members or not, often operated in some respects as if they belonged to very compact societies." What Viner says of the British, Commons echoes in discussing the American movement. The earliest strikes are "unorganized" and "such were the majority of the strikes that occurred prior to the decade of the thirties in the nineteenth century."

To paraphrase Aristotle's dictum, the worker is, by nature, a union creature. The more conscious worker pays dues in the same way that the more involved citizen pays taxes; the more conscious worker is active in his union in the same way that the more civic-minded citizen votes. The less active union member goes along. And outside the formal union ranks are masses of workers who, despite their nonadherence, are willy-nilly part of a movement, unconscious and sometimes unwilling members of the workplace culture.

In countries other than the United States the tightness of the "worker" culture is starkly apparent. In India, it was the long-recognized base of the society, with frozen castes, allowing neither geographic nor occupational transfer. In Europe, the formal caste system did not exist, but the relative immobility of the classes, with the child following in the trade of the parent, set up an informal caste system. In the United States, the culture of the workplace is considerably diluted by both horizontal and vertical mobility: movement of wage earners from place to place and from job to job, including movement from proletarian to capitalist status. Because lines are smudged in America, however, it does not follow that they do not exist. The culture of the caste does exist in America even if the boundaries are constantly blurred by an army of transients.

This tap root of the labor movement need not be nourished by grinding poverty or despair. Indeed in the United States the first solid organizations were those of the skilled craftsmen, a prideful crew who decided to battle employers to avoid sinking to the level of the European workers. "It is our belief," declared an assembly of Boston workers in the 1840s, "that the same causes of evil and suffering are operative in this country that in the Old World are developed to giant magnitude, and are crushing the producers of wealth to the very dust, and that unless a speedy change can be effected in our social condition the time is not far distant when the laborers of the United States will be as dependent, as oppressed, and as wretched, as are their brethren in Europe." Through the generations of organized labor in America, the higher-paid crafts have been the backbone of the movement. And even today, the poorest and most oppressed of American workers—the agricultural workers, to wit—are among the most poorly organized.

After all, why should working people in a given craft or industry organize only in response to maltreatment? Kings and queens organize; doctors and lawyers organize; bankers and managers and middle-managers and consultants organize—though most of these tradesmen are neither impecunious nor impotent.

This tap root of the labor movement—an organized expression of a subculture—is still alive, creating new unions, actions, protests, and aspirations daily. This root does not feed any single sector of the labor population—the skilled craftsman, the factory operative, the movie star, or the five-and-dime-store counter girl. It feeds all who work and therefore allows the reasonable presumption that working people in the future, like workers in the past, will organize, whether they create computers, manage automated machines, or shuffle social security cards in a vast government building.

Im Anfang war die That, insists Goethe. In the beginning of the labor movement there is the *deed,* the coming together of workingmen. Once this natural grouping takes on organized form—as in a political party, a fraternal society, or a trade union —the organizers seek stated purposes. The member who pays dues wants to know why he is paying dues. At this point, the labor movement in general—and especially the individual trade union—begins to articulate its program.

"No one will dispute the beneficial results attendant upon harmonious and intelligent action," declared the Cigar Makers' International Union of America grandiloquently in 1864, "and it is imperatively the duty of man to do all in his power to secure these results through organization and unity of action. In the performance of that duty we have formed the Cigar Makers' International Union of America, with a view to securing the organization of every cigar maker, for the purpose of elevating the *material, moral* and *intellectual* welfare of the craft." (Italics mine—G.T.)

In the promotion of the material, moral, and intellectual welfare of its members, the union discovers resistance—from the employer and from society. To overcome this resistance, the union becomes involved in a struggle in the workplace and in the community. Whether this is a "class struggle," implying a united effort of a whole class, or just a "trade conflict," indicating the narrow effort of a craft or shop, is a secondary matter: what is primary is the fact of conflict. Whether the struggle sets a fixed programmatic terminus, such as socialism, communism, anarchism, or is just an unending struggle for daily advances and ameliorations is also secondary: primary is the fact of *movement*.

This struggle, whether limited to the workplace or extended to government, whether involving a dozen patternmakers or a million auto workers, whether fought over a half cent for setting a sleeve or over nationalization of the steel industry, is "political." It is political because it concerns the basic question of all political strife: "Who gets what, when and how."

Collective bargaining consists of discussion, sometimes followed by strike or lockout, over the ancient interrogatives of the *who* and the *what*. The strike or lockout, the stoppage or firing, the sabotage or physical beating are merely continuations of the discussion by less diplomatic means. And conversely, the settlement of disputes by amicable means is merely a continuation of the struggle by more sensible means. But the struggle goes on and makes all collective bargaining a political struggle in the society of the workplace.

The struggle is not limited to money matters—the economics of the labor-management contract. It covers a broad spectrum of items: recognition (the right to a voice), security (protection of the job), wages and hours and fringe benefits, work conditions and work load, grievance procedure. The debate over the dollar, which sometimes appears to be the sole object of unionism, is often not the most important item.

Primary in this political struggle is the right to be heard. In formal union language, this is called *recognition*. This right is basic, taking precedence over wages, hours, working conditions. It is the right to talk with the employer as an organized group. It is, of necessity, preliminary to any discussion.

Recognition in collective bargaining is equivalent to the right to vote in a democratic society. With recognition comes the right to express grievances—to make a complaint, to have that complaint discussed, to settle the grievance. With recognition comes the right to make formal demands, similar to a platform presented by a political party. With recognition comes a tacit admission by the employer that the representatives of his employees have the new status of equals or, at least, of people who must be given the public treatment of would-be equals.

In discussing the strike policy of American trade unions in 1899, Samuel Gompers, then president of the American Federation of Labor, in testimony before the U.S. Congress saw the obvious parallels between the struggle for union recognition and the struggle for basic rights in a democracy.

"It required 40,000 people in the city of New York in my own trade in 1877 to demonstrate to the employers that we had a right *to be heard* in our own defense of our trade, and an opportunity *to be heard* in our own interests. It cost the miners of the country in 1897 sixteen weeks of suffering to secure a national conference and a national agreement. It cost the railroad brotherhoods long months of suffering, many of them sacrificing their positions, in the railroad strike of 1877, and in the Chicago, Burlington and

Quincy strike of the same year, to secure from the employers the *right to be heard through committees,* their representatives— that is, their committees of the organization, *to secure these rights. . . .*

"A strike . . . *is to industry as the right that the British people contended for in placing in the House of Commons the power to close the purse strings to the Government.* The rights of the British people were secured in two centuries—between 1500 and 1700—more than ever before, by the securing of that power to withhold the supplies; tied up the purse strings and compelled the Crown to yield. A strike on the part of workmen is to close production and compel better terms and *more rights* to be acceded to the producers." (All italics mine—G.T.)

Recognition really means that the workers are now involved in decision-making in the plant. In government, the participation of the common man in decision-making is the essence of political democracy; in the workplace, it is the essence of industrial democracy. The push and pull of the forces within this industrial democracy make collective bargaining a political phenomenon.

In response to the question of "who gets what," recognition offers, in partial reply, that workers get the right to a voice and a vote in connection with their circumstances. The struggle for this voice—this recognition—was at one time a revolutionary upheaval, challenging the whole established concept of "who" is to be in charge of "what" happens in the plant. At one time that matter was settled and closed: the boss was the man who decided what. As one self-righteous industrialist, inspired with his own illusion of divine mission, put it: "The rights and interests of the laboring man will be protected and cared for—not by the labor agitators, but by the Christian men to whom God in his infinite wisdom has given the control of the property interests of the country." The fight for recognition is based on the assumption that God in his infinite wisdom has also given a voice to wage earners.

Once trade unions are in the politics of the workplace, over how wide an area shall they extend their power? In other words, what are proper grounds for bargaining?

The answers vary, elude sharp definition, and will continue to do so for years to come. Paul R. Hays, then Nash Professor of Law at Columbia University, refused in 1959 to set any limits. "If the purpose of unionism is the dispersion of the power of the decision, then unions should be able to bargain about anything over which management has that power." Frank Tannenbaum, in his *Philosophy of Labor*, agrees that "the argument over the separate prerogatives of management and trade unions is largely beside the point. . . . Every activity of management bears upon the well-being of workers. . . . The end is participation by the trade union in all of the affairs of management."

The limits cannot be set because the relationship between employers and employees is, like life itself, a set of constantly shifting permutations and combinations. To freeze it is to kill it. And to try to freeze it is futile. In getting to the life force behind bargaining, Jack Barbash of the University of Wisconsin evolved a generalized approach. The company works out a "system" for a "rational" program to maximize efficient production. But, he says, "while the systematization of things offers no special problem, systematizing people does. People tend to resist systematization." And there's the rub.

One of the first points of bargaining involves the complex question: *whose property is the job?* Where there is no union, the job is the sole property of the employer—to give or take away as he pleases on any terms he pleases. Where there is a union, the worker insists that the job belongs to him. The worker wants job security: that he may not be fired without cause, that he may not be laid off except under some prearranged logic such as seniority. If the employer wishes to pick up the job and move it to some new location, perhaps in a different part of the country, the worker—through his union—proclaims his property right to the job: a first crack at the job in the new spot, a formal confrontation with the union before the job is removed. If an employer wants to wipe out a job by some new machine or system of production, the worker painfully proclaims his right to the job: the union insists that the worker have a voice in deciding whether the job may be liquidated, how it shall be liquidated, or who shall be liquidated.

On this one point of job security, the *corpus juris industrialis* laid down in contracts, board findings, and court decision is voluminous, recording landmarks in the political struggle over a piece of property known as the job.

In crafts where the job is not pinned down to a specific spot in a specific plant, the unions have devised a kind of collective-ownership approach to the jobs. These unions are in the journeyman trades where skilled craftsmen move about from day to day, working on construction or road building, sailing ships or playing a saxophone. How can any one of these workers claim property to the job when the job disappears at one nightfall while a new job blooms the next morning? In such trades, the union workers have traditionally developed the closed shop and the hiring hall. The jobs collectively belong to the workers who are union members, and the hiring hall is the instrument for an equitable distribution of each member's share in the job collectively. In these trades, no matter what the law may be, the worker instinctively looks to his union to get him a job, to keep him on the job, and to get him a new job if the old one falls away. As he sees it, the jobs in the craft collectively belong to him through the union.

The third major item of collective bargaining, following recognition and job security, is the division of the company's income: how much shall go for wages in general, and for the wage of each worker. Over the years, this matter of economics has become increasingly complicated. Once it was a matter of the dollar wage. Now we talk about the package, which means the wage plus fringe benefits such as holidays, vacations, medical plans, retirement, supplementary unemployment insurance. The bargaining over such items is what normally gets headlines that give the public the impression that the wage package is the be-all and end-all of unionism. In reality, it is only one of many items and, unless seen in perspective, perplexes the onlooker who sees workers ready to turn down a higher wage in favor of steady work or greater work satisfaction.

This last item is a sensitive subject, often least understood by the formal spokesmen for labor and for management and most appreciated by professors and by workers themselves. To the typical wage earner, his work is not simply a way to earn money; it is his life; it conditions his behavior in the post-working hours, right into his hours of sleep; it leaves its wear and tear on his bones and nerves. The job shapes so much of the man that it is often possible to tell a man's occupation by simply looking at him.

The subject of work satisfaction has fascinated scholars who have tried to study the worker as a whole man: not only as an economic function but as a psychic complex. By these measurements, the "happy worker," who should be happy because he is earning $150 a week, may not be so happy after all. The frustration accumulated in the shop explodes in the home or at the bar. The punishing pace of the belt beats a few years out of a man's life, and he feels it happening. His dollar happiness means unhappiness, with his bigger earnings coming right out of his own hide.

While these anthropologists of work and the workers themselves are sensitive to this problem of satisfactions, most officials of labor and management tend to be less aware. The latter tend to concentrate on production and earnings, on rights and prerogatives, on average input and output. They tend to think in terms of the contract and its provisos wherein work satisfaction,— precisely because it is often personal, subjective, and intangible —goes undefined and unstated.

In much of basic industry the employer has a mathematical answer to an increased hourly wage package. If you pay the worker more, get him to produce more. The greater production is to be obtained in two ways: (1) by introducing labor-saving devices; (2) by getting the worker to work harder. In modern terms, the first idea is automation; and in old-fashioned talk the second idea is speed-up. Both are aimed at stepping up the individual productivity of the worker.

To the worker, this is a nerve-racking business. Automation often means no job. Speed-up often means no nerves. Under the high pressure of speed-up, the belt moves faster; the latest average work load becomes the minimum; the rest break that once seemed adequate is inadequate under the new pace; the job reclassification often means a downgrading with the same worker working harder and earning less; the stop watch becomes a whip. Trips to the toilet are timed and the toilets photographed to make sure that nature's time is not playtime; if the prying camera eye is outlawed, the doors are removed from the washrooms. The worker who does not meet his quota is put on the demerit list. In short, the higher wage comes out of the worker's hide. And when he screams, nobody knows why, because the contract looks so good.

Work satisfaction, however, is not based solely on such matters as pace and privacy. In certain positions, satisfaction is measured by the degree of leeway for autonomous decision; it may also be measured by authority and responsibility; it may be measured by office decoration, system of promotion, window space; it may even be measured by status conferred on the job while away from the job.

Actually, the term "work satisfaction" is quite unsatisfactory. Very few people are truly happy with their work. What we have been discussing, so far as the mass worker (either blue or white collar) is concerned, is work dissatisfaction. Most employees are ready to put up with quite a bit of this as part of the job for which they get paid. To many, the wage is a compensation for discomfort. Dissatisfaction becomes a problem when it crosses the worker's threshold of tolerance and gets under his skin. And in the attempt to find relief from the ulcerating ambience of the workplace, the worker demands changes. He is no longer ready to put up with the society of work within which he moves just because he is well paid; he wants to organize that workplace to make it more livable.

In early union contracts, this problem of work satisfactions and dissatisfactions fell under the prosaic heading of "working conditions." Then it meant a toilet, a light, a window, and similar simple items. Today, in basic industry and in the white-collar world, the content of working conditions has become much more complex, involving fewer physical conditions and more psychological conditionings. But the struggle over working conditions is just as fierce as it has ever been, even if the words used to define the issue are more refined.

The best-concealed and the subtlest power play in the shop—the most basic, in some ways—is the political competition of union and employer for the loyalty of the worker. The existence of this profound political play, similar to the rivalry of Democrats and Republicans for the favor of the voter, is often denied by the easy declaration that the worker can be equally loyal to both employer and union, giving the employer the best of his talents as producer and giving his union the fullness of his heart as dues payer, rendering to the employer what is the employer's and rendering to the union what is the union's. While this statement contains some truth, it confuses the issue. The rivalry occurs when union and employer seek to be the voice of the worker in the matter of earnings, job security, work hours, shop conditions. The employer would like the worker to leave it to the boss because the boss knows best. The union wants the worker to voice his desires through the union. Both seek the worker's vote of confidence.

This process of competition for the worker's vote is actually formalized under American law. The labor board conducts an election to determine whether a majority of the workers will elect a union to represent them or whether they prefer no union. At a later point, an election may be held to decertify a union. And, in between, employer and union are at quiet war, campaigning for votes.

This political struggle in the society of the workplace is a second live root of trade unionism. Its presence has meaning for the future. The vast areas covered by bargaining, with their shifting boundaries, with their reappearance in new forms, with their applicability to all human beings in all work situations, almost guarantee that the coming years will give new grist to the bargaining mills. The nature of bargaining may change; the subject matter may alter; the kinds of employees may be transformed. But the process will go on—the eternal effort of "parties" in any community to advance and protect their own interests.

Curiously, this struggle does not postulate that the interests of employers as a class and the interests of workers as a class are necessarily contradictory. The interests of both, as classes, may be the same. Yet the conflict will continue at the plant, craft, and industry level, because here the confrontation is not class against class, but individual workers against individual employers, a struggle in which the part cannot act like the whole.

It may very well be that American society is gradually working out a way for everybody to live better: to make the pie bigger so that even if everybody gets the same proportion of the pie as formerly, everybody has a bigger piece. The scheme seems to be working. Unions no longer believe that for the rich to be richer, the poor must be poorer. Unions now argue that good wages mean good business for everybody—a spur to the economy, creating many jobs and much profit. The experience of the post-depression period gives credibility to the theory: jobs increased, wages rose, millionaires multiplied, and profits soared.

At the plant or industry level, however, an employer cannot and does not think that way. He will grant that his business will do best when his customers have money. He will grant that high wages make good consumers. But, since his customers are not exclusively or mainly his own employees, the wages he pays represent higher costs but not necessarily greater sales of the particular product he manufactures. Hence he wants to keep costs as low as possible to promote profits. And precisely this makes the conflict inevitable in the plant or industry.

It may appear paradoxical that a process as *economic* as collective bargaining should be described as *political*. But the paradox disappears when one considers the nature of all government and politics and their heavy concern with economic matters. The struggle of parties and factions is heavily—Karl Marx might have said "exclusively"—economic. The decisions of legislatures and courts are fraught with economic significance. Rights and privileges are sought out, fought out, and sometimes bought out by economic groups. Collective bargaining is a political struggle over economic goals—just like most other political struggles in the world.

The labor movement is political in the common use of the term;　*3*
that is, a participant in elections, legislation, governmental processes. Its political bent, in this third sense of the term, is inherent.

"From the beginning," notes labor historian Philip Taft, "organized labor has been interested in politics, although sharp differences have arisen out of tactics and the policies to support."

Some groups of organized workers have favored a labor party; others favored trade unions acting as pressure groups on existing parties. Some groups reached out politically for a brave new world; other groups sought politically to make life more comfortable in this sorry old world. Some groups were concerned with national, even international policy; others with protective legislation at the state level; and still others with the puny politics of survival at the local level. But one way or another, all have been concerned with politics.

Trade unions as a distinct expression of one aspect of the broader concept covered by the term "labor movement" turn to politics for a variety of compelling reasons: to organize; to enjoy legal status; to maximize employment; to legislate protection against the hazards of accidents, unemployment, illness, old age; to express the viewpoint of a body of citizens on its own state and the state of the world.

The least common denominator of labor's political interest—and, incidentally, the least discussed in genteel journals—is involvement with those primary political potentates: the police and the courts.

The active trade unionists, especially those on the picket line, learn early that the greatest lawmaker in the land is the cop on the beat, with the power to make law with the club in his hand

and the power to unmake law by closing one eye. With him rests the power to be present or absent, to see or not to see, to arrest or not to arrest, to testify as it was or as he thought it was. Sharing such primary power with him is the judge—the police magistrate sentencing pickets or the more august court issuing injunctions to bar all picketing. Political action at the local level, reaching the men on the beat and on the bench, is basic, therefore, for the practical trade unionist.

To function freely, a union seeks the status of legality. Without such public standing, a union must operate as a conspiracy, outlawed and underground. To gain the legality that allows life and growth in the open, a union must turn to politics—to the election of judges who will not (as judges did for many decades) see the union, or the act of collective bargaining, or the strike as an illegal conspiracy; to the election of legislators who will not (as legislatures have done) banish the union shop, or restrict the union's right to strike or picket or act in concert with other unionists; to the election of executives who will not (as some have done) appoint agency heads whose interpretations of existing law diminish the free action of unions.

Throughout the nineteenth century, the fight for legality revolved around the courts. In the absence of any clear body of federal legislation on unions, the courts made legislation from the bench. In labor matters, the common law was turned against the common man. Conspiracy trials held successively that unions per se were outlaw; that unions were legal but that concerted action to force a given wage was outlaw; that unions and wage scales were legal but that coercion of nonunionists was illegal. Over the years, the law as spoken by the courts has accumulated. Yet almost daily new interpretations are handed down on what a union may do and may not do—delimiting its latitude of freedom, the scope of its legal behavior.

In the twentieth century, labor law has increasingly been formulated in the federal legislature: the Clayton Act liberating human labor from the commodity category; the Norris-LaGuardia Act restraining the use of injunctions in labor disputes; Section 7A of the National Recovery Act encouraging workers to join unions of their own choosing as an act in the public interest; the Taft-Hartley amendments to the Labor-Management Act limiting some of the rights and privileges granted to unions; the Landrum-Griffin amendments to the same act limiting and defining union actions with special regard to the internal conduct of unions. This body of law—written by elected representatives—has been further spelled out by labor boards—appointed by elected executives.

Out of their long experience, trade unionists know that the political struggle for the legalization of unions does not end with the simple recognition that a union is a legal entity. The struggle goes on for two reasons: first, because law is a reversible reaction and what is legal today may be illegal tomorrow; second, because the *scope* of legal action is often almost as vital as *bare* legality itself.

Unions also go into politics to maximize job opportunities—for everybody and especially for their dues-paying members. The fight for full employment is the pivotal point in labor's political program for America. This emphasis on "jobs for all" flows from the great trauma of 1929 to 1932, which was followed by the New Deal and other welfare-state programs aimed at expanding production and jobs. But long before 1932, before the trade unions officially recognized the vital role of the federal government as a spur to the economy, labor organizations turned to political action to get and guarantee jobs for their members. Railroad unions fought for "full crew" legislation; building and construction unions sought "codes" to stabilize employment for their skilled crafts; a variety of artisans demanded licensing provisions for the practice of their specialty, with stipulations for apprenticeship; unions facing foreign competition petitioned for tariffs and quotas and, on the other hand, unions in export trades favored free trade. More recently, labor organizations in nationally competitive industries employing marginal populations have worked for higher minimum wages to halt the drift of plants from high-wage to low-wage areas; maritime unions have insisted that government promote the use of American shipping. Each union tends to wage a double political fight for more jobs: first, by joining all other unions to work for such legislation as will produce a full-employment economy; then, by working for special legislation to get more jobs for the dues payers in the particular craft, trade, or industry. While emphasis and program vary from union to union, they all turn to political action as one major means to create a full-employment economy.

An interesting and revealing aspect of this political concern is the deep involvement of some crafts and trades with key positions in *local* government. Certain unions have a membership largely dependent for employment on contracts from local government. These unions make it a prime point to get their man into a position to "set" the contracts. By such influence, unions can maximize both jobs and standards. Ironically, such unions, whose absorption in local matters dulls their interest in national affairs and makes them appear nonpolitical, are actually, in terms of their backyard bailiwicks, among the most political unions in America. Like most practical Americans, they politick hardest where it counts most.

Unions also go into politics to get special legislation, usually at the state level, to protect their specialized membership against the hazards of job, economy, and nature. Much of this legislation appears almost comically petty, except to the man on the job to whom it may be a matter of life and death.

In describing the work of the New York State Federation of Labor between 1894 and 1918, Philip Taft catalogues support for the "closing of barber shops on Sunday, licensing, and sanitary standards. Thirty-four laws affecting building tradesmen were sponsored. Among them were those requiring enclosed elevator shafts in construction work, regulating apprentices, giving building mechanics and laborers preferred wage claims, compelling supervision of plastering by mechanics, and requiring thirty-four-inch safety railings on scaffolds. Thirteen laws affecting metal tradesmen, foundry employes, molders, polishers, and blacksmiths were supported; twelve affecting hotels, liquor and brewery workers; seven requested by printing tradesmen; and twelve sought by employes in the retail trades. Some of them required inspection of premises, and Sunday and holiday closing laws requiring one day's rest in seven. Twenty laws were supported which regulated the employment conditions of stationary firemen, engineers, and electrical workers; twenty-nine laws, including full crew legislation for workers on steam and electric railroads: seven laws governing theatrical and motion picture establishments; and twenty-eight laws regulating mining, tunneling, subway and caisson workers. In addition ninety-six laws affecting women and children in industry were sponsored."

In 1962, the New York State federation was still carrying on similar work. Its program called for proposals to require a contractor to provide an elevator in construction exceeding six stories; to require sanitary facilities in similar construction; to outlaw power-activated tools in construction, repair, and demolition; to amend Code Rule 23 to require catch platforms of netting on the exteriors of all multiple-tiered buildings; to require protective netting and lifeboats under bridges; to require a statewide license law for stationary, hoisting, and portable engineers and stationary firemen; to make it a misdemeanor not to pay vacation monies as per contract; to require bidders on public work to have operating safety programs; to require a first aid station with competent person on duty at places of employment with at least 50 workers; to make it illegal to require Sunday work, etc. Minuscule as such items appear to the nation at large, each little act is no minor matter to the individual worker who is involved. To him, it may mean the difference between a broken back or a sound body, between endless anxiety or relative security on the job.

This level of politics, affecting the literal survival of the worker and the union, is the oldest, most continuous, and most effective area of labor political action. Ironically, it is the most neglected in writings on labor.

For all these reasons then—to organize a union, to win legal status for the organization, to maximize employment, and to enact special legislation for special categories of workers—trade unionists turn to politics as *unionists*. The same people, however, are citizens of a community, concerned with transportation and communication, hospitals and clinics, education and prejudice, air and water pollution, delinquency and crime, taxes and tariffs, bombs and birthrates, riches and poverty, rights and wrongs, democracy and dictatorship. While each trade unionist brings his individual view to these problems, the members of trade unions, brought together by their common stake in work and often living in the same neighborhoods, develop a group point of view. The union in politics tends to become a vehicle for a class view.

In the earliest political efforts of American trade unionism, there was considerable awareness of the differing attitudes of classes in America: the innate clash between owner and worker, employer and employee, common man and bigwig. To the Work· ingman's Party of 1828, the clash was between aristocracy and democracy. "There appears to exist," the party states in one of its declarations, "two distinct classes, the rich and the poor; the oppressor and the oppressed; those that live by their own labour, and they that live by the labour of others; the aristocratic, and the democratic; the despotic and the republican . . . ; the one seeking to introduce and perpetuate amongst us invidious and artificial distinctions, unnatural and unjust inequalities, while the other party declares that all men are created free and equal, enjoying a perfect uniformity of rights and privileges."

This early workingman's declaration, recognizing the instinctive incompatibility of top and bottom, laid the groundwork for political organizations of labor to express a given point of view. Over the decades, this point of view has been spelled out as labor's program for the *community*, the momentary details of a proletarian *Weltanschauung*. By the mid-twentieth century, this program has developed into a complex platform, covering such varied items as a traffic light at Broadway and Broome, a labor attaché to Honduras, a civil rights law, or the reapportionment of state legislatures.

What does labor's instinctive involvement with government at all levels mean for the future of labor—and of the country? If it is assumed that the country will become more political in coming generations, then it must also be assumed that labor will become more political. The more deeply government goes into regulation of the economy of unions, of industrial relations, the more deeply will unions go into politics. This will not be a new policy for trade unions, but the intensification of an old habit.

The labor movement is political in a fourth sense: the 4 Machiavellian sense of men manipulating men. Policy-making in unions is a political function. All the laws of political science apply to unions as thoroughly as they do to all other human organizations: nations, parties, churches, clubs, clans. Unions, like nations, are constituted and run in varying ways: some are intensely democratic; others are dictatorships; some are run like constitutional monarchies; others like feudal states; some are clean; others are crooked; some rally around purposes; others rally around personalities. But they are all political.

Many factors shape the political traits of unions: personalities, the composition of the membership, the nature of the trade, traditions and aspirations, the stage of development. Unions tend to be most factional when they are still forming, with many activists striving for leadership in the absence of established authority. This factionalism tends to crop up again whenever a union is going through a transition or crisis, whether industrial or political. Unions with all-male membership live a fiercer factional life than those with female members: women usually shy away from full-time paid union posts. In unions with a high degree of local autonomy, the national head reigns more than he rules. In unions with national contracts, power is usually centered at the top, where the patterns of economic and political power are designed.

Political style varies. In some unions, even the most trivial gain is presented in the grandiloquent language of the social revolution; in other unions, the most sweeping economic reforms are ticked off like cold clicks on a dutiful cash register.

Whatever else a union leader may be, he must be, in the first instance, a politician. This term is not used derogatorily, although sometimes the ugly connotation is quite applicable. The union leader must be a politician because only thus can he remain in office, whether democratically or bureaucratically, since the laws of politics are not inert in a bureaucracy; only thus can he hold the organization together. Whatever his dogma, his industrial program, his personal predilections, his choice of cronies, he must adjust them all to allow for the real political pressures in and around his union. He must do what circumstances make necessary and possible as well as what he considers desirable.

In this generation, the political task of the union leader has become more complicated because the labor chieftain must keep his eyes on the outside as well as the inside: the outside being the law and the public. In previous generations, the main outside that the union leader had to watch was the employer and the local government with which he had to do business. Nowadays he has to operate within a body of federal law and within a body of national opinion. Hence, he is increasingly compelled to develop sensitivity and skill in dealing with this greater outer world.

Because policy-making within a union is a political process, it is futile to forecast the future of labor by mechanistic references to "bargaining patterns," or "market pressures," or governmentally defined "guidelines," or even such old stand-bys as "productivity" and "a fair day's pay for a fair day's work." None of these is irrelevant. But precisely because they all are relevant, the union leader must pick and choose and make his own mixture. In considering a new contract, the union leader does consider the productivity and the profits in his trade; he also considers the earnings and edginess of his membership. He will consider government guidelines but is more likely to view them as a minimum goal rather than a maximum limit. He will be influenced by what a brother or sister union has recently written into a contract but is unconcerned about the attainments of unions in unrelated trades. He will measure his strength and the readiness of his membership to fight. And he will make a similar estimate of the employer. He will try to foresee and perhaps influence the role of the government in any coming struggle. He will try to gauge public opinion. The policy he makes will ultimately have to be submitted to his membership for approval. In the end, he will write a set of contract demands that will sit well with his membership but will not lose him his own seat when he has to make his ultimate settlement.

Before calling a strike, the union leader must consider all the factors and consider them well. A big strike is a Pandora's box. A strike can unleash every demagogic oppositionist in the union, whose fervor may make an ultimate settlement impossible. A strike may turn public and government against the union. A strike may harden, rather than soften, the employer. A strike may be lost, and, with it, the union, or the leader's post, may be lost as well. Before calling a strike, a leader must balance all these political considerations in the same way that a President of the United States must weigh similar considerations before calling upon Congress to declare war.

For all these reasons and for many more, to predict the future of trade unionism in the United States is not an exercise in econometrics. Union policy is not made on a slide rule. The unions are political organisms responding to a complex social order around them and to a complicated political psyche within them.

The ancient political roots of the labor movement are still alive. They bring new nourishment to the trade unions. They feed its futures. Because the union is the natural community of the professional polis, the future promises new unions among hitherto unorganized, even hitherto unorganizable, occupations. Because the political struggle of the union in collective bargaining covers a wide area of relationships going far beyond wages and hours, it can be expected that, in the future, unions will move into hitherto undefined bargaining jurisdictions—both in the content of contracts and in the type of workers covered. Because the labor movement has become an increasingly political-minded force in an increasingly politically oriented social order, it may be presumed that in the future trade unions will have to be reckoned with increasingly in American government. Finally, because unions are *internally* political, it is inevitable that they will produce new leaders with new ideas to meet both the external and internal pressures of the future.

The four-fold political character of the labor movement has also made it one of the great pillars of American democracy. Because a union is the political expression of the workplace polis, it constitutes a separate and special locus of power. In a society whose democratic vigor depends upon a pluralism of powers, the labor movement constitutes a significant independent center of decision-making. Indeed, in the century from 1864 to 1964, the trade unions may well have been the basic counterforce to the prevailing Establishment of wealth.

"Unions were deliberately and consciously fostered," wrote Paul Hays, "for the very purpose of furthering the dispersion of power and preserving the pluralistic character of our free institutions."

Labor through its collective bargaining function—the political struggle over rights and riches in the workplace—has established a measure of economic justice, a prerequisite for democratic progress. Extremes of wealth and poverty have been reduced, although not eliminated. The ill-will, the sullen anger, and the wild outbursts characteristic of civilizations damned by extremes have been tempered by the existence and accomplishments of the American labor movement.

A democracy is more than a constitutional form. It is also a nation of people who, despite conscious conflicts, are prepared to do battle on a common ground, in a tolerant atmosphere. The majority, in a democracy, rules but it must also tolerate the rights of the minority. The minority, in a democracy, enjoys certain inalienable rights but it must also tolerate the rule of the majority. This mutual acceptance of rules and rights is not possible when the opposing parties act out of agonizing hunger or obsessive arrogance. The heat generated by the friction of extremes dissolves the fiber of a free society.

If America does not suffer from the politics of extremism, this is to a large extent owing to the work of the unions that have curbed the arrogance of the industrial rulers and abated the hunger of the industrial workers. Consequently, the boss has come to respect the rights of his workers and the workers have come to tolerate the rules of the boss. Organized labor has created the economic middle class and the emotional middle ground that provide inner strength and cohesion to our democracy.

Labor has promoted literacy and won the leisure to enrich and employ literacy—a *sine qua non* of a democracy. Organized labor has been a prime mover for general literacy and especially for political literacy. A century and a half ago, the trade unions pushed hard for free, universal, public education through the workingmon's parties in our Eastern cities. The movement was successful. The almost utopian hope that such a broad educational system would totally democratize both our economic and political life was not realized. Yet the Herculean impact of public schools on industrial development and political participation is largely responsible for our present strength—as an economy and as a democratic culture.

Organized labor is also primarily responsible for the ever-shortening work week, the well-spring of leisure time for the non-leisure class. This free time is necessary for a free society, providing the opportunity for cultural blossoming and self-education of the adult. At the same time, the hours made available for reading, for bull sessions, for barroom politicking, for electioneering, provide breathing time for democracy.

The unions have helped create a machinery for the adjustment of conflicting interests through a regularized process of law and order—a process that is indispensable for the smooth functioning of an industrial system in a democratic society. Without regularized and institutionalized channels for the expression and adjudication of conflict, collective grievances and aspirations could be ventilated only through a recurrent series of disruptive explosions, endangering both the productive flow and the legal processes of a democratic industrialism.

The unions have also made a basic contribution toward the

creation of orderly machinery for the expression and adjustment of social relationships, a spelling out of rights and obligations. The contract does not eliminate conflict; it recognizes conflict and then proceeds to contain the conflict by the creation of industrial constitutions.

The body of labor law that has evolved in the United States is an extension of the same concept. These laws and the body of official and unofficial umpires lay down the ground rules of conflict, as interpreted and modified by human need and understanding.

Without the contract, the mediator, the arbitrator, the body of labor law, industrial strife would be jungle warfare. No better measure of the extent to which labor relations has become a codified form of behavior can be found than the growing legion of labor lawyers. And none of this would have come about without the labor movement.

By participation in the political life of the nation, the unions have helped to democratize the entire political process. The wage earner in this country is not, by history and habit, an active participant in politics. The professional and business elements of our society contain a much higher percentage of active voters and doers. The basic work of labor-in-politics in the last decade has been to convert the heavily immobile labor electorate into a dynamic factor. Millions of wage earners and their families who were inert in the past are presently active, interested, and informed voters.

The methodology of labor in its politicking means the democratization of politics. The basic operative assumption of labor is that wage earners should urge platforms on candidates and parties in line with a broad liberal program. The emphasis is on *issues*—not on people, labels, or geographic and ethnic habits. The prime instrument for making issues the basis of votes is education. The continuing work of the labor movement in educating its members, their families, and the public to study issues, make up their minds on them, and thus cast their votes tends to build a broad base of principle for American politics. No other organized force in American life carries on such political missionary work among blue-collar workers.

The fund-raising activities of the labor movement are a further contribution toward the democratization of politics, helping to balance the financial scales in political struggles. All legal attempts to limit contributions and expenditures to candidates by law have thus far failed. People of wealth can pour as much money as they wish into political campaigns. Limits on campaign contributions to a candidate do not really apply to all his committees. And limits on contributions somehow do not limit "expenditures." And finally, wealthy individuals can always buy or establish a newspaper that day in and day out can cultivate a point of view, endorse candidates, and publicize aspirants for public office, without any accounting under any corrupt practices act. This failure to control money in politics by laws means that wealth in America can subsidize a commanding voice in elections. Some financial counterweight to the generally conservative position of the money lords is vital for democracy. And it is the labor movement that, in recent years, has moved toward supplying some, even if not enough, financial counterbalance to the voice of our moneyed aristocracy in elections.

Finally, because unions are internally political, the labor organization provides working people a workshop in the arts and crafts of statesmanship. As shop stewards, workers learn the ways of tribune and ward-heeler; in local executive boards, they compose a miniature parliament; as business agents, they become craftsmen of the contract and composers of majorities. And so the learning goes up the line to national union presidents who are often called upon to be commander-in-chief of the union at war and chief magistrate of the union at peace. Millions of American workers have learned the skills of government on the playing fields of the local union.

By their very nature, then, trade unions have been vitalizing forces in the American democracy. In the future it is likely that this long-lived movement will continue to help shape the contours of our economic and political life. What the exact impact of trade unionism will be on our institutions depends upon the changing character of both social order and unions.

CHAPTER 4

The Challenge of Automation

"Two per cent of the population—by implication the two per cent at the upper administrative levels—will in the discernible future be able to produce all the goods and services needed to feed, clothe and run our society with the aid of machines."

This is the prophecy of a Rand Corporation computer expert. Two per cent will do the world's work! While the forecaster is quite definite about the infinitesimal group that is to run the show, he is not quite so definite about the date of the "discernible future," although it is "discernible." Let us, then, for discussion purposes assume a date about twenty years away.

The Census Bureau projects a population in the United States of 265,575,000 by 1985. Two per cent of that figure—about 5 million—would compose the total labor force. In a population that will have expanded by 72 million over 1965, the labor force will have shrunk by 65 million. Work would be out of style. At present, four out of ten people are in the labor force; in the "discernible future" only two people out of one hundred will work. The rest of the population will be either voluntarily or involuntarily at leisure.

The implications of this cyberculture have been explored in a cascade of predictions—gay, glum, and gruesome. What will the impact of such an economy be on the labor movement?

If human nature does not change by 1985, the 5 million cerebrating drones who will be running the economy will be organized. They will organize because they are members of the economic elite, and the elite always is the first to be aware of its special status and interests. In the past, the skilled workers were the earliest to compose guilds, associations, and unions. They are likely to perpetuate this clannish tradition in the future.

This American Federation of Laboring Upper Administrators—AFLUA, for short—will be the most powerful collective-bargaining agency the world has ever seen. The high skills and inevitable esprit de corps of its members will make strikes effective and scabbing difficult. On the backs of these workers will be riding mountains of capital. On the results of their collective labor will hang the fate of the whole civilization. An attack of upper-administrative flu might crimp an industry. A key local of the AFLUA could seriously damage the economy with a work stoppage. A strike of a million in 1985 would have the impact of a strike by 14 million workers now and would paralyze the nation. With this kind of leverage, the members of AFLUA could command whatever they wished—by a mere threat to withhold their rare and indispensable talents.

Politically, this labor federation would be conservative. Its members—few as they would be—would be the mass base for the "haves." Outside their ranks, there would be only the idle rich and the idle poor. The "have-nots" would compose 95 per cent of the population—a standing army of disemployed, dispossessed, and disgruntled, with nothing to do but contemplate their own rot and conspire for revolution. The 2 per cent of the enjobbed would have to keep the political as well as the economic institutions on an even keel; they would be the rock of conservatism, defenders of the status quo.

This, then, would be the labor movement of the future, if the world's work falls to the chosen two out of a hundred: a social elite that is industrially militant and politically conservative—the ultimate in a labor aristocracy. To paraphrase Karl Marx, these workers, once united, would have nothing to lose but their brains, and a world to gain.

There is a school of thought that looks forward hopefully to the world without work—provided society makes a *volte-face* in its values and system of remuneration. If 2 per cent do the creative work, the other 98 per cent should, without shame and as a matter of right, receive the fruits of that labor. The Ad Hoc Committee on the Triple Revolution proposes rather plainly that it is the responsibility of society "to provide every individual and every family with an adequate income as a matter of right." Under this proposal, it is society's duty not to find a job, but to provide an income.

Robert Theobald is quite explicit about this: "We must develop a new, human and constitutional right—the right to an income. At this time such a right is not only economically feasible and socially necessary, it is also prerequisite for the preservation in the United States of Western ideals of human dignity and freedom.

"Every citizen of the United States and everybody who has resided in the United States for a period of five consecutive years should be guaranteed the right to an income to enable him to live with dignity. No government agency, judicial body or other organization whatsoever should have the power to suspend or limit any payments assured by this guarantee.

"This right would apply equally to every member of society and carry with it no connotation of personal inadequacy or implication that an undeserved income was being received from an over-generous government. On the contrary, the implication would be one of responsibility by the total society for ensuring that no member of the society lived in a manner incompatible with the standards acceptable to his fellow men merely because he lacked purchasing power."

The idea here stated is not new. It has always been the dream for a future when man has so completely conquered the material world that he is liberated from the need to work—or, according to this new prospectus, can turn over the workload to 2 per cent. For such a land of plenty, the slogan has always been: from each according to his ability, to each according to his need.

Under such a system, the great societies of mankind would

probably be composed, not of the few who work, but of the many who do not. These latter would be grouped not by vocation but by avocation—by the predilections, indulgences, and creations of their leisure time.

How closely do these prophecies correspond with what has actually been happening in the last quarter-century?

Question No. 1: Has the size of the labor force in the United States been shrinking? The answer is no. In 1949, there were about 44 million in the *civilian* labor force. In 1954, there were 64 million. In 1965, there were 75 million. In short, the labor force has not been shrinking; it has been growing steadily.

The phrase "labor force" includes those who have jobs and also those who are unemployed and looking for jobs. This distinction between the working and nonworking members of the labor force raises the next question:

Question No. 2: Has the number of *employed* in the United States been shrinking? Again, the answer is no. In 1939, there were 45 million employed; by 1954, the number had risen to 60 million; by 1964, to 70 million and, by 1965, to 72 million. In sum, the number of employed people in the United States has been going up steadily.

The undisputed fact, then, is that both the labor force and the number of employed have been climbing upward. It is, however, mathematically possible that, while the number of gainfully employed is going up, the *percentage* of such a labor force as part of the total population is going down. This would certainly be true if the population were growing more rapidly than the labor force. This then brings us to the next question:

Question No. 3: Has the percentage of the labor force as part of the total population been shrinking? The answer is hardly at all.

Between 1939 to 1964 the population of the United States rose from 130 million to 192 million. But the labor force has been growing at about the same rate. In 1939, the civilian labor force was 40 per cent of the population; in 1954, it was still 40 per cent;

in 1965, it was 38 per cent. In sum, the civilian labor force in relation to the population has remained about the same.

The preceding figures, however, are somewhat misleading. In the population are included those under the age of 14, who are not properly part of the job-seeking population. A better measure is based on that part of the population above age 14 which is described as "noninstitutional"—that is, outside prisons, hospitals, homes for the aged, etc. By this measure, the civilian labor force was 56 per cent of the noninstitutional-above-age-14 population in 1940; 58.4 per cent in 1954; and 57.5 per cent in 1965. In short, despite rapid population growth, the civilian labor force has not fallen behind: it, too, has grown.

Experts at the U.S. Bureau of Labor Statistics expect that the labor force will continue to grow as the population grows. By 1970, the labor force will be 85,999,000 or 57.5 per cent of the above-14-year-old population; by 1975, it will be 973,646,000 or 57.8 per cent; by 1980, it will be 101,408,000 or 58.3 per cent.

Thus far, all seems in balance. But there is a disturbing factor. While the labor force has grown and while the total number of employed has grown, so has the number of *unemployed*. In the period since World War II, there has been an over-all climb: about 2 million in 1947; about 3 million in 1957; and about 4 million in 1964. Along the way, there have been ups and downs but the long pull shows a gradual growth in the jobless.

And this brings us to the decisive Question No. 4: Has the *percentage* of unemployed been growing—that is, as part of the civilian labor force? The answer is yes.

Because the percentage of unemployed varies with each year and each month, it is handier to look at five-year averages to get the long-range trend. From 1950 to 1954, the jobless were 4.04 per cent of the civilian labor force; from 1955 to 1959, they were 5.04 per cent; from 1960 to 1964, they were 5.76 per cent. The percentage of unemployed is growing—slowly but perceptibly. Our experience from 1950 to 1965 shows that every five years the percentage of jobless increases by about one-half a percentage point. In twenty years, if the present rate continues, the percentage of jobless would stand at 7.76. By the year 2005, it would stand at almost 10.

Although any such percentage of unemployed—10 in 2005, or 7.76 in 1985, or even between 5 and 6 in 1965—constitutes a social problem of serious dimensions, such rates of unemployment hardly square with the augury of an economy sans employment.*

The figures do not justify any prediction that the future will operate with a tiny labor force and therefore a tiny labor movement. The trend thus far shows an ever bigger labor force, ever more employed, accompanied by a gnawing problem of upward crawling unemployment. There are real problems ahead, but no cataclysm.

But why do present trend lines show no such sudden and catastrophic end to work? Automated, cybernated mechanisms are undoubtedly doing work once done by people. These mechanisms are, after all, labor-saving and thought-saving devices. Surely, they must be a replacement for muscle and mind. How is it that *employment* increases and *unemployment* rises so slowly?

Testifying before a Senate Committee in 1963, John I. Snyder, Jr., the chairman and president of the U.S. Industries, Inc., stated that "automation is a major factor in eliminating jobs in the United States at the rate of more than 40,000 a week." This adds up to more than 2 million jobs per year. The rate portends speedy catastrophe.

But unemployment has *not* been rising at 2 million a year. What is the reason?

To begin with, Snyder, despite appearances to the contrary, was right. Improvements in our method of productivity are, in a way, eliminating more than 2 million jobs a year. (We speak of "improvements in productivity" rather than "automation" because the latter is an inseparable and hardly independently measurable part of the former.)

---

* In early 1966, the jobless figure was down around 4 per cent—indicating the response of the job market to internal government policy and to international events.

These 2 million jobs are "eliminated" by our improved productivity. At present, our productivity rate goes up about 4 per cent a year. Each year, each worker, on an average, can turn out 4 per cent more than he could in the previous year. If each worker each year turns out as much as he did the previous year, the economy can do with 4 per cent *fewer* workers. In a total employed labor force of 70 million, this 4-per-cent increase in productivity makes unnecessary the work of more than 2 million workers, hence the conclusion that improved productivity knocks out 40,000 jobs a week.

The conclusion, however, depends upon a big "if." There are 2 million fewer jobs each year only if our economy is turning out each year only as much as it turned out the previous year. In that case, the same amount can be turned out by fewer people. But if the total economy creates each new year a greater amount of goods and services, then the total number of jobs need *not* decline. Indeed, the number of jobs may actually increase in spite of increased productivity.

Let's take an actual example. In 1954, there were about 61 million employed. They turned out a gross national product (GNP; standing for the total of goods and services) worth 363 billion dollars. Between 1954 and 1964 the GNP rose to 622 billion dollars. As a result, the GNP in 1964 involved the efforts of 70 million people, in spite of the fact that in 1954 each of the employed was responsible, on the average, for turning out a value of about $6000 a year, and in 1964 each of the employed turned out a value of about $9000 a year. (In 1965, the GNP rose to 675 billion dollars.)

If the gross national product rises as rapidly as productivity, then automation need not create unemployment: if everybody on a job turns out 4 per cent more next year and simultaneously 4 per cent is added to the GNP, then all is well. And something like that has been happening—our productivity is greater and we live better.

Actually, if we are not to be bogged down in unemployment, we must see to it that our economy grows even faster than our productivity. We must find added jobs for the young, for the addition to the labor force. To keep down or wipe out unemployment, the GNP must grow faster than our productivity: we must grow to provide new and added jobs as well as to take up the slack created by automation.

In fact, that is happening too, although the economy is still not growing fast enough. And that is why unemployment is an embarrassing 4 and 5 per cent in the 1960s.

Let's take a look at the facts on productivity and the growth in the economy:

In his Manpower Report of 1964, the Secretary of Labor laid out the mathematics of "full employment." The increase in productivity "of 2.75% between 1962 and 1963 in the total economy represented roughly the equivalent of almost 2 million jobs. That is, in 1963 the economy could have produced 1962's level of GNP of $555 billion with nearly 2 million fewer workers. In order merely to have kept employment from declining in the face of this productivity increase, it was necessary to raise GNP in 1963 by an amount equivalent to almost 2 million jobs."

To make room, moreover, for all the new additions to the labor force, it was necessary to expand the economy even further: by the equivalent of 3 million jobs.

Now what actually happened? The GNP rose by 30 billion dollars between 1962 and 1963. (About 8.5 billion dollars can be disregarded because it represented a price rise: higher prices for the same amount of goods and services.) Of the remaining 21.5 billion dollars, about 15 billion went toward maintaining the old level of employment. Between 6 billion and 7 billion dollars went for new jobs. As a result, "the net increase in employment was slightly short of the almost 1.1 million growth in the labor force."

In sum, growth in the economy saved the jobs of the 2 million who might otherwise have been displaced by improved productivity and created an added 1 million jobs over that. (The growth still was unsatisfactory since it did not create enough jobs to move the unemployed back to the work bench.)

The theory behind the mathematics of full employment maintains that, if the growth of the economy is great enough, the expansion can absorb those displaced by technology, plus new workers added to the work force, plus the presently unemployed. The key is the speed of growth.

Just how fast the American economy must grow to provide this opportunity for full employment is a matter of some debate: the experts wrestle with figures that run from 5 to 7 per cent. Thus one group of specialists concludes from an examination of "the American experience" with "the impact of technological change," that "a booming economy with a growth rate of five to seven percent would have facilitated and hastened the readjustment of . . . displaced workers. A normal economy with a growth rate of two and one half to three percent creates a problem of persistent and hard core unemployment by failing to provide opportunity for rapid readjustment to job displacement."

Economist Leon Keyserling does not feel that 5 to 7 per cent would do the job. He foresees (December 1964) the need for a growth rate of 8 to 9 per cent for a couple of years to absorb the present jobless as well as to create jobs for the new additions to the labor force and for those displaced by technology.

The different growth rates proposed by various economists depend, in part, on their definition of unemployment. The technical definition of "unemployed" refers to those who are looking for work and do not have jobs. But, in addition, there are those who do have jobs but are only at work half a week. Translating part-time unemployment into its full-time equivalent adds to the number of unemployed. Then there is the category of those who are out of work, who could work, who need work, but who are not looking for work. They have withdrawn from the labor force—either out of despair or out of apathy. In this last category is a large group of young people who, after dropping out of school or after a vain search for a job, give up the hunt for work to join their equally idle companions in the limbo of no school, no work. These are statistically not counted as unemployed. The addition of this group increases the count of the actually unemployed. The difference between this "true unemployment" and the formally reported unemployment is considerable. By one count, at a time when the formal figure stood at 5.3 per cent, the true figure was 8.5 per cent. To overcome this true and higher level of unemployment obviously requires a greater growth rate.

Whatever the differences may be in the computation of growth rate—4 per cent or 9—the theory is the same: a proper rate can offset the displacement of technology, can make jobs for the newcomers, and can absorb the jobless. This stands out in contrast to the forecast that, regardless of future demand, the jobless will mount and the work force will shrink almost to the vanishing point.

These contrary conclusions flow, in part, from contrary ways of reasoning. The optimists reason from what has been happening; the pessimists reason from what will be happening. The former note the growth of the labor force right along with the growth of the population and, by extending the graph of the past, conclude that in the future the ratio of labor force to population is likely to remain constant. Indeed, this "participation rate" (working-age population divided by labor force) is so constant that two recognized economists have concluded that it is one of the "great ratios of economics." Those who see a vanishing labor force note the *potential* of future technology and foresee a productivity rise that will far outstrip growth in the economy. The Research Institute of America, for instance, argues that "automation has just begun to bite in. Up to now, technicians have been in the process of development: today, the major systems are complete. From this point on, they'll be spreading. The effect will be revolutionary on everything from office and plant to society itself."

The great debate, then, is between those who measure what has been and those who forecast what can be. The former insist that the latter are permitting their imaginations to run away with them. The latter insist that the former just do not have imaginations.

The two schools have vastly different visions of the future world. Those who see the new technology merely as a variation on the old envision a future society not radically different from the present: about half the population of working age (above 14 and not institutionalized) at work, operating with improved and increased productivity, lifting the civilization to new high standards of consumption and living by its efforts. Those who see in the new technology something qualitatively as well as quantitatively different from the old envision new civilizations—cybercultures—in which only a small percentage of the population works and wherein the mores are readjusted to income without employment and leisure without guilt. The cybercivilization will have solved the problem of making and can turn to the problem of living.

A conclusion offered by Solomon Fabricant, director of the National Bureau of Economic Research, suggests that "there have been both a revolution and no revolution. There is always a question of degree. But to say simply that there has been a revolution in technology is not justified. Perhaps there will be a revolution, but we have not yet seen one, according to the records on productivity and all the other relevant statistical records of the economy as a whole."

Although the American labor movement has never made an official statement in regard to the great debate on the future economy, it has, in typical fashion, taken an unofficial stance that falls midway between the two views of automation's impact on our society. Labor shares the pessimistic view of those who see automation squeezing men out of employment. How could labor think otherwise? Union leaders see work lost and membership dwindling in one industry after another. They see the machine come in and the men go out. They see whole trades, and consequently whole unions, wiped out by the new technology. Extrapolating from their own experiences, they clearly see a world of jobless. Yet, simultaneously, the labor movement asserts that there is an answer to automation, an answer to be found through social action and reorganization. The response to the challenge of automation is to be found in skillful collective bargaining and in legislation. And, here, the unions tend to line up with the optimists who feel that automation need not mean mass unemployment so long as the economy as a whole expands.

Labor's attitude toward automation appears contradictory. The unions see technology foreboding a nation of unemployed; yet the same unions insist that proper social adjustment can guarantee full employment.

Thus Perry S. Heath, Grand Chief Engineer of the Brotherhood of Locomotive Engineers, cites with approval the conclusions of Norbert Wiener "who knew very well that yesterday's lessons count for no more than water under the bridge. Professor Wiener was the man who first called the attention of the world to the revolutionary implications of 'machines that think,' what we refer to today as automation. He knew—and tried to tell the policy makers of this country—that we are entering an age when machines would simply take over all the jobs performed by common and unskilled labor." Yet, in the same booklet, Heath proposes a program of social and legislative action for full employment: shorter work week, increased purchasing power, etc. As a trade-union leader, neither Heath nor anyone else in a similar position is likely to yield to the inevitability of extinction.

Walter Reuther, for instance, has testified before Congress again and again on the dangerous potential of advancing technology; and simultaneously, he has proposed programs to turn automation from a doom into a boom.

"The technological revolution is going to be accelerated and accelerated and accelerated," Reuther declared at the AFL-CIO 1963 Convention. "We will make in the next few years more technological progress than we made since the beginning of our republic . . . 41 million new jobs must be created in the next ten years just to be certain that unemployment does not become more severe." With this projection, Reuther joins those who see in technological advance a real job threat. But, undaunted by the challenge, Reuther went on to state that "the labor movement has made it clear that we are not opposed to scientific and technological progress. We want the best tools that science and technology can give us. We know that you can only have higher living standards, better housing and education, better medical care and an increasing measure of human pleasure, only as you create the wealth to make these things possible." Then, reasoning from that assumption, Reuther proposed a long-range program of economic growth and planning to "relate the tools of abundance to the basic needs of all the people" through trade-union and political action.

George Meany, in blunter fashion, lashed out at automation at the same convention:

"There is no longer any question in my mind as to the direction in which automation is going today. There is no element of bless-ing in it. It is rapidly becoming a real curse to this society. When you study what's happening, you realize that this is a real threat. This could bring us to a national catastrophe. Every big corpora-tion in America is in a mad race to produce more and more with less and less labor without any feeling as to what it may mean to the whole national economy.

"Competent technologists in this field think of the day a few years hence when all the production we need will be furnished by less than 25 percent of the manpower we have."

Having emphasized the negatives of automation, Meany then moved into the peroration of his keynote address with a positive program. "Our job is to wake up the nation, take every possible step to improve the vital purchasing power that means jobs, tax relief in the lower income brackets, public works of all kinds, a higher minimum wage for those covered and also to bring the millions uncovered under coverage, a 35 hour week or less now and later on, God knows only how short it will have to be."

The labor movement, by its very nature, is stung by automa-tion; labor's natural response is to continue doing what it has been doing but more so. Labor looks at the menacing machine monster and fights back—with shorter hours, higher wages, creat-ing jobs by doing the unfinished work of the nation.

While the labor movement as a whole works on its program to get maximum employment in America, the individual unions must wrestle with a much tougher, more immediate, more personal problem. They must face the threat of automation in a given industry, branch of an industry, or even in a given factory, and must deal with the threat here and now. To a union faced with the direct threat, generalizations about stepping up the growth rate of the economy, or increasing aggregate demand, or cutting taxes to unleash buying, or new credit devices for encouraging investment are of little consolation. To such a union, it is of no use to know that jobs lost here will be picked up there: the jobs lost here are the immediate problem for the representative of the people who live here. New jobs for other people elsewhere may produce a tranquilizing statistic for the sociologist. But those other jobs do not lessen the tragedy for the head of a family who has just lost—or feels that he has lost—his whole future.

The immediate challenges of automation in the union's jurisdiction are far more real to the given union than is the general problem of percentage of unemployed in the nation as a whole. The union must find immediate answers: to hold on to jobs, to cushion discharge, to speed transfer, to facilitate transition. When the head of a railroad union writes that "in the 17-year span from 1947 to 1964, railroad employment in the U.S. was just about sliced in half—from 1,350,000 to less than 700,000 workers," he is talking not only of declining membership but of a major calamity to hundreds of thousands who saw in railroading the way to a good life. To the railroader, there is little balm in the knowledge that, in the same years, the number of workers employed in truck and air transport may have picked up by 700,000 or more. The displaced worker turns to his union for protection and relief, and the unions have responded by trying to evolve and enact meaningful programs for those under the ax of automation.

This threat in the specific work area opens a second front for action by the labor movement. (The first front is the broad campaign for full employment in the nation.) This second front requires specific formulas that are applicable realistically in given industries or with given firms. In subsequent chapters, these arrangements to deal with technological displacement in given crafts and industries through collective bargaining are examined in greater detail.

Technological changes open up still a third front for the unions, again almost solely at the plant level: new systems of production create new kinds of jobs, wipe out old types of skills, reassign personnel, compel a reassessment and re-evaluation of old employees shifted to new posts, and thereby open a Pandora's box at the local bargaining level. How much shall a man be paid for the new job? Shall remuneration be determined by what the man earned formerly or by what he is doing now? To answer these and related questions, unions often find that they must start the bargaining process afresh. Old firms with old workers now pose the problems of newly organized firms. In the process, some workers may be upgraded; many feel downgraded. Sometimes earnings fall and quite often work load rises. Old contracts and established job descriptions and evaluations are suddenly anachronisms. Agreements written for old categories prove untrustworthy guides for newly created assignments. Rank-and-file discontent rises in the frustrations of shifting classifications. Willynilly, the unions are driven to fight a fresh war on this third front, measuring and weighing the worth of the new posts created by automation.

Technological changes also change the character and behavior of the labor movement. The push for a full-employment economy politicalizes unions. Formulas for contract safeguards against the hazards of automation require a revolution in labor-management agreements. Disturbances at the plant level as a result of job changes—new skills, new posts, new definitions, new evaluations, and new pay scales—create fresh tensions and frictions between membership and leadership, demand better lines of two-way communications, open new frontiers in contract interpretation and enforcement. For the unions, these new confrontations create a new character.

The greatest and most meaningful of labor's confrontations in the coming years, however, may very well be with the *new labor force.* The composition of the working population is changing. The percentage in blue collar and manufacture will be smaller and that in white collar and service larger. As industry relocates, there will be boom towns where there were once prairies and ghost towns where there were once thriving cities. The demand for skilled workers may outrun supply while the supply of unskilled may far outstrip the demand. Inventions and innovations will wipe out certain trades and skills, create new ones, and totally confuse jurisdictional lines. Some unions will appear, others disappear, others merge. Employment in the private sector may continue to shrink in relation to increasing employment in government. And as the labor force changes so will the composition and character of the labor movement.

For the American labor movement, in its response to technological change, the 1970s may be a reprise, with variations, on the 1930s. During the 1920s, the unions were shaken and shattered by changes in production systems. Master mechanics were being replaced by workers who performed simple operations on a division-of-work basis; autos were being assembled on a moving belt; ancient skills were declared obsolescent. Jobs were threatened en masse as the rate of productivity leaped forward by more than 4 per cent a year—a faster rate than that in the 1960s. Taking advantage of these developments, employers launched their anti-union, open-shop campaign (a direct ancestor of the right-to-work drive of the 1950s) to weaken and almost destroy the trade unions.

During the 1920s there developed a new work force: the unskilled and semiskilled in the mass-production industries where modern technics had made their greatest inroads. These millions were not schooled in unionism. They had none of the traditions and none of the bottleneck positions of the former skilled artisans, craftsmen, and skilled unionists. These new millions stood outside the labor movement through the 1920s and the early 1930s.

In the mid-thirties, a double revolution took place in the United States—a political revolution that expressed itself in the election of Franklin D. Roosevelt and an economic revolution that expressed itself in the Committee for Industrial Organization. The mass-production industries were organized. New union forms became popular. Political action was intensified. New parts of the country were organized. A new element came into the movement as Negroes, recent arrivals in the basic industries of the Midwest, joined their workmates in the union halls. Younger men rose to positions of leadership. Progressive-minded intellectuals were attracted to the vigor, romance, and opportunities of the new labor movement. Out of the difficulties and setbacks of the 1920s arose the opportunities and the advances of the 1930s.

In the 1960s something similar is happening. The nature of the economy is changing: from blue collar to white, from manufacturing to service, from low skill to high skill, from private industry to government, from North to South, from hand to brain. Unions in the established areas feel threatened; unions in the newly emerging areas are germinating. It may not be until the 1970s that the sprouts take root and not until the 1980s that they will flower. But if the past is a guide to the future, it is likely—virtually inevitable—that out of the changes in the economy, caused largely although not solely by changes in technology, there will arise a new labor movement, a creation of the past and a creator of its own future.

CHAPTER 5

Labor's Economic Program

In their retort to the challenge of automation, American trade unions are convinced that their self-interest coincides with the social weal. What is good for labor is good for America. The unions reach this conclusion by instinct and by reason. By instinct, unions reach out for higher wages and a shorter work week. By reason, they conclude that higher wages pave the way for more work and that a shorter work week makes way for more workers.

This basic labor philosophy is not startlingly new. Ever since the Lord cursed Adam by forcing him to live in the sweat of his brow, man has been seeking and finding ways to soften the eternal edict—to live better while sweating less. Labor's simple dedication to a richer life with less toil is just a natural continuation of this ancient desire. The idea is as old as it is inevitable.

Labor's case for the higher wage is a many-sided argument. Its ramifications are ethical as well as economic, tapping the Judeo-Christian tradition as well as the theories of Keynes and Keyserling. The major segments of the labor brief are divided into three main categories: impact on worker, on economy, on productivity.

Labor's primary appeal for a higher wage is an appeal to the humane. No one should be forced to work for starvation wages. And it is only by force—the force of circumstance—that people do work for such wages. In a democratic society pledged to the ideal of individual dignity such poverty appears a mockery.

This basic appeal is ethical, a plea to end man's inhumanity to man. It is strongest when advanced on behalf of the poorest. It is most effective when addressed to the rich—to an affluent society that feels a sense of guilt and can afford the costs of conscience.

Once unions get beyond this primary plea (although there are always depressed groups for whom this appeal is as valid today as it was a hundred years ago), labor advances a broad economic argument in which ever higher wages become the key to economic growth and full employment. In this argument, the worker appears not as a worker but as a consumer, part of the ever-expanding American market without which new economic growth is impossible and with which such growth is inevitable.

"In recent years," argues *Labor's Economic Review*, an official voice of the AFL-CIO, "about 63 to 65 percent of all goods and services produced by the American economy has been bought by consumers. An additional 4 to 5 percent of total national wealth has gone for home-building. Approximately 67 to 70 percent of the nation's total output, therefore, has been directly related to consumer buying power.

"The American consumer, then, is the American economy's major customer. The economic system rests to a great extent on the purchases made by families."

Of these families, whose purchase of daily bread, weekly hairdo, or annual car is the mainstay of the economy, the overwhelming majority depend on wages and salaries. Such earnings, in recent years, have accounted for about 70 per cent of total income, according to U.S. Commerce Department figures.

These households, with their massive buying, stimulate other sectors of the economy to buy. Family buying stirs business buying; family income stirs government buying. Buying undertaken by business (as distinguished from buying by individuals and families for personal consumption) constitutes about 10 per cent of the nation's total. Such buying by business—investment in buildings, machinery, raw material—is vigorous when the market outlook is good, when the public has the wherewithal and the will to spend. Hence big buying by families booms bigger buying by business.

Government activity in the economy also is dependent on the income of the wage-earning families. When the taxpayer is broke—and workers are at the base of the tax pyramid—governments find it hard to raise funds with which to make their purchases of goods and services, with which to buy asphalt or pay teachers.

Since direct private consumption plus business buying plus government purchases add up to almost 100 per cent of the American market (the small remaining portion is net foreign buying), labor argues persuasively that the worker's pay envelope contains the elixir of the American economy. A thick envelope makes for a sanguine market; a thin envelope means an anemic market.

This economic argument of labor—high wages mean high employment—takes on an ethical overtone when social conscience and policy are directed at raising the income of the poorest third or fifth of the nation. These mutually reinforcing arguments are strengthened by a third line of logic: higher wages make for greater productivity. ("Productivity" is used here, as in the previous chapter, to measure the output per man-hour.)

Labor's oldest argument along these lines goes back to the truism that a healthier and happier worker is a better worker. The toiler who is underfed, unrefreshed, and underpaid is an underachiever. Better pay makes for a better man able and willing to turn in a better day's work. High wages are also an incentive to management to maintain and improve the efficiency of the company's operations.

A more sophisticated argument rests on the parallel rise and fall of productivity and employment. In periods of recession, productivity increases slowly; in periods of prosperity, productivity rises rapidly. The reason appears to lie in the increased efficiency and output per worker when there is a steady and long flow of work. When things are slow—little or no work—the production line goes slack: idle overhead, slower work tempo, loss of momentum. When things pick up, man and machine begin to hum.

In the Annual Report of the Council of Economic Advisors to the President in 1964, it is noted that "during recessions, employment falls proportionately less than output." Put differently, if employment sags by 1 or 2 per cent, the gross national product sags by much more, indicating that when the market and employment go slack, productivity—output per man—also falls. The Council attributes this parallel behavior to lags in "employer reaction, uncertainty about the future, the need to retain the same supervisory and maintenance personnel over wide ranges of output, and hiring and firing costs. Employed manpower is not fully utilized, and the *level of output per man hour is depressed.*"

When the economy starts to bounce up again from its trough, an increasing portion of productive capacity is utilized, and productivity rises. The system becomes more efficient, with each man turning out more.

There is still another way in which higher wages—stepped-up purchasing power—increase productivity. By providing a mass market, high wages make possible our modern system of mass production, with all its economies and efficiencies. In the absence of a mass market, mass production is unlikely, if not impossible. Low-wage, low-income, limited-market countries do not develop systems of mass production. In such wage-laggard countries, production is on a "custom" basis, limited manufacture for a small clientele. If such a country does develop mass-production methods, it does so for a foreign market, since there are not enough customers at home.

In the United States, where the home-grown customer composes the base and bulk of the market, mass production was a natural and instinctive response to the challenge and opportunity. And with mass production, along with the prodding force of high wages on management, came research, invention, innovation, investment. All of these were costly but justified by the mass market: the child of the high wage.

The high wage not only encourages efficient production; it

forces efficiency, including technological revolutions. When wages are coolie-low, an employer lacks incentive to invest in labor-saving devices. The cost of labor is so low that he feels no compulsion to save labor. He can go along with old-fashioned methods, with inefficient systems, with waste and mismanagement. A multitude of sins are covered by cheap labor.

But when wages rise, management must begin to think about better ways to produce. It uses steam and electric power to replace bones and muscles; it puts production on a belt; it invents devices that will see and hear and respond; it automates, computerizes, and cybernates. High wages goad management into progress.

Samuel Gompers recognized many years ago that high wages are a spur to improved productivity. "Whenever men are cheap," he wrote, "no machinery is used in industry or any other way. It is only when men are dear, when wages are high, that machinery is brought in." When a coal operator was asked some years ago why he did not install props in a mine to ward off a disaster, he answered, "Wops are cheaper than props."

Higher wages need not mean higher production costs. If, indeed, the higher wage steps up productivity to compensate for increased hourly pay, the unit cost of production may even fall. According to labor's official argument, precisely such a drop in unit costs took place between 1959 and 1965, in spite of higher hourly pay. "Factory production in recent years," points out *Labor's Economic Review*, "increased faster than factory payrolls. Factory workers received wage increases, but productivity rose faster."

The September 1965 issue of the *Monthly Labor Review*, published by the U.S Department of Labor, states, "Unit labor costs for production workers, therefore, actually fell slightly throughout the last five years (1959–1964), at a rate of 0.2 per cent a year." This trend of declining unit labor costs for factory production and maintenance workers continued in 1965.

Labor's case rests on the triple argument that a higher wage raises the standard of living for the worker, employment for the economy, and productivity in a factory or industry. Ergo, higher wages are a central retort to automation.

The case for the shorter work week strongly resembles the argument for the higher hourly wage. Indeed, in one sense, the logic is identical, because a shorter work week is, among other things, an hourly wage increase.

When unions ask for a shorter work week—a reduction from forty hours to thirty-five, for instance—they do not mean, in modern times, that take-home pay is to be cut accordingly. They mean that the weekly pay is to be maintained, if not increased. Hence a reduction in hours must be accompanied by an increase in hourly pay.

To modern trade unionists, this goes without saying. But it was not always so. An early union agitator recalls his dismay when his advocacy of an eight-hour day instead of the prevailing sixteen was greeted with groans of objection by his overworked listeners. Later, one of the more sophisticated workers in the audience explained the reason for the groans. "Those workers are fools," he explained to the speaker. "They say that if they cannot make a living on sixteen hours of work how can they make a living working only eight hours. But I understand you. If we work only eight hours, I can then go out and get another job for the remaining eight hours."

The cry for shorter hours has always been a rallying point for unions, a great unifier. Workers of different callings cannot agree on a uniform wage, but they can agree on hours—that is, on a limit on hours.

Before the Civil War, the great push was for the ten-hour work day (seven days a week of course: "If you don't come in Sunday, don't come in Monday"). After the war, labor rallied around the demand for the eight-hour day. At the turn of the century, the drive was toward the six-day week. (Even Judge Elbert Gary, head of the U.S. Steel Corporation, proclaimed *ex cathedra:* "The commandment says, 'Six days shalt thou labor and do all thy work.' The reason it didn't say seven days is that the seventh day is a day of rest and that's enough.") In the 1920s, labor moved toward a second day of rest. (Now labor had to fight both Judge Gary and his interpretation of Scripture.) In 1940, the legal forty-hour week became one of the pillars of the New Deal. In the coming years, shorter hours will continue to be a great uniter of unions as labor pushes for thirty-five hours and the four-day work week.

As early as the 1820s, the function of the demand for shorter hours as a natural cement among unions became apparent. The earliest instance was in Philadelphia, where carpenters complained that the ills of long hours were both real and psychosomatic. "A man of common constitution," read their protest, "is unable to perform more than ten hours faithful labor in one day. . . . Men in the habit of labouring from sun until dark are generally subject to nervous and other complaints." The campaign of the carpenters became the rallying point for other unions. They set up a central body, the Mechanics' Union of Trade Associations, that in turn led to the formation of the Philadelphia Workingman's Party, the first labor party in the world.

In New York, in 1829, a similar political party was organized, with shorter hours as one of its major planks. In 1831, the New England Association of Farmers, Mechanics and Other Workmen called for a convention to "mature measures to concentrate the efforts of the laboring classes, to regulate the hours of labor, by one uniform standard." When the National Trades' Union—a federation of unions—was organized in 1834, it demanded a reduction in work hours. At its second convention (1835) it appealed specifically to Congress for a reduction of hours on public works, expressing the opinion that "ten hours a day is fully sufficient for any laboring man to work." At its third convention (1836) the federation reached out boldly to request "of the President of the United States his interference for the adoption of the [ten-hour] system." The plea was rewarded. President Martin Van Buren issued an executive order establishing the ten-hour day for mechanics and laborers on government works. The National Trades' Union had won its point, after which, assisted by the depression of 1837, it folded up.

In the 1840s the campaign for a shorter work day was renewed, with special emphasis on the dangers of long work hours for the women who were employed by the cotton textile industry in New England. In 1842, women workers of Fall River petitioned the Massachusetts legislature to limit work hours because "in many manufacturing establishments more hours of labor are required than can be made consistent with the bodily health and the proper intellectual and moral improvement and well being of adults." Out of these efforts arose the New England Working Men's Association, later known as the Labor Reform League.

In this early period of agitation for the ten-hour day, the argument revolved solely around the worker: his health, his moral and intellectual growth, his freedom. There was little or no appeal for shorter hours on the grounds that such a system would make for greater efficiency or for greater employment. Workers wanted the ten-hour day because a longer work day was intolerable. Thus, one woman worker, testifying before a Massachusetts legislative commission in 1845, pleaded for a ten-hour day for women workers "even if they had to take a wage cut."

The simple human appeal—the right to live in the image of God—has always been on the lips of workers fighting for shorter hours. In the 1880s, in the sweeping drive for the eight-hour day out of which was born the American Federation of Labor, the marchers sang:

> We want to feel the sunshine
> And we want to smell the flowers;
> We are sure that God has willed it
> And we mean to have eight hours—
>   Eight hours for work,
>   Eight hours for rest,
>   Eight hours for what we will.

By shorter hours, the worker is liberated from the machine: he takes his first step toward the democratization of leisure.

Some employers fought the sociomoral appeal with like weapons. The president of the Pettibone Mullikan Company prophesied that, under a five-day work week, workmen "would abuse the additional time; would waste it in unnecessary pleasures, if not in vicious habits; it would mean a waste of the workman's energy; encourage a disposition to loaf; create a desire for many things that would be not only unnecessary, but burdensome as to purchase and payment and involve men in debt. It would also create among their families a desire for luxuries and to use the additional holiday for display and injurious amusement."

The last portion of A. H. Mullikan's argument concerning the "desire for many things"—minus the pejorative adjectives—later became one of labor's major arguments in *favor* of the shorter work week. Leisure does create a desire for many things. Precisely these desires have brought whole industries into being. The American family, with a weekend on its hands, jumps into a car for a nearby beach, park, or countryside. The weekend habit is one of the pillars of the Saturday-Sunday economy of the nation: autos, gas, hot-dog stands, roadway restaurants, toll roads, freeways, guns, fishing gear, and boats. The apparel trades provide sports clothes, leisure wear, bathing suits, athletic costumes. The movies, television, radio, newspapers, books, bars, and ballet all vie for a portion of that free time. People work weekdays to live weekends. The shorter work week, as Mullikan anticipated, brought on a cultural change in the habits of America. Working people are free to develop new desires and, in the attempt to indulge these fresh interests, to get and spend money on new products and new services in a new way of life. No doubt, workers with leisure often get sucked into buying unnecessary goods, burdensome to pay for, just like their richer compatriots, who do the same on a larger scale. But what about the profits to the descendants of Mr. Mullikan and their fellow manufacturers from these unnecessary products and services for the pleasures of a nation with leisure?

Shorter hours, which create jobs in new work, also create jobs in old work. When hours shrink, the work force expands. Under shorter hours employers have one of two alternatives: they can start paying overtime at time and a half or they can employ additional workers at straight time. It is calculated that for every hour cut off the present normal work week, an additional 500,000 to 1 million workers would be needed to fill the gap. One hour less means half a million to a million jobs more.

In the 1920s, some employers moved voluntarily for a shorter work week because they were convinced that the abbreviated work day made for more efficient workers. Employees appeared to be healthier, happier, and—above all—more productive, when they worked at top speed and accuracy before weariness set in. It was Henry Ford who moved most dramatically toward the shorter day, perhaps inspired to do so by the fatigue factor that set in quickly with a man on the belt, drearily repeating the same deadly dull motion. Labor has added the argument of increased efficiency to its arsenal of weapons for the shorter hour cause.

The trade unions thus had three big guns in their war for the shorter work week: (1) the health of the worker; (2) increased efficiency; (3) full employment. The power of the first two of these arguments has dwindled somewhat over the years as the length of the work week has been reduced to a standard forty hours. The eight-hour day in a five-day week is no such threat to mental and physical well-being as was the twelve- or sixteen-hour day in a six- or seven-day week; the work day is no longer so wearying as to impair efficiency. The main argument now is economic: shorter hours for fuller employment.

Partly because two out of the three good reasons for a shorter work week have lost their force, the length of the work week has not been reduced appreciably since the mid-1930s. This is in sharp contrast with the experience of the three decades before 1930. In 1900, the average work week was sixty hours. Between 1900 and the mid-1930s, it was reduced by about five hours per decade. In the three decades since, the prevailing number of hours worked per week has remained unchanged.

In the near future, however, organized labor will renew its drive for a shorter work week. The renewed effort will stem in part from a push for full employment. The greater the leisure that automation makes possible, the greater will be labor's demand for its share of that leisure, primarily as a way of avoiding disemployment.

Some unions have already pointed the way. A work week of less than forty hours is already embodied in contracts in ladies' garments, rubber, construction, brewing, printing, and coal mining. Increasingly, a work week of less than forty hours is moving into the service trades. The inevitable result of the trend will be a major legislative campaign by labor for the thirty-five hour work week for the whole economy. And before the century ends, the emphasis is likely to shift from the number of hours per day to the number of days per week; namely, to the four-day work week with its longer weekend.

Such a campaign may very well gain added impetus from the fact that, in some industries, the introduction of automation may also reintroduce some of the now neglected reasons for cutting hours. Even a forty-hour work week may appear "inhuman" to workers who must speed up their movements or concentrate their attention to keep pace with faster-running mechanisms. Efficiency may be impaired, too, if a new intensity of demand per minute is applied to the nervous system of the worker. Increasingly, in such plants, where the screw has been tightened—demanding sharper attention and swifter movement—workers have been crying for more "allowance time," a longer "break" per hour. In some of the automated industries, the unions have been turning their backs on overtime, not because workers do not want the extra pay but because they feel that the extra time now takes too much out of them. Such unions now insist that overtime under these conditions deserves double-time pay. Hence, automation has spurred the drive for the shorter work week not only to hold on to or to add jobs but also to protect the physical and emotional health of the modern worker against the grueling demands of the automated pace setter.

In recent years, a new reason for the shorter work week has evolved: to give workers time to learn new skills. Automation, by wiping out some skills and creating others, has created a need for learning while earning. The worker must, if he is provident, acquire new skills while practicing old ones. To allow for such "schooling," unions have negotiated contracts to reduce work hours and to allot the "free time" for learning. This application of the shorter work week helps workers keep up with sudden and swift changes in the productive process.

Since 1938, the foundation on which American trade unions have been building their wage and hour programs is the Federal Fair Labor Standards Act. When it was first enacted, in 1938, some unions took a dim view of the act, fearful that workers who got 25 cents an hour through government edict would lean on Washington, D.C., rather than on their local union for their wages. The fear, a holdover from the Gompers attitude that social legislation is a poor substitute for union action, was rapidly dispelled, however, as a result of experiences after 1938. With the legal minimum as a base, the unions erected their wage pyramid. The higher the base, the taller the pyramid. In the subsequent years, it was the labor movement that made the big push to raise and reraise the legal minimum to 40 cents in 1940, to 75 cents in 1949, to $1.00 in 1955, to $1.25 in 1961, to $1.40 in 1967, and to $1.60 in 1968.

While the legal wage has been going up, the legal work week has been almost stationary. In 1938, the work week was set at forty-four hours, to become forty in 1940. The overtime rate was set at time and a half in 1938 and has not changed at all. By 1965, labor was demanding double time for overtime by law; and it was insisting on a thirty-five hour work week.

The greatest lag in up-dating the Fair Labor Standards Act has been in the area of "coverage." Not every employee in the country comes under the umbrella of the federal law.

Not everyone in the excluded categories earns less than the federal minimum. But in all the trades there are some and in some trades there are many. These are the millions of working poor, fully employed but living in poverty.

Extension of coverage would have a triple effect on the economy: (1) lift the lowest earners in the nation out of the poverty swamp; (2) stabilize the earnings of the better paid (including union members) by lessening the competitive gap between high- and low-wage units in the same trades; (3) stimulate growth in the total economy by pumping fresh blood into the most anemic sector of our nation's earners.

Although higher wages and shorter hours are traditionally labor's mainstay in the crusade for full employment, they are by no means the sole union instruments. Common variations on the theme of the shorter work *week* are the shorter work *year* and the shorter work *life*.

The shorter year is accomplished by more holidays and more vacations. This trend has been marked in recent years and is discussed around the bargaining table as one direct answer to disemployment through automation. In the 1930s, the paid holiday was an executive and white-collar privilege, uncommon among hourly employees. Indeed, this was one way to distinguish "salaries" from "wages." By the 1940s, the paid holiday began to find its way into union agreements. By 1950, the standard was six paid holidays a year. In the 1960s, it rose to seven and it is now moving to eight. By 1965, 90 per cent of the significant collective agreements contained paid holiday provisions. In communications and utilities, holidays may be nine or more. Where holidays fall on Saturdays or Sundays, it is not uncommon to have them observed on Friday or Monday, even if the community does not do so. In other instances, the Saturday or Sunday holiday is replaced by the day after or the day before a regular holiday, to stretch the pause. There are also "personal holidays" in honor of John Doe, Worker, as well as George Washington, President. Cumulatively, paid holidays presently average about a week and a half of work days.

The elongated vacation is gaining popularity to make way for more workers. The steel workers' thirteen-week vacation for certain employees is virtually a proletarian sabbatical. *The Wall Street Journal* reported in the spring of 1965 that "longer vacations forced more employers to hire extra help. Last year, Inland

Steel took on 1,300 men for summer maintenance work because of the drop in its regular labor force." The *Journal* also reported that "more companies now give three weeks off to 10-year employees than give two weeks, and 23% of the companies grant four weeks to 25-year employees, up from 14% only two years ago." A fully employed worker in 1965, as contrasted with a fully employed worker in 1900, enjoys a work year that is about 40 per cent shorter, thanks to a shorter work week, to more holidays, and to longer vacations.

The shorter work life is accomplished by encouraging workers to retire early and to enter late, by stretching the golden days of the senior citizen and the salad days of the student. Of the 1,040,000 Americans who chose to retire in 1964, 56 per cent were under 65. In 1960, the percentage was only 21, and in 1956, a mere 12. Early retirement has now become the norm.

The reasons for retirement before 65 lie in the constantly expanding structure of security for the elderly. Before social security, the average worker did not even think of retirement. After Federal Old Age and Survivors Insurance, the citizen over 65 thought about retirement if he had some savings and loving children. As unions set up pension funds to supplement federal payments, retirement at 65 became a real possibility.

Recent contract trends, however, have begun to place a real premium on *early* retirement. Under some of the older plans, the worker who retired early could do so only on a reduced pension. Under new contracts, the early retiree is rewarded by an increased pension. The 1964 auto contract, for instance, gives a hefty supplemental allowance to a man who retires between the ages of 55 and 65. This allowance is made because between the ages of 55 and 62 the retiree gets no federal benefit. Medicare, paid for out of social security funds, also speeds retirement. Many who wanted to retire in the past hesitated to do so for fear of medical expenses.

In some management circles, early retirement, despite the increased cost to the company, is viewed as a blessing. Companies have been complaining about "age-imbalance" in their work force, with seniority rules weighting the balance for the elderly. Management argues that this reduction in younger workers has impaired efficiency and slowed production. The investment in early retirement freshens the work force.

In ratifying an agreement with the Oil, Chemical and Atomic Workers Union, an official of Sinclair Oil stated, "This is one of those rare instances where both sides see eye-to-eye." The contract provided for full retirement pay at 62, whereas formerly the retiree lost 5 per cent for each year under 65. The company assumed an added cost but by encouraging early retirement it pepped up the work force.

In industries demanding endurance under trying physical conditions, early retirement pays for itself. Says an official of Unitcast Corporation, "We pour metal at 3,250 degrees. That's a hot, nasty job. We had an excess of older people who could only do light work under their doctor's orders but couldn't handle their regular jobs. We feel we'll increase our plant's efficiency by this plan."

Providing further impetus for early retirement are the preretirement training programs. Some workers do not retire because they do not know how to. They would not know what to do with themselves if they left the job; they have no other skills, no hobbies, interests, or companions. They fear—and quite properly— loss of *raison d'être* by loss of job. To counter this fear and to enrich retirement, unions and other agencies have moved to set up programs to prepare workers for nonwork. Although these programs in their initial purpose are directed at filling the vacuum of leisure, in the long run the spread of these new "prep schools" will undoubtedly increase early retirement.

While early retirement cuts down the percentage of people over 60 in the work force, extended education reduces the percentage of those below 25. To unions, there are several good reasons to push for longer schooling. Working people know that if their children are to find worthwhile jobs in the newly evolving economy they will need more formal education. The expansion of the school system will mean additional jobs: building schools, printing textbooks, training teachers. And the longer the young stay in school, the fewer young people will be crowding the labor market.

In plugging for more education, American unions are doing what comes naturally. In the 1820s, the workingmen's parties that mushroomed into being in Philadelphia, New York, Baltimore, and other early urban centers made free, universal public education a major demand. Education was to be the "open sesame." Education would mean better jobs at better pay. Education would mean background for wise voting and for holding public office. In sum, education would mean both industrial and political democracy.

The original labor push was for elementary schools. Then unions began to demand "higher education"—namely, secondary schools, with vocational and technical education as part of their training. Then unions associated themselves with the movement for land-grant colleges, to provide education at the college level for the children of working-class families, again with a focus on occupational skills.

In the many legislative battles of recent decades to get federal funds for education, for raising teacher salaries, for special attention to depressed areas, for integration of schools, for tuition-free universities, for government-financed scholarships and low-interest loans, the labor movement has been a major and sometimes the main lobbyist. Indicative of this intense traditional interest was the centennial conference organized by the AFL-CIO in collaboration with the Association of State Universities and Land-Grant Colleges in January 1962 in Washington, D.C.

The theme of the conference was equal opportunity for higher education. "What we ought to have in this country," said George Meany in a major address, "is a program that will finally eliminate financial barriers to higher education; a program that offers each student freedom to choose both his college and his course of study; a program for which ability is the only requirement." Such a program would, of course, flood existing overcrowded institutions with new students, requiring more classrooms, more dormitories, and more teachers.

Another indicator of union interest in higher education is the proliferation of union-financed scholarships for undergraduate and postgraduate study. More than 1000 scholarships were in existence by 1965. With each year, new scholarships are added.

The labor movement is concerned not only about the quantity but also about the quality of education. Here again, the unions continue an historic interest in vocational education. This special interest takes on poignant meaning in a rapidly changing economy where old jobs die and new jobs are born. "Our labor force cannot absorb all the people who—untrained—are available only for unskilled jobs," testified the AFL-CIO in 1962 to a House of Representatives Subcommittee on Vocational Education. "Opportunities for jobs are expanding in occupations that require more education and better training. In addition old skills often become obsolete and new skills must be acquired to keep a job."

In relating education to employment, the unions have been pointing up a sad irony of our economy: unfilled jobs and unemployed workers. Skilled work lacks callers and unskilled workers lack takers. In 1963, for instance, one-third of those chronically out of work had not gone beyond elementary school.

In short, the educational system is out of gear with the total economic machinery. The educational wheel is not big enough to develop the manpower potential nor is it geared for the kind of work that will become available in the coming world. There is not enough preparation for future jobs and too much preparation for nonexistent types of jobs. Labor proposes to redesign and enlarge the educational system for the manpower requirements of the cybernated society.

In advocating more and more appropriate education, the labor movement is reinforcing an existing trend in the nation. In 1940, less than 16 per cent of the youth between 18 and 21 were in college; by 1950, 30 per cent were; in 1960, 38 per cent; by 1970, half the youth of that age are expected to be in college. This trend will be further reinforced by the increase in postgraduate work.

This rise in the academic population, coupled with a rise in the apprentice population, can ease some of the crowding in the labor mart. But the trend must be accelerated to keep up with the population explosion and the expectations of the new economy.

While labor's proposals for earlier retirement from and later entry into the economy are intended, among other reasons, to cut down unemployment, the unions simultaneously push for more *work*. In doing so, labor turns to the unfinished business of America: housing, roads, hospitals, clinics, schools, libraries, the rebuilding of our metropolitan areas, urban mass transit, reforestation, river development, and training of doctors, nurses, paramedical workers, and teachers.

Consider the magnitude of the unfinished work in just one area: housing. By the year 2000, the population is expected to reach 340 million, a rise of 150 million over 1965. The pressure will be felt in the cities, since 80 per cent of that growth will take place in urban areas. To meet this need, about 2.5 million new housing units will have to be built each year—about 87.5 million units in the period from 1965 to 2000. Failing that, we are likely to enter the twenty-first century as one great slum. In the decade before 1965, new housing ran at about 1.5 million units or about 60 per cent of what is needed. At this rate, we will enter the year 2000 about 52.5 million units short. Our housing shortage, moreover, is a problem not only of the future but of the present. One-fifth of America lives in substandard housing. "Substandard" is a euphemism for subhuman.

The shortage pinches the poorest hardest. New housing is mainly for those with money. Those without money are sometimes pinched even harder by new housing that drives slum dwellers out into other already overcrowded slums. Too often, tearing down slums means tearing up people.

To meet the need, labor proposes a thirty- or forty-year development program. The strategy operates on many fronts. The measures proposed cover public housing for low-income families: special financing for middle-income families too poor to buy on the private market at going rates and too rich to be admitted to subsidized public housing; mortgage arrangements on cooperatives and privately financed rental units to make them available to modest-income earners; housing for the elderly; college housing; urban renewal; farm and rural housing.

Such a long-range housing program would have a dual purpose: homes and jobs. The National Association of Home Builders estimated in 1961 that 10,000 new homes represents roughly 20,000 man-years of employment. The ratio is two man-years to a house. Another million homes per annum would mean another 2 million at work. Construction also has a high multiplier effect on lumber, metals, paints, transportation. Where new projects arise there is a call for roads, sewers, schools, lighting, water. As new families move in, they purchase refrigerators, stoves, furniture, garden supplies, and other household wares.

Such a housing program is but one of the many "must" items on labor's agenda for America—an agenda with a half-century reach. There are, for example, rivers to be tamed and developed for flood control, navigation, electric power, and recreation.

A full-scale war on illness and ignorance in America requires the recruitment, training, and employment of vast civilian armies. We must call on the construction trades for hospitals, clinics, libraries, and schools. We must tap the intellectual potential of America with scholarships and better-paid internships; we need more teachers to turn out more teachers, more doctors, more nurses, more paramedical people. The need would extend to secretaries and clerical workers, as well as to sweepers, cleaners, and carriers.

The process of making America healthy, wealthy, and wise—as a civilization should be—would mean jobs for added millions for many years, automation or no automation.

Few Americans will argue against the desirability of these good works, often referred to as "public works." Yet whenever the nation gets around to doing these necessary jobs, we tend to awaken late. We depend on private enterprise to meet our national needs. We expect the profit motive to goad investors into meeting public demand. And we do not wish to discourage private initiative and investment by setting up government-financed or government-owned competition.

Yet, in the great areas of housing, urban redevelopment, health and education, valley development, care of the aged and infants, the profit motive may be inappropriate and inadequate, especially when these services are intended for the poor. What private entrepreneur would put his own money into a new school or library for the poor? There is no profit in such a venture. An entrepreneur might put money into a professional and technical school where tuitions yield a profit; or he might run a publishing house. But a business without profit is just bad business. Consequently, to meet some of our greatest social needs social investment is required. While such public funding may yield no direct gain to the investor, there is an inevitable social profit that more than justifies the outlay.

Consider education, for one example. The government obviously is not enriched directly and immediately by the tuition income from students, even when tuition is not free. But there are huge hidden profits. Putting up the school plant means work, fuller employment, a growth in the economy, and a gain in tax income. Turning out texts means work for authors, publishers, printers, paper and binding industries—still more employment and greater tax income. But the greatest national gain lies in the education of the otherwise uneducated. Illiteracy, incompetence, inadequate training in the needed skills are massive wastes of manpower. Idle people or people working at fractional capacity are a drag on the economy. They are not good earners or good taxpayers. They may fall out of work and become a burden on the tax rolls. They needlessly fill our jails, hospitals, and institutions. Their lack of education has a great social cost. The initial investment required to educate these uneducated may in the long run represent our most profitable move.

Opposition to social investment is a reflex for any taxpayer. What homeowner would not prefer to pay a few dollars less on the local school tax? Yet, suppose school taxes were eliminated entirely and our public schools were abolished, would the nation be richer or poorer? Or suppose that we agreed to put secondary and higher education on a privately financed basis, where would our economy stand today? In the final analysis, our educated population—our managerial genius, our inventiveness, our skilled workers—composes the broad firm base of our economy. To establish that base costs money. To widen that base will cost more money. But such costs are investments made by society in areas not profitable to private entrepreneurs but highly profitable to the society as a whole.

To fund the unfinished business of America, governments (federal or local) have two devices: to tax or to borrow. Both moves are politically unpopular. Nobody prefers to pay out more in taxes. And when the government goes into debt, there is the inevitable cry to balance the budget, which means either to raise taxes or to cut expenditures.

To meet this problem, the American labor movement has evolved a "fiscal policy" that is likely to govern its thinking for a long time. Although this policy did not begin as an economic doctrine, it has, by bits and pieces, become a sort of philosophy of public finance, much of it an updating and simplification of Keynesian economics. In this view, taxing and borrowing are not considered as "good" or "bad" per se. They are useful instruments in speeding economic growth and employment. "A rational fiscal policy" argues the *American Federationist,* official publication of the AFL-CIO, "would require concentrated attention on the state of affairs in the national economy rather than focusing solely on whether or not the books are in balance. Needs of the economy for maximum and balanced growth would come first."

Hence, continues the labor view, "the amount of deficit or surplus in federal fiscal operations should vary with the needs of the economy. When unemployment is high, the deficit should be great enough to add to sales, production and jobs as rapidly as possible in order to achieve maximum use of manpower, plants and machines. When the economy is operating at full blast and shortages threaten, the surplus should be great enough to restrain effective demand and reduce the shortages without throwing the economy into a recession."

On this basis, to unbalance the budget—to create a deficit—is not a frightening prospect. Indeed, it is even highly desirable and necessary to spur jobs. The purpose of fiscal policy is to create a *balance* in the economy, to raise demand when it is too low and to lower demand when it is too high. Instead of trying to balance the budget, labor proposes to budget the balance.

Once more, this proposal meets a reflex resistance. To the householder who must budget the family's expenditures to fit into the family's income, it runs counter to common sense to suggest that you can continuously spend more than you earn without someday going bankrupt. To the provident American, a mounting debt casts a dark shadow of fear.

Labor seeks to counter this fear of debt with three intertwined arguments: first, a nation is not a family with a fixed income; second, the national debt is money we owe to ourselves and not to others; third, when measured against the gross national product, the national debt has been shrinking rather than growing.

The American nation more closely resembles a huge corporation than a little family, in that indebtedness for investment by the nation, like the borrowings of a company, can create jobs to yield income. When a corporation borrows money from banks, insurance companies, and private investors to launch or expand its business, such indebtedness is unexceptionable, although the loans may total millions of dollars. The only concerns of the men running the corporation are whether they will have a lively market, can show profits, and can pay dividends. The borrowing is wealth-producing and the debt becomes dangerous only if the company is unable to sell its product. The same is true of our nation. If deficit spending boosts demand to create more buyers, more production, and more jobs, there is no need for fear. The economic growth resulting from such deficit financing means a broader and heavier tax base for the country. Without raising the tax rate, the government increases its income because there are more taxpayers and they are earning more. Hence, for the country, as for a business, borrowing can be the very cornerstone of growth.

A family with a more or less fixed income does not of course think in such terms. A family with an annual income of $10,000 would be in serious trouble if each year it kept spending more than it earned. In the family, borrowed money does not go into building a plant, creating jobs, or selling a product to increase the family income. Therefore, endless borrowing can lead to bankruptcy.

The government, however, unlike the family, does not owe money to an *outsider*. The people who compose the nation owe the money to themselves: the federal debt is owned by Americans. Interest paid on this debt goes to Americans who can use the added income for added spending. This in turn spurs economic growth and raises government income.

Finally, the constant growth of the economy, resulting from increased demand, shrinks the relative size of the federal debt. In 1946, the federal debt was 132.8 per cent of national production. By 1962, it was 55 per cent of the gross national product; and by 1965 only 48 per cent. The total debt rose, but as a percentage of the total product the debt fell.

The real meaning of this should be clear to the householder. A family with an income of $5000 a year is in trouble if it has a debt of $5000, especially if the money borrowed is doing nothing to increase the family income. But a family with an income of $50,000 a year can easily carry a debt of $5000, especially if the money is being put to use to give the family an income of $60,000 the next year.

This sophisticated view of public debt—increasingly acceptable and popular among the economists of the mid-twentieth century —is not labor's sole fiscal device. A tax cut for lower-income groups is one of the staples of the program. The theory is that such a cut would increase consumer demand among people who normally spend everything they make. Such a tax cut need not force a cut in federal expenditures. First, the income gap can be closed by other taxes hitting more favored earners. Second, the government can go ahead with expenditures even with a tax cut because government borrowing could spur total growth and thus prove to be a new source of income for the government.

From all the foregoing, it is evident that labor is presenting a comprehensive program for dealing with the problem of unemployment. From a daily reading of the press, the over-all plan is not quite so clear, since the headlines feature only the one or two issues that the unions are immediately plugging. Casual readers get the feeling that at one time labor's only suggestion is shorter hours; at another time, public works or accelerated public works; at still another time, a tax cut or deficit spending. In general, the unions are commonly believed to be primarily interested in higher wages. Actually, no one of these alone constitutes the labor program. Collectively these planks make the platform; plus additional proposals such as earlier retirement, longer schooling, greater training, foreign trade. And precisely because the program is many-sided and not likely to be embodied in any one piece of legislation, it may be expected that the unions will be working for this program for a long time to come.

In recent years, there have been stirrings in labor's ranks toward federal action to establish some sort of national agency to give coherence and direction to national economic policy, to stimulate and map democratic planning. At its 1963 convention, the AFL-CIO concluded that "experience has shown that we cannot rely upon the blind forces of the market place for full employment, full production and effective use of our resources to meet our most urgent national needs. Other advanced free and democratic industrial nations have found that they can achieve their economic and social objectives only through a rational national economic planning process involving the democratic participation of all segments of their populations together with government. We urge the creation in the United States of a National Planning Agency, which through similar democratic mechanisms will evaluate our resources and our needs and establish priorities in the application of resources to the meeting of needs."

Although this statement is the very first resolution listed in the printed booklet of policy positions taken by the AFL-CIO 1963 convention, the move for a national planning agency did not rate top priority on labor's legislative agenda. The coming decades, however, may cause labor to take this resolution more seriously, because of the impact of war and peace on the American economy.

In January 1966, President Johnson reported to Congress that "the rising defense needs of the Federal Government are an important new force in the economy." The war in Vietnam undoubtedly contributed to rising employment: men in uniform and workers in armament industries. Now the Administration began to talk of shortages and the danger of inflation.

From Washington came talk of converting wage "guidelines" into a wage pattern to check rising costs and prices. The guideline concept was first advanced under President Kennedy. The central idea was that wages should not go up faster than productivity, because if they did the result would be inflationary. Although this concept was advanced by the Kennedy Administration more as a theoretical footnote than as a federal edict, the unions expressed their disagreement almost from the very beginning.

The unions argued, first, that such a generalized guideline (set at 3.2 per cent) was not realistically applicable. In the aluminum industry, productivity might go up as much as 6 per cent. Should the workers still be limited to 3.2 per cent? In a certain small unit handicraft trade, productivity might not go up at all. Should these workers still get 3.2 per cent? In other words, how was it realistically possible to apply an average for the economy to every skill and industry?

Second, if there is to be a wage guideline, why not an effective price guideline that enforces price cuts in high-profit industries to offset price increases?

Third, if ceilings are to be slapped down on wages, why not slap them down on profits as well?

Fourth, the unions pointed to workers who, because of past neglect, were lagging far behind the rest of the country. Should a worker making only 60 cents an hour also be limited to an increase of 3.2 per cent per annum?

Fifth, the unions argued that an increased wage resulting in greater buying power was itself a factor in stepping up productivity.

Finally, they pointed out that the numerous exceptions admitted under the guidelines (many of them taking the preceding objections into account) were enough to make the whole idea meaningless.

So long as the guidelines were a conversation piece, union objection to the idea was mere talk. But as the war in Vietnam warmed up and the Administration became serious about the guidelines, the conversation became a bitter debate. Behind the guidelines was the threat of controls, backed up by new legislation and executive action.

Should the coming decades involve American armed forces more deeply in world struggles, wartime controls such as those in World War II may be imposed. It will then not be unlikely that the AFL-CIO will dust off its resolution on national planning. If wages are to be limited or frozen, then labor will demand the same sacrifice from other sectors, especially from management and investment. Should there be shortages in material and manpower, labor will ask for some over-all plan—with labor participation—for a rational allocation. If a lid were to be clamped on strikes, unions will seek procedures to ward off total prohibition and to speed nonstrike settlements. In sum, labor will resist a veto on its own freedom to bargain and, if it must make concessions because of world pressures and defense needs, will only do so in exchange for a voice in an over-all planning of the economy to democratize sacrifice.

Always lurking behind the threat of war is the threat of peace.

Should the world situation radically change (and it can), the nation would be faced with the challenge of reconversion from a military to a civilian economy. Whole industries and millions of jobs can disappear. Entire communities can become ghost towns. The dislocations will be far too great to be handled by unions over bargaining tables, and the reorganization of the economy far too complex to be left to individual entrepreneurs.

In this sort of radical reform of the economy, the 1963 resolution on national planning may once more become a most meaningful program for the labor movement. If and when this happens, the American unions will once again find themselves working for a major and radical change in the management of the American economy, not out of ideology but, as in the past, out of necessity.

CHAPTER 6

The Resurgence of Collective Bargaining

While labor's political program for full employment takes care of employment *generally*, it does not provide employment opportunities in specific trades and for individual workers. Total economic growth means more jobs, but it does not protect the job of the individual worker in any given trade or plant. To protect the specific job (rather than general employment) and to protect the individual's income (rather than the average income) becomes the responsibility of the union as a bargaining agent (rather than as a generalized social force). It is for this reason that technological change simultaneously enlarges labor action on two fronts: on the political front to promote fuller employment and on the bargaining front to promote individual protection of the union member.

The need for more effective industrial action to parallel greater political action is perfectly clear to the worker who experiences both. Consider the case of a railroad fireman who has just celebrated the victory of re-electing a national Administration whose policies have expanded the economy. The unemployment rate, according to the newspapers, has just dropped from 4.7 per cent to 4.5 per cent and appears to be continuing a downward trend. To the fireman this is a cause for rejoicing; he is naturally disturbed by unemployment and he worked to elect an administration that would stimulate fuller employment. His joy, however, is somewhat marred by the fact that he is about to lose his job, forever. His craft is being wiped out by the Diesel engine. Because this worker is fifty-two years old he sees hardship ahead: learning a new craft, landing a job at his age, paying his mortgage, and sending two kids through college. He wants job security—the number one reason why he has been paying dues to his union. And so he resolves to go down to his union office to find out what they are going to do to protect him against firing.

Or take the case of a girl who has been employed assembling transformer parts in an electronics firm. She, too, is happy with the election. But she, too, is worried about her fate in this full-employment economy. She is not about to be fired, but she is about to be "transformed" as a result of a big reorganization in the plant. Management has decided to turn out the same product in a different way. The girl's job has been automated out and other jobs have been automated in, and she does not know what her new job will be, how she will learn it, what her earnings are likely to be, and what her standing will be alongside former peers. To speak her piece and to restore her peace of mind, she goes to the union.

Because it is a union's traditional duty to protect the job and to protect the worker's standing on a job, technological changes in the coming decades will vastly widen the scope of collective bargaining. The more rapid and drastic the changes, the more comprehensive the areas of bargaining. Certain labor-management relations that have become as stylized as a minuet will be thrown into wild disorder. To recompose a *modus vivendi,* unions will demand a voice in areas traditionally marked as management prerogatives—such as introduction of new techniques, job description and evaluation, hiring and firing, plant movement, in-training and upgrading, separation and severance procedures, relocation allowances. To the present lengthy agenda of items covered by negotiations there will be added items arising from the new modes of operation.

As management seizes upon the momentary disarrangement brought on by new processes to redefine jobs "scientifically" and to reset wage rates "objectively," unions will simultaneously move in with their counterstandards to prove that "scientific objectivity" is often just a euphemism for "profiteering subjectivity." Each new job will become a battleground; each new rate will become a battle; and each new reorganization of the production process will become a war.

The coming years will see a vigorous resurgence of collective bargaining in major industries in which, in recent years, negotiations appeared to be a ritual. The value of certain jobs will have to be defined. Rates will have to be set anew with one eye on the task and the other on the jobholder. A refined system of firings and delayed firings, of hirings and belated hirings, will have to be negotiated. In the process, the men around the bargaining table will have to do some fresh thinking, thereby making what might have looked like the end of collective bargaining actually its beginning in the era of rapidly revising technology.

Item One on the new agenda will be an old question: "Shall the complex of problems arising from the introduction of new techniques be a matter for bargaining or shall this be a management prerogative?"

In recent years, labor-management contracts recognize a bilateral interest in automation. For instance, in an agreement between the International Union of Electrical, Radio and Machine Workers and the Emerson Radio Corporation, there is explicit recognition that the entire subject of automation is an appropriate matter for *joint* concern. "The parties mutually express their interest and concern about the impact on manpower and conditions of employment, resulting from technological improvements and automation. The parties desire to utilize to the best advantage of the company and the employees scientific improvements. The Employer and the Union, therefore, shall establish a committee known as the Committee on Automation . . . a) to study the effect of such changes on the utilization of manpower; b) to study the data on technological changes as they occur and the effect on manpower requirements; c) to make such recommendations as are agreed upon to extend the benefits of automation to Employer and Employee." Other contracts, to be discussed later, are even more specific, making concrete and binding proposals on how to handle automation problems.

Many generations before there were such *formal* approaches to technological problems, however, organizations of artisans were laying down their work rules to protect their jobs. By the middle of the nineteenth century, printers insisted (1) that the number of copies run off one set of type be limited in number; and (2) that the type be redistributed one-by-one and by hand. Without a committee on automation, the old guilds were protecting their men against the machines.

In the twentieth century, the same craftsmen instinctively moved to protect their jobs against the precast mat that made their skill as linotypists obsolete for certain newspaper advertisements. They insisted on setting the type and being paid for it, even if the type was then discarded. In trade parlance, this is "bogus type."

It is customary to denounce such practices as "featherbedding." Featherbedding—payment for nonwork or needless work—is assumed to be both inefficient and immoral, and simple proof that the practice exists is considered sufficient cause for abolishing it.

As far back as 1869, John Stuart Mill assailed the immorality of what we now call featherbedding: "All restrictions on the employment of machinery or on arrangements for economizing labor deserve moral censure. Some of the unionist regulations go even further than to prohibit improvement; they are contrived for the express purpose of making work inefficient; they positively prohibit the workman from working hard and well, in order that it may be necessary to employ a greater number. . . . It is palpably for the good of society that its means of production, that the efficacy of its industry, should be as great as possible, and it cannot be necessary to an equitable division of the produce to make the efficacy less."

The case against featherbedding is obvious. Why do things inefficiently when they can be done efficiently? Why use two men where one man will do? For society as a whole it is patently wasteful to the point of being sinful to pay people for nonwork or make work. Yet before any one group in American society is condemned for such wasteful practices, it might be well to note the universality of the practice—not to excuse it but to understand it.

Consider, for a first instance, American governmental policy vis-à-vis the farmer. In certain instances, Uncle Sam pays the farmer *not* to produce. Indeed, if that farmer does produce, he may be penalized. If he does not produce, he is rewarded out of the public coffers and rewarded in almost direct ratio to his nonwork. This practice is not called "featherbedding"; it is called support or price stabilization. The theory behind it is simple: if every American farmer were allowed to produce at top speed and at full acreage, the supply would be so huge as to make crops almost worthless on the market; as a result, farmers would go bankrupt and the economy would be ruined. So we pay farmers to hold back production—to "featherbed" on the farm.

Consider, for another case, the "production" policy of large companies, especially when they are, singly or in combination, in near monopoly position. It is common for such huge operations to make a careful survey of the market. After measuring demand, they decide whether they will run their plant at 100 per cent of capacity or at 50 per cent or not at all. They make the decision not in terms of social need, but in terms of optimum profit, although to limit production may injure the total society, causing employees to be without work, great plants to be idle, suppliers to go without sales, and, above all, the consumer to pay more for the product.

Companies do not consider such action as immoral or inefficient. To withhold or limit output is considered prudent, proper, and efficient. Indeed, to do otherwise—to run the company at full steam regardless of demand—would be considered inefficient and downright stupid, if not suicidal. Yet, stripped of euphemisms, the company that limits its plant and product to maximize return is doing exactly the same thing as the worker who is withholding top output in order to maximize *his* return. In the case of business, this is called farsightedness; in the case of labor, it is called featherbedding.

Or, to add an example of another type which has the same ultimate effect, consider the case of an automobile manufacturer who plans obsolescence in his cars. He puts good brains to work to make certain that something breaks down at 40,000 or 60,000 miles. He turns out new styles every year to make the old car aesthetically and socially obsolete, even if it is not mechanically so. He plans to turn out a product far inferior to what he can turn out for the same or even less money in order to maximize his own return. He may not be holding back on the quantity of his output, but he plans to downgrade quality to get optimum profit. His planned obsolescence is his special form of featherbedding.

In the same genre as planned obsolescence is the withholding of certain discoveries and inventions from the market. What maker of razor blades, left to his own devices, wants to turn out a blade that will never wear out? Or what hosiery maker will turn out an everlasting pair of hose? To protect themselves against such misfortunes, great and respected companies have for years bought up discoveries and inventions in order to keep them off the market. They search high and low for scientific progress—to buy it and to bury it. This is their special form of featherbedding.

These are all forms of waste. And to the extent that waste is immoral in a culture raised on the maxim "Waste not, want not," these practices are immoral. Yet they are widely and deeply rooted in an economy where individuals as diverse as farmer, steel producer, automobile manufacturer, and worker fear that without such waste they would indeed be in want. The motive is the same in all cases: to get optimum return on output.

Confronted by a technological change that will do him out of a job or curtail his earnings, the instinctive reaction of a worker is to say no. And if the change is inevitable, the worker will seek work rules for maximum self-protection. Thus was it in the time of John Stuart Mill and thus it is in the era of the electron. And to ask the worker to accept unemployment or a cut in income as his personal contribution to social progress is about as effective as to ask all farmers to produce full crop on full acreage for the open market, or to ask automobile manufacturers to make cars to last forever, or to ask steel plants to run at 100 per cent of capacity regardless of demand.

If technological change brings on social progress, the individual worker sees no reason why society, the ultimate beneficiary, should not protect the worker against injury. The individual worker sees no reason why he should be singled out to become *the* victim of progress. Hence he demands relief from society, whether "society" be represented by his employer, the government, the union, or a combination of these. And until such relief is forthcoming, he will use his organized strength to block that "progress."

This fact of life, which is actually nothing more than the law of self-preservation applied to the job, is a central bit of wisdom for any trade-union leader. He knows that technological change threatening jobs in a given spot in his trades poses a tough problem. He is confronted with a nearly impossible situation if he must ask his members to ratify a contract that will leave them jobless. And the more democratically run the union is, the more difficult the effort. No matter how statesmanlike the union leader, he is not likely to recommend self-extinction to his members and, if he did, the result would probably be his self-extinction instead.

While the member expresses his opposition to the menacing machine quite directly, the leadership is compelled to find a rationale. The more exposed the union is to public opinion, the more acceptable must be the rationale. Union leaders will, then, explain that new devices are dangerous to the worker's health, that they turn out shoddy results, that they are being used solely to break the union or to reduce income. In many instances, these arguments are true; in others, they are not.

When a union spokesman runs out of sound arguments he may simply resort to sound, to a loud noise. He knows the value of a raucous shout. He knows from experience that people who do not complain are the forgotten people. To be remembered, one must make a tumult. As a result of the shouting, somebody will be

awakened to do something—maybe the company or the community or the federal government. "Society"—the great beneficiary
of technological advance—will be under pressure to act, to oil the
wheel which squeaks. The union spokesman may know that his
noise sounds like nonsense, that his obstinacy is an irrational objection to rational progress, but he also knows, or hopes, that his
stubborn opposition will compel a rational society to find a way
to ration the benefits of science to include the affected worker.

Opposition to new techniques and protection against their impact are a kind of policy, but at best a negative policy that in the
long run can only delay the march of the machines or cushion the
shock of technological change-over. A positive policy makes the
union a party to the change. And it is toward this kind of positive
policy that we may expect the American labor movement to be
moving in the coming decades. Negotiation of the *terms of the
change-over* is the next new frontier in collective bargaining.

The first step in the process of change-over bargaining is open
recognition by management that the union is entitled to a voice in
the handling of innovations.

Thus, a clause in a contract between the International Brotherhood of Electrical Workers and Niagara Mohawk Company
states simply that "when a decision is readied by the management
to install electronic data processing equipment, the Brotherhood
will be informed of the decision and any changes that affect the
members of the Brotherhood shall be negotiated." A clause in a
contract between the Brotherhood of Maintenance and Way
Employees and the railroads calls for negotiations "minimizing
adverse effects upon the employees involved." A contract between the Textile Workers Union of America and Berkshire
Hathaway Inc. calls for two weeks' notice between changes,
followed by a trial period, followed by the right of the union to
submit grievances that, in the event management and union can
not agree, will go to arbitration.

Whether a union is usurping management prerogatives when it
insists on bargaining over technological displacement is a question that came before the U.S. Supreme Court in 1960. In a case

involving railroad telegraphers, the Court held that "in the collective bargaining world of today, there is nothing strange about agreements that affect the permanency of employment." The Court specifically rejected an opinion of the Court of Appeals that a union's efforts to negotiate about job security for its members "represents an attempt to usurp legitimate managerial prerogatives in the exercise of business judgment with respect to the most economical and efficient conduct of its operation."

Where unions are weak, management specifically reserves to itself all rights to make changes. The only concession to the union may be a few days' or weeks' notice to give workers a chance to hunt for jobs. Where unions are strong, the contract makes the entire question of new devices and job changes a subject of negotiation and arbitration.

The key question is always the same: how to hold on to the job and to the income during and after the change-over? The broad formula is "attrition." This is a commitment by the company that nobody will be fired as a result of the change, but when a worker leaves, retires, or dies, he need not be replaced; the post goes out with the worker. Hence, although no worker is discharged immediately, the number of jobs in the plant may ultimately shrink.

The policy of attrition means that companies will often be carrying on their payrolls workers who no longer have any real function. This is, of course, an extra cost to management that may well be worthwhile if it smoothes the way for the introduction of new technologies that will cut over-all production expenses. The added pay of the supernumeraries is just so much added cost for the new process.

A rationale behind the attrition principle was outlined by the emergency board appointed by President Johnson to look into work rules on railroads then in dispute with six shop craft unions. "Job protection," they reasoned, "is favored generally by public policy. Public opinion is sensitive to the need for gearing the pace of disemployment stemming from automation and generally rising managerial efficiencies to the rate of growth of the economy as a whole. In recent years, the former outstripped the latter and public policy has increasingly favored arrangements to cushion the impact. The results can be seen in the growing number of stabilization, technological displacement and job protection agreements in outside industry." In 1964, the Council of Economic Advisers referred specifically to the attrition concept as a major device for dealing with technological displacement. "Human adjustment problems are minimized," the Council declared, "when needed workforce reductions can be accomplished by normal attrition and reassignment."

A highly publicized plan to induce workers to go along with technological change is that worked out for the Kaiser Steel Corporation in its Fontana Plant. The basic idea is to share the gains of increased productivity with the workers. Coupled with this is a measure of protection against unemployment by the creation of a plant-wide employment reserve. Employees who choose to join the reserve plan are guaranteed at least the average number of hours worked that week in the plant or forty hours, whichever is less. Because the specific formulas devised to measure input and output and to apportion the gains of automation are drawn especially to meet the specifications of this plant and industry, the experience may not be transferable. But the general idea of a joint approach that will allay the employee's fear of being fired and provide a positive incentive to go along with change is applicable elsewhere.

Another approach to the change-over was worked out by the International Longshoremen and Warehousemen's Union with the Pacific Maritime Association. For many years, the union had insisted that the longshoremen had to remove cargo from the pallet and place it on the dock before teamsters could load cargo on to trucks. Another rule limited the pallet load to 2100 pounds. Still another rule called for gangs of eight, with four working while four were resting. These rules were running up the costs of shipping to the point where it was cheaper to ship by truck and rail than by water. Both longshoremen and their employers were suffering as a result.

To meet the problem, union and association negotiated an

agreement in which the former withdrew all opposition to mechanized operations on the docks. The four-on, four-off practice was dropped. Load limit was maintained, for safety reasons, but could be changed under new circumstances. The employers, on their side, agreed to the establishment of a fund to which they were to contribute 5 million dollars a year. Longshoremen were guaranteed a minimum number of hours of work per week. The rest of the fund—after payment for guaranteed hours—was to be used for retirement benefits or to encourage early retirement. The employers, in this case, were prepared to pay a premium for the right to introduce mechanized loading and unloading and to eliminate certain wasteful work practices. The premium went to protect workers and to modernize the docks. The extra investment by the companies proved profitable all around.

In writing a contract with an attrition clause, it is not uncommon to set a limit on *rate of attrition*. Thus, a contract of the Railroad Telegraphers with the Southern Pacific places a 2-per-cent limit on the number of reductions in the work force that can take place annually by attrition. The contract of this type with the broadest impact was one signed in 1965 between an employee group and railroads to cover some 300,000 workers. It was agreed that the total number of jobs cut out by attrition in any one year should not exceed 6 per cent of the force. Such clauses put a brake on attrition.

When management undertakes certain special obligations, under contract, to cover change-overs in the process of production (or sometimes in the location of plants), a variety of special clauses covering the affected employees have to be worked out. Some examples of these specific problems and responses will illustrate the breadth and complexity of such bargaining areas.

When jobs are abolished and new jobs created, what employees if any, shall be transferred to the new positions? "The Company shall fully consult with the Union respecting any transfers made necessary by reason of technological improvement . . . and shall exert every possible effort to effect such transfers with a minimum of detriment to employees," reads the contract of the

Transport Workers' Union with the Brooklyn Union Gas Company. Without spelling out the details, transfer is made a subject of joint discussion and decision.

Seniority is invoked in a contract between the United Automobile Workers and General Motors to determine who shall be transferred, and seniority is applied on a plant-wide rather than on a department-wide basis. "When changes in methods, products, or policies would otherwise require the permanent laying off of employees, the seniority of the displaced employees shall become plant-wide and they shall be transferred out of the group in line with their seniority to work they are capable of doing, as comparable to the work they have been doing as may be available, at the rate for the job to which they have been transferred."

A contract of the Utility Workers Union with the Cleveland Electric Illuminating Company states bluntly that when an employee of ten or more years of continuous service finds himself and his function surplus as a result of "automation," he shall nevertheless "receive no reduction" in his hourly rate. And in addition, such a worker will be entitled to "one half of future increases." In this, as in many other union contracts, seniority becomes a bulwark against discharge resulting from automation.

In a contract of the International Brotherhood of Electrical Workers with the Pennsylvania Electric Company, "no regular employee with five or more years of continuous service shall be laid off because of lack of work." This is a real job guarantee. Should the job be wiped out, the affected worker will be offered another job with the company "at no reduction in his wage rate" —that is, his personal wage rate. If the worker accepts the offer, he must be given the job, even if this means taking it away from another worker with less than five years of continuous service.

While an arsenal of seniority clauses serves to save the job for the worker with maximum continuous service, further terms have to be worked out to arrange for the training or retraining of an employee when he is shifted from one job to another. Merely to say that a worker, because of his seniority, shall have the first crack at a job, even if it means bumping another worker, does not equip the senior man with the needed skill for the new assignment.

To meet this problem head on, the International Brotherhood of Electrical Workers in their contract with International Good Music, Inc., set up a "Re-Education Fund," whose function it is to "re-educate eligible employees displaced as a result of automation equipment and program services made and sold by the company."

In a contract with the Corn Products Refining Company, the Oil, Chemical and Atomic Workers spell out the process of retraining in considerable detail. The proviso covers "employees . . . displaced from their jobs due to technological improvements or automation." To be eligible for this retraining, employees must have three years of continuous service in the plant. While in retraining, such employees "shall have their base rates maintained for a period not to exceed one year." To determine what employees are eligible for retraining, the company may run tests on applicants. A score of 70 out of 100 points shall be considered as passing. The union may, upon request, review these tests, presumably to check on their fairness. The union may also "be a party to the administration of the testing program."

In clauses such as these, the union becomes a party to selection of trainees, to the testing process, to a determination of the "passing grade." Other clauses in other contracts deal with such matters as the length of the training period, amount of payment during schooling, adjustment of training length to years of work.

A whole family of clauses relates to plant location. In some cases, the company has no responsibility to offer jobs in the new location; in other cases, the company is bound to extend job opportunities in the new location to its former workers. There may be clauses stipulating how the job offer shall be made, limiting the obligation on a mileage basis, or holding the employer responsible for the expenses of relocation, with a listing of reimbursable expenditures.

Another family of clauses relates to severance pay arising either from the discharge of the individual worker or from the closing of a plant. Some contracts call for a lump-sum payment, usually determined by length of employment. Other contracts call for a lump sum plus weekly or monthly payments over a stipulated period of time. Sometimes these periodic payments are limited to a certain number of weeks of unemployment after severance, generally accompanied by the designation of a maximum period. Closely related to this latter form of severance pay is the provision for supplementary unemployment benefits (SUB), a system of payments added to the regular state-federal system of unemployment compensation.

Technological changes daily provoke a proliferation of new, ingenious, and often unpredictable ideas to provide by contract for continued employment or for transitional assistance to affected workers: to keep the worker on the job, move him over to another job, or, *in extremis,* to help him with some cash while he is trying to find another job.

There is a second major front, however, along which unions must move as a result of changes in business systems. (The term "business systems" is more useful than such a phrase as "productive process," because technological changes are not and in the future will be even less limited to manufacture or the turning out of a commodity. New devices invade retail establishments, offices, government, executive suites, stock and inventory management, etc.) This second front deals less with preserving employment or easing the shock of unemployment than with the terms of continued employment under changed conditions. How much shall the employee earn in a traditional job when the nature of that job changes as a result of some technical innovation? And how much shall a worker earn on newly invented jobs for which there is no traditional scale?

Where a worker is accustomed to a certain level of earnings, the trend is to preserve these earnings. A typical clause calls for "displacement allowance." As spelled out in a contract of the Brotherhood of Railway and Steamship Clerks, this proviso calls for monthly extra compensation to make up the difference between current earnings and average earnings prior to displacement, for a worker transferred from one post to another.

Similar safeguards are provided for workers who, though they remain in the same post, must work under changed conditions of operation. To protect such a worker against reduced earnings, the furniture workers wrote a contract stipulating that the "rate for such changed or modified job shall be adjusted so that the earnings of the employees involved shall not be reduced." Likewise, in a rubber workers' contract with Goodyear, the "piecework price of an operation [is] increased to the extent necessary to prevent loss in the normal piecework earnings as the result of imposing a machine, specification or cycle limitation on an operation."

In seeking such clauses, the union has several motives. First, the worker should not be victimized by technical progress. If the new device promises to promote business and profits, the older worker should be entitled to a portion of that progress. If his income cannot be increased, as it is by the Kaiser Steel Corporation formula, something should be done to see that it is not decreased. Second, the worker, as an individual, has a certain status in shop and community—economic and social—and that status is to be protected. In the neighborhood, he perhaps has mortgage payments to meet, a car to keep up, a child in college, an insurance policy to maintain. In the shop, he has a known rank in the pecking order of the workplace. Both are endangered by a wage reduction. His whole manhood is in the scale. Third, the moral and psychological resistance of the average worker to surrendering his status for some boss-enriching bit of machinery makes a loud rumble in the union hall. And the union leader knows it.

Employers are not altogether opposed to these union demands. In the first place, employers do not want their workers to think increasingly of technical change as the enemy. If each change were to bring about a wage reduction, employees would think of all machines as devices to cut wages and every innovation would be fought, no matter the toll. Second, a wise employer knows that there is no wisdom in multiplying the number of unhappy employees. And nothing makes a worker so uncooperative and rebellious as a downgrading in earnings and standing. Hence, the expanding trend toward clauses that protect the worker's status as well as his job during technical change-over.

Technological change compels unions to find ways to protect the job and income of the old employee caught in the change-over. The same technical changes, however, also force unions into an even broader arena of collective bargaining: the rate of pay for all the new workers—ultimately for all the workers—in the new business system.

In the normal process of setting wages for certain crafts, skills, trades, a great role is played by tradition. Indeed, tradition and scarcity may be the two greatest determinants. Certain craftsmen are very well paid only because they always were and because they have learned the ungentle art of making themselves scarce. Sometimes, of course, they are scarce because their skill requires many years of training and experience. But in other instances, organizational and institutional devices promote such scarcity. Yet even this fails to explain the choice position of certain craftsmen whose position seems like inherited wealth, like a title in the landed aristocracy.

Technological change in a shop is like a revolution. It wipes out old orders. It creates new professions. It weakens and almost destroys tradition as a major determinant of wage rates. And in this new setting, both unions and management are hard put to find rational ground for new wages and salaries. Under the old order, wage patterns were set by the past, with varying crafts continuing a relatively orderly procession. Under the new order, who shall say how much a job is worth?

The generalized gauge used traditionally by unions is embodied in the slogan, "A fair day's pay for a fair day's work." Once labor and management can agree on the meaning of "fair," the bargain is concluded. But what is "fair?"

In recent years there have been many attempts to arrive at an objective measurement of fairness. Jobs in general are broken down into genus and differentia. The genus is the classification of a worker by his basic skill: pattern maker, tool-and-die maker, operating engineer, cutter, assembly-line operative, linotypist, oiler. The differentia is the rate of pay for the *individual* worker in his craft or skill: Is he fast? Is he accurate? Is he experienced?

Because various systems have been elaborated to arrive at a scientific determination of job classification and individual performance, a belief has grown up that calculating machines can replace collective bargaining. If we can feed a man's classification into a computer and follow it up with data on his individual performance, the machine should be able to come up with an answer to make traditional wage and salary haggling obsolete. The very multiplicity of the systems, however, casts some doubt on the scientific objectivity of all of them. In addition, some systems quarrel with others. In general, the outcome—the final determination of wage rate—depends on what system is used and who is using it.

What has been happening, in effect, as companies have made management engineers a staple of their staffs and unions have come to do the same, is that "job evaluation," "time and motion" study, "predetermined times" measures, and other "systems" have become weapons in the struggle over rates. Engineers use the jargon of the trade to challenge one another's theoretical systems and to challenge the use of any given system. The haggling over rates is not ended by the "scientific systems"; the weapons are changed. Bargaining finds a new language.

Dr. Pearce Davis of Illinois Institute of Technology set forth the subjective nature of these allegedly objective measures in an opinion as arbitrator in a case between Magnavox and the Industrial Union of Electrical Workers. "There is no purely scientific system of setting production standards." he said. "All who are competent and conversant with this field recognize this fact. Such industrial engineering procedures as MTM (Methods-Time-Measurement) are not pure science; they are at best 'scientific art.' The exercise of human judgment in all methods of standards setting is inevitable and inherent. *Nor is it ever likely to be otherwise* because of the nature of the procedures themselves. In addition to the continuing presence of human judgment, there is always the further problem of the degree of variation in the exercise of human judgment. This degree of variation depends fundamentally upon one's philosophy of life, on one's conscious or unconscious evaluation of the goals of workers versus the goals of management, on the individual's level of impartiality, and upon numerous other similar conditioning factors."

While the unscientific character of the scientific systems for wage determination is apparent to the experts in the field, the reasons that these objective measures are so subjective can be appreciated by the layman as well. Consider two basic systems for setting the wage: time-and-motion study and predetermined time.

In time-and-motion study, a worker performs a task and is timed. If the task takes an hour and the worker is supposed to make $2 an hour, then that task (piece of work) is paid for at the rate of $2. At this point, two major subjective decisions must be made. Why should this worker get $2 an hour and not $3 or $1? The answer is that the contract calls for $2 an hour. But in the next contract that worker may be entitled to $2.50 or $3 an hour for no reason other than the fact that such a new level of earnings was agreed upon as a result of collective bargaining: reasoning, shouting, pleading, bullying, striking, and compromise. The time study did not and does not set the general rate of compensation. The man with the stop watch can at best set a piecework rate for a worker in order to make it possible for the average worker to make the average wage *set in the contract* for this kind of work.

But here another "unscientific" factor enters: is the worker under study by the engineer really an *average* worker? Suppose he is a superior worker who habitually works twice as fast as his fellow operatives. If he gets $2 for the job, thereby making $2 an hour, his fellows, who work about half as fast, would only end up making $1 an hour. And by the same token, if the worker under study is a slowpoke and gets $2 for finishing that piece of work in one hour, his fellows who work faster will be making $3 and $4 an hour. Hence, the industrial engineer must "rate" a worker under study: Is he faster than average? Is he slower? Is he just right? In management lingo, is he a 100-per-cent, a 50-per-cent, or a 150-per-cent worker? The results of the study based on an individual performance must be adjusted to get a norm.

Now, who decides whether the worker under study is average, above, or below? That is a subjective judgment based on the knowledge, the feel, the insights, the prejudices, and the purposes of the management engineer. The union man has another set of measures and motives. The study is the beginning of the debate. When the stop watch stops, the argument starts. Exit computer; enter disputer.

A second major set of systems for rate-setting derives its authority from time-and-motion study but does not enter the workplace with a stop watch in hand. The study is done outside the given workplace on the amount of time needed to perform a given function: a simple movement. The rate of pay is then set for a given operation by breaking it down into its component movements, for each of which a predetermined rate has been set. Kermit K. Mead, Director of the Time Study and Engineering Department of the United Auto Workers, describes the predetermined-time system as follows:

"These systems analyze any manual operation into basic motions . . . and assign to each motion a predetermined time value which is determined by the nature of the motion and the conditions under which it is made. They contain such basic elements as reach, move, turn, crank, apply pressure, grasp, release, position, disengage, eye motions, body-leg and foot motions and simultaneous motions. The time values are supposed to represent normal times and therefore no rating factor is applied."

Now, why cannot this scientific-sounding system be used for cybernated setting of wages? First predetermined time (PDT) measures *time* value. The question of how much one hour of a worker's time in a given skill shall be worth is outside the PDT system. The dollar value of an hour's work is an item in the contract worked out at the bargaining table.

Second, PDT assumes that the whole is equal to the sum of its parts. PDT assumes that if it takes a second to reach, two seconds to crank, and one-half second to release, an action involving all three of these motions will take three and a half seconds. But it does *not*. The reason lies in the fact that the amount of time it takes to perform any one motion is always dependent on what goes before, what happens after, and what is going on at the same time.

In attacking PDT as an "atomistic concept of human behavior" that originates in an "engineering or mechanistic approach to the study of human phenomena," Eugene Jennings, Professor of Industry at the University of Pennsylvania, challenges the notion that the whole is equal to the sum of its parts. After reciting numerous experiments to disprove the atomistic view, he concludes that "time required to perform a motion among other motions in a total pattern of movement will vary with preceding and following motions and will be substantially affected by conditions either directly or indirectly associated with it."

In addition, the time value set on a motion by the creator of any PDT system is determined by the study of some worker somewhere. That worker, like any worker under time-and-motion study, must be rated as average, or above or below, and by how much. And once more, we are back to a subjective decision.

As a result, time-and-motion study and predetermined-time systems have not eliminated the haggling over the rate. As a matter of fact, these systems have themselves become a bone of contention. Many unions flatly refuse to abide by any rate set by any such system. Others insist that the application of any system be subject to bargaining and grievance procedures.

As far back as 1949, Walter Reuther, president of the United Auto Workers, assailed the scientific systems as a way to avoid collective bargaining. "PDT systems," he said, "are being promoted as a new and improved substitute for present time study practices. Its practical effect is virtually to abolish collective bargaining on production standards and piece rates. Management has never been happy with the necessity to bargain on production standards and piece rates. It has long been looking for a way to end such bargaining by convincing the workers that there is a 'scientific' way to set fair standards and rates. Time study was at first promoted on that basis. Now that experience has made workers increasingly skeptical of standard time study practices, management welcomes PDT systems as a new scientific excuse to eliminate or stifle bargaining."

In the years since that statement, union after union has challenged the "engineered" rate and standard. The systems have become a point of friction; when new contracts are concluded, the basic decisions about future earnings are made to *confine* and *define* the purposes of the systems. In recent years, for instance, the International Ladies' Garment Workers' Union—the first union to have a management-engineering department of its own to confront its opposite number on the employer's side—has been revising its contracts to protect its members against the "engineered" piecework rate. These contracts call for "craft minimums," to make certain that the "scientific" rate is not so low as to force all workers, regardless of their craft skill, down to the "floor" or basic minimum of the contract. In addition, these contracts call for rates that will yield average earnings of the crafts at some set percentage—such as 20 per cent—above the minimum. And if, after a fair time of trial, the engineered rate does not yield that average, the entire rate structure is reviewed. Within this framework, of course, individual rates must still be set for individual operations on the garments and, once more, these become highly bargainable items.

The skepticism of unions and of professionals about the scientific or objective character of the systems does not, however, discourage their inventors from proclaiming their virtues or employers from trying to apply the methods. In a society that increasingly prefers mathematics over language and mechanics over judgment it may be expected that there will be an increasing interest in the engineering system that claims scientific validity. In selling such scientific frauds to a science-minded society, the system inventors develop a special huckster style. "The king-size label, 'scientific management,' is attached to the over-all management function," according to Dr. Adam Abruzzi, Professor of Industrial Engineering at Stevens Institute of Technology, "in the hope that it will persuade the recalcitrant. To be fully effective this technique of proof by proclamation requires that the proclamation be achieved by noise level rather than by verifiable content. Proof by proclamation must decree that results can be verified but only 'if properly applied' by 'properly trained observers' using 'proper methods.' It must decree that the results can be stated in multi-decimal terms arrived at by arbitrary, whimsical or shallow methods. It must decree that assumptions and hypotheses be mentioned either not at all or phrased in terms of pontifical gibberish." By such scientific salesmanship, the systems are peddled and sold in a society mad about mathematics but unable to distinguish true from false formulas.

Hence, it may be expected in the future that as systems are invented and peddled, as management tries them on for size, and as the public is told that the computer has displaced the disputer, the unions will increasingly be engaged in opposing the systems, challenging their application, and applying to their evaluation the rules of thumb common at the bargaining table and in the grievance procedure.

In sum, the age of the new science will be a renaissance for collective bargaining: to block firings, to regulate training and new hiring, to protect traditional earnings and status, to formulate classifications and earnings for new types of work and jobs, to determine individual rates and standards. New techniques may cause an old order to pass. But a new order is being born. And in this new order, the union finds new grist for its bargaining mills.

CHAPTER 7

The New Labor Force

The labor movement in America is a "mix," about as heterogeneous as the United States itself. Its members are of many nationalities and religions; it represents intellectuals, illiterates, and everything in between; it is based in all fifty states and in the District of Columbia; it is well organized in some trades, badly organized in others, and unorganized in still others; it exists in urban, suburban, and rural areas; it is jostled by conflicting goals and ideologies. And its character depends largely on who is in it, on the ingredients in the mix.

These ingredients are especially important in the American labor movement because it consists of a "down-up" rather than an "up-down" structure. At the top is the parent body, the American Federation of Labor-Congress of Industrial Organizations, with which most national and international unions are affiliated. But the parent has no authority beyond its moral and financial influence and some of the children are richer than the parent. The AFL-CIO cannot name or remove the officers of a national or international union; it cannot set the economic or political policies of its "children." All the parent can do—if sufficiently provoked —is to order a child out of the family. As often as not, the child disowns the parent.

This fundamental autonomy of national unions is repeated, though to a lesser degree, among the local affiliates of these

bodies. Although national unions do as a rule have tighter constitutional controls over their locals than the AFL-CIO has over its
affiliates, the national bodies are not as almighty as they appear.
Top leadership of national unions must be elected by locals and
so the former respect the voice and will of the latter. Some locals
are richer than the national with which they are affiliated and can
get their own way because of their importance to the national
treasury. Sometimes, locals secede from national affiliation to go
their own merry way, often with success.

Because the American labor movement is composed of free-
moving parts, the character of organized labor in the future will
of course be largely shaped by the nature of the future mix. And
the key to that coming mix is the coming labor force—the body of
people, employed and unemployed, who occupy seats in and
move through the labor market. Some of this labor force has always been well organized, easily responsive to labor's call to join
the ranks. Other sectors have resisted unionization. Still others are
now toying with the idea of organizing, not quite certain whether
they should be professional organizations, guilds, independent
unions, or dues-paying members of the AFL-CIO. And there will
be other groups, twenty years from now, who will be confronted
with the appeal of unionism for the first time: employees in
newly created trades or crafts or workers in areas of the country
hitherto immune to unionism.

Let us, then, consider the shape of the labor force to be. (In
the next chapter, we will explore the meaning of such a labor
force for the trade unions.) The American labor force circa 1975
will be bigger, younger, and more feminine. It will wear a white
collar, be better schooled, and work in a service trade. Its muscles
will have shrunk and its brain will have grown. It will be drifting
away from the farm and countryside for factories and stores in
the neighborhood or for jobs in cities and suburbs. It will reduce
the crowding of the Northeast and the Midwest by moving to the
South and Far West. If it finds employment in a newly created
job, it is likely to be working in a nonprofit institution, probably
local government. It will, in the process of homogenizing Amer-

ica, itself become homogeneous: it will lose any lingering trace of a foreign accent and speak American.

The evidence for the changes is at hand. Let's start with the size of the coming labor force. The simplest way to predict the size of the labor force is to make an estimate of future population and then take 55 per cent of those 14 years of age or older. The result is the labor force figure.

The 55 per cent seems to be a magical figure, for reasons that nobody has yet spelled out. The figure is derived from experience: that is what it always has been and, for easy calculation, it is reasonable to assume that it will prevail for some time. Economists have come to call this rate of participation in the labor force by people age 14 or over one of the "great ratios of economics." Whether this ratio is eternally valid is doubtful. But, for the moment, it is a good rule of thumb. After all, in 1900, when the population (14 and over) was 51.2 million, the labor force was 28.1 million or 54.9 per cent; and in 1960, when the population was 126.3 million, the labor force was 69.9 million or 55.3 per cent. This figure of 55 per cent has been valid for the past seven censuses.

With a projected population of 173,908,000 by 1980, we may anticipate a labor force of about 95,600,000 by applying this rule of thumb. This would be an increase over 1964 of about 18,000,-000 in the labor force. Experts in population and labor-force figures do not, of course, rely on this rough measure. They forecast the size of the labor force, at least up to 1980, by an examination of present age groups, their sex, their age in 1980, and their probable rate of participation in the labor force at that time. Such a forecast does not depend on future birthrates since all the candidates for the labor market in 1980 have already been born.

On this basis members of the United States Bureau of Labor Statistics conclude that in 1980 there will be a labor force of 101,-408,000. If this figure is put alongside the rule-of-thumb figure, the labor force in 1980 can be estimated as between 95 million and 102 million. The difference is really too small to warrant a quibble.

The rising percentage of married women in the labor force is one of the distinguishing marks of the future. In 1900, 3 per cent of the labor force consisted of married women. By 1910, the figure rose to 5 per cent and then kept climbing every decade so that by 1960, 18 per cent of the labor force consisted of married women. This increase took place among women between the ages of 25 and 64, whose rate of participation in the labor force rose from 9 per cent in 1900 to 24 per cent in 1960.

Why are married women going to work outside their homes? Families are smaller than they once were and women are free to seek work when their children grow up. Labor-saving devices—dishwashers, driers, canned and frozen foods, blenders, pressure cookers, vacuum cleaners—liberate the housewife from the house. The expansion of white-collar and service-trade employment has opened job opportunities to women who would not as readily fit into blue-collar jobs in a factory. The shift of families from rural to urban areas has permitted wives once burdened with typical farm chores to find time and opportunity in the city for jobs. The growth of part-time jobs—in itself a product of a service-oriented economy—has made it possible for many women to combine home duties and jobs in the same day.

As a result of the increasing participation of married women in the labor force, about one out of every three employees in the United States is female. Interestingly, there are today more *married* than *unmarried* women in the labor force. The percentage of unmarried women in the labor force (about 15 per cent in the total force) has remained unchanged since 1900. In the coming mix of the labor force, we may expect that more than one-third of the workers will be female, that a majority of these will be married, and that two-thirds of them will be between 25 and 64 years old.

Here is the typical work life of a female American, as uncovered by the Bureau of Labor Statistics. "Most unmarried girls will go to work at age 17 or 18 (unless they go to college). Within 3 or 4 years, most of these girls will marry. Some of them will then stop working for pay in order to get a new home organized, but a majority will continue to work, either to help put a husband through school, to supplement a husband's income, or to permit purchase of a home, a car, or labor-saving equipment. Then, when the first baby arrives, the vast majority of young mothers give up their jobs and remain out of the labor market until their youngest child is old enough to go to school. It is true that as many as 1 in 5 women with preschool age children do continue to work, usually because of economic necessity, but the general pattern is that the age group 25-35 supplies the lowest proportion of women workers.

"When the youngest child no longer needs constant care, the trek of mothers back to paid employment begins. This usually happens when the women are approaching their middle thirties, after they have been non-wage earners for about 8 to 10 years. Once back, the tendency is for them to remain in the labor force, perhaps not continuously, but certainly for a substantial proportion of their years to age 65. By 1975, nearly *half* of all women between 35 and 65 will probably be either working or looking for work."

This growing movement of women into the labor force is one of the reasons that experts forecast for 1980 a labor force of more than 100 million, instead of the routine 55 per cent of the work population. Another reason for the forecast is the boom in births after World War II which produced an unusually large brigade of babies in the 1940s. This brigade, as its members come of working age, proceeds into the labor force, swelling the army of workers and job-seekers beyond the normal. As a result, from 1960 to 1975, the labor force "will grow faster than the population as a whole." In the 1960s, these war babies will endow the labor force with a percentage of young people much larger than that in the past. After 1975, of course, as this group grows older, the great increase in the labor force will come not from the younger workers but from those now aged 25 to 34.

The Bureau of Labor Statistics predicts that "young people

under 25 will account for almost half of the net increase of 12.5 million in the labor force between 1960 and 1970. Their proportion in the labor force will rise from less than 19 to more than 23 per cent." By 1970, about one worker out of four will be under 25 years of age.

This is even more remarkable when it is recalled that each year more and more young people seek extended education. The turn to school by teenagers cuts down the percentage turning to jobs. To use the technical phrase, the "participation rate" of the young is reduced. In spite of this, however, the percentage of young workers in the labor force will be high, at least up to 1975, simply because there are so many of them.

Statistically, the BLS reports that the participation rate of those between 14 and 19 will fall from 46.3 per cent in 1960 to 44.4 in 1975. Also, the rate for those 20 to 24 years of age will fall from 88.9 per cent to 86.7 in the same period 1960–1975. Nevertheless, this age group (below 25) will hold one place out of every four in the labor force by 1970.

The participation rate of this group might be even more reduced if it were not for the growing number of part-time jobs that make it possible for these young people to earn while they learn. These part-time jobs provide special openings for women and youth to enter the labor force. Part-time jobs have grown with the industries in which part-time work is common. Selling, for example, is a trade in which 25 per cent of the employees voluntarily work part time. Of household workers, 50 per cent were on part time in 1962. And in a variety of other service trades—at gas stations and parking lots and hotels—almost 20 per cent were on part time. One out of every eight clerical workers was part time. In the wholesale and retail trades part-time jobs rose from 46.2 per cent of the jobs in 1953 to 52.5 per cent in 1962. The continued growth of part-time jobs may further step up the participation rate of young people in the labor force.

The growth both of part-time jobs and of jobs congenial to married women is largely due to the growth of service industries in America. These include retailing, wholesaling, finance, insurance, government, real estate, and personal, professional, business, and repair services. The service category excludes the production of food, clothing, houses, and other tangible goods. As of 1965, the United States was a service economy, with more than half the labor force engaged in occupations other than turning out tangibles, according to Dr. Victor R. Fuchs, associate director of research of the National Bureau of Economic Research. And, he adds significantly, the United States is the first nation in the history of the world to have attained such a status.

The "service revolution" may carry with it changes as profound as those accompanying the shift from hunting and fishing to agriculture, or from agriculture to industry in the industrial revolution. A minority of our work force is producing *things*. Automation may enable an even smaller percentage to do that job and to produce even more and better things. A majority of the work force is distributing those things, or curing the sick, or amusing the well, or managing the relationships of people to people, or tutoring the mind, or moving money from one place to another. The focus of our civilization has shifted from making things to making them available at a given time and place, from turning out products to turning out beautiful women, from production to peddling, from hiring people for the factory to hiring people for the home.

Sometime late in 1956, the number of workers engaged in services caught up with the number engaged in goods. By 1957, services were ahead: there were 33,807,000 in services and 32,767,000 in goods. By 1963, services had a long lead: 37,962,000 were employed in services and only 31,445,000 in goods. The race was not too difficult for services since goods has been running backward. In 1953, more than 33 million people were engaged in the production of goods. A decade later, only 31 million people were in goods industries, a decline of about 2 million. In the same period, the number of people in service trades increased by about 6 million.

The growth in services is not attributable to growth in any single sector of that front. Each branch has moved forward. The following table shows the trend by comparing three selected years:

PERSONS ENGAGED IN SECTORS OF SERVICE TRADES
(by thousands)

	1929	1953	1963
Wholesale trade	1,744	2,971	3,391
Retail trade	6,077	9,311	10,537
Finance and insurance	1,207	1,705	2,437
Real estate	368	615	763
Household and institutions	3,249	3,246	4,316
Professional, personal, business, repair services	3,235	4,780	6,182
General government (including armed forces)	2,775	9,151	10,336

A breakdown of the sectors in goods reveals no such broad advance in employment. Indeed, in many sectors, as in the category as a whole, there is a retreat. In 1929, there were more than 9 million employed in agriculture, forestry, and fishing; by 1963, that number was cut in half. In 1929, more than a million were in mining; by 1963, about 650,000 remained. In transportation, over the same period, there was a decline of half a million workers. The two areas in which there were gains were manufacture and construction: from 10 million to 16 million in the former and from 2,300,000 to 3,300,000 in the latter.

Where did the new jobs come from in the last decade? From the service sector of the economy. While certain sectors of the goods industries have grown—the space industry is one striking example—the sector as a whole has actually come to offer *fewer* jobs than in the past. The added jobs to absorb the new additions to the work force and to find a spot for those displaced by automation have all come from the service trades.

Government has led the service trades in providing new jobs. "During the past half dozen years," stated the *Manpower Report* of the President in 1964, "the growth in state and local government employment has provided 4 out of 10 of the net additions to nonfarm payrolls in the economy." State and local government, it should be noted, are not the sole sources of government employment. In addition, there is of course direct employment by the federal government as well as the jobs that result from government expenditure in the private sector. "The public sector," continues the *Manpower Report*, "has, in fact, been the major source of job growth in recent years." Since the end of World War II, employment in state and local governments has leaped upward. Between 1947 and 1957, jobs in these areas rose by 185,000 a year, about 4¼ per cent. From 1957 to 1904, these jobs rose by 285,000, or 4¾ per cent, annually.

The job explosion in state and local government shatters two myths: first, that the private sector of the economy is the great creator of jobs; second, that the federal government—as contrasted with state and local governments—is the ever-growing octopus. In the past decade, and probably for the next, quite the opposite is true. The big maker of jobs is government; and the biggest maker of jobs is local, not federal, government.

In a society dedicated to the idea that private profit is the spur, the real spur to jobs in recent years has, ironically, come from the nonprofit sector. The evidence, contained in a provocative table of the *Manpower Report* of 1964, tells the story.

Between 1957 and 1963, total nonfarm employment rose by 4,300,000. Of this, nearly 2 million can be accounted for by jobs in government. This leaves about 2,400,000 in private employment. Of these, about 800,000 jobs came into being because of government procurement. This leaves about 1,600,000 jobs stimulated by private investment. Of these, there were about 700,000 jobs generated by nonprofit institutions. This left about 900,000 jobs that were brought into being by the private profit sector of the economy. But, since most of these were in the service trades where part-time employment is common, the number of full-time jobs generated by the private profit sector comes down to 300,000 jobs. These figures dispose of the myth that new jobs are brought into being by the private enterprise of companies in pursuit of profit. The opposite has been true for the recent past: the entrepreneurs have fallen down on the job while government has moved on to become the big jobmaker.

The growth of employment in the service trades and in government has helped change the collar of the American worker from blue to white. Up to the mid-1950s a majority of the labor force was blue-collar. Then, just about the time that the service trades moved past the goods industries in job opportunities, the white-collar worker moved past the blue-collar. Alongside the service revolution, the 1950s experienced the white-collar revolution.

Curiously enough, these "revolutions" of the 1950s were not seriously discussed or even noted until the 1960s. And the organizational consequences—for trade unions and for politics and for the society as a whole—will probably not be felt until the 1970s. The revolutions in our work force have quietly sneaked up on the nation.

The white-collar revolution has several origins. First, the growth of service trades; second, the growth of professional and technical occupations; third, the increase in nonproduction workers in manufacturing. The increase in white-collar workers from 1940 to 1960 is a steady upward movement—absolutely and as a percentage of the labor force. In 1940, there were 44 million white-collar workers; in 1950, there were 55 million; in 1960, 61 million. As a percentage of the work force, the white-collar people were 32.9 in 1940; 37.4 in 1950; and 43.3 in 1960.

During the same period, manual workers also multiplied but not so rapidly, with the result that while there are more of them, they are shrinking as a percentage of the labor force. There were 16 million in 1940; 22 million in 1950; and 23 million in 1960. The real slowdown came between the censuses of 1950 and 1960, when the percentage of manual workers fell from 40.3 to 38.6. It was during that decade that the white-collar group outran the blue.

The forecast is that this trend will continue. "Over the 15 year period 1960–1975," according to the *Special Labor Force Report* of the BLS (March 1963), "employment may increase by about 31 per cent in all occupations taken together, 46 per cent in white-collar occupations, and 21 per cent in blue-collar jobs." On the basis of this projection, in 1975 blue-collar workers will compose only about one-third of the work force and white-collar workers almost half—35 per cent and 47.5 per cent respectively, to be more accurate.

The occupational group that has been most responsible for this boom in the white-collar sector is the professional, technical, and kindred workers. They are, according to the *Special Labor Force Report* just noted, "the fastest growing occupational group during the past decade." The forecast is that this group will grow even faster. They "may increase at more than twice the average rate for all fields of work between 1960 and 1975. The increase in professional and related employment is projected at about 43 per cent over the 1960 decade and another 16 per cent between 1970 and 1975—which would raise the number of workers in the group to more than 12 million by 1975."

These workers are engineers and scientists, doctors and nurses, lawyers and accountants, teachers and technicians. Engineers, for instance, whose number ran to 850,000 in 1960, will probably count a million and a quarter in 1970—an increase of 65 per cent. The same rate of increase is expected to apply to scientists and technicians. Teachers, for another instance, who counted about 2 million in 1960 will count 2½ million by 1970. Among them, the greatest percentage growth will be at the college level. "In 1960, the total number of full-time college and university teachers in the country was about 175,000," notes the *Special Labor Force Report*. "By 1970, this number will need to be about 80 per cent greater to take care of the unprecedented numbers of young people expected to be seeking a college education."

Even in manufacturing, the traditional stronghold of the blue-collar worker, the manual worker is losing ground. "Between 1953 and 1962," reports the AFL-CIO Department of Research in October 1963, "the employment of production and maintenance workers [blue collar] in manufacturing fell from 14 million to less than 12.5 million. At the same time, employment of non-production workers [white collar] in manufacturing industries—professional, technical, clerical, sales—rose from 3.5 million in 1953 to 4.4 million in 1962."

The rapid growth of professional, technical, service, and government elements in the labor force compels a higher level of education. All these occupations require more learning. And even in manufacturing, among the production workers, a higher level of education is in demand. "The occupations that require the most education and training have grown the most rapidly," notes the Manpower Administration in its booklet, *People, Skills and Jobs.* This declaration is followed by the ominous warning that "employment has dropped in unskilled jobs." The forecast is that "among blue collar workers, the craftsmen, foremen and kindred workers will have the most favorable employment outlook. The number of these skilled workers may increase by nearly two and a half million over the 1960–1975 period—to more than eleven million by 1975." On the other hand, the unskilled laborers who made up 5 per cent of the work force in 1960 are expected to compose only 4½ per cent in 1975. In short, the uneducated will be the unemployed, or maybe even the unemployable.

Responding to the demand for workers with more education, the labor force has been going to school. Consider the number of workers who complete high school. In 1940, only 32 per cent made it; in 1952, the percentage rose to 45; in 1959, it rose to 51; and in 1962, it rose to 55. Workers have also been going to and graduating from college: 8 per cent in 1952; 11 per cent in 1962.

Because of this education, the men in the labor force are becoming almost as learned as the women, who were out in front in 1952 with an average of a year and a half more schooling. But in the following ten years, the males caught up—the median for men was now 12 years and for women 12.2—in good part because of the GI Bill of Rights and its liberal educational benefits.

The forecast is that the labor force of the future will be even better schooled. "By 1975," says the *Manpower Board of the*

President, "the proportion of younger workers (25 to 34 years old) with four years of high school or more may rise to about 73 percent, from 65 percent in 1962. The number with four years or more of college is expected to show a substantial rise in this period—from about 2.2 million to about 3.8 million, or from 16 to 19 percent of all workers in this age group." Graduate degrees are also on the climb. In 1961, the number of master's degrees was 79,000. The forecast is that by 1970, master's degrees will rise to 150,000. Doctorates stood at 10,575 awarded in 1961. In 1970, 18,000 doctorates are expected to be awarded.

The profile of the new labor force must also consider its residence. It is a mobile force, despite the fact that portions of it are painfully immobile, ready to perish in some exhausted area of our economy rather than move. The force in general does move about: from farm to town, from town to city and suburb, from north and central to west and south.

Employment on the farm goes down and down. Between 1930 and 1965, the labor force in farming has been cut in half—from 10.3 million to 4.5 million. The forecast is that by 1970 the number will have fallen to 4 million. The number on the farms is falling in spite of the fact that our soil is producing more food, feed, and fiber than ever before. The farmer, not his urban cousin, is the real victim of technological progress. Using machinery, modern fertilizers, feed additives, new strains of food and cattle, each farmer can produce more. In 1860, a farmer could produce for himself plus four people. Now he can produce for himself plus twenty-eight people. His productivity is increasing so that he can take care of about one additional person per annum. And as a result, he is working his way out of a job. He can produce faster than the population can reproduce. The small farmer is, of course, the first to be pushed off his land. To keep up with technological advance, he needs machinery that he cannot afford. So he quits and sells out to the larger farmer. As a result we have fewer farmers and larger farms.

Agricultural employees—those who work in the factories in the field—are also fewer in number. There were 2.1 million in 1940, 1.6 million in 1950, and only 1.4 million in 1960. The outdoor proletarian is a vanishing American.

Where do these displaced sons of the soil go? Some stay and rot where they always were, festering away in pockets of perennial agricultural poverty. Many of them stay on in the same rural county to find jobs in newly opened factories, stores, gas stations, construction gangs. These assorted jobs in the home county are sometimes a stepping stone to jobs in the big cities and their suburbs. In the transition from farm to factory, many work at both simultaneously: living on the farm, handling farm chores, but taking on a factory or store job for what may be the best cash crop in the farm household.

As the farmer leaves the soil, manufacture, trade, and services move in to provide new work. The surplus of labor in these once-agricultural regions makes such areas attractive to entrepreneurs. The labor is cheap. The land is relatively cheap, as contrasted with footage in urban areas. The steady inpouring of folk from the farm creates a buyer's market for the purchaser of labor. The town fathers are supercooperative in their dealings with prospective employers: free buildings or cheap buildings, often sold on a lease-buy plan; free training for employees; free protection against unionization. In short, as agricultural areas move toward industrialization and urbanization in the second half of the twentieth century, they repeat the history of all societies beginning to taste the bittersweet fruits of the industrial revolution.

A dramatic indicator of the areas into which nonfarm employment has been moving since the end of World War II is the list—in order of rank—of states where there has been the greatest percentage change upward in jobs off-the-farm. One notes the heavy, almost exclusive, focus on the West and South. The states are Arizona, Nevada, Florida, New Mexico, California, Colorado, Utah, Texas, Mississippi, Georgia, North Carolina, Maryland, Virginia, Delaware, South Carolina, Arkansas, Oklahoma. For the leader in this group of seventeen states, Arizona, the percentage of increase in nonagricultural employment between 1947 and

1962 was 149; for Oklahoma, it was 37. The national average was only 26 per cent. The forecast is that jobs off the farm will continue to increase more rapidly in the West and South than in the rest of the country.

What kind of industry and trade is locating in these newly urbanizing states? Among the first to move in is light industry: textiles, apparel, and any other easily assembled, easily transported item. The reasons are the same here and now as they have been in the past for Pennsylvania, when coal collapsed, or for Southern Illinois or West Virginia or Appalachia. The labor was there in supersupply. The work could be taught easily. The machines could be set up quickly. The raw material and the finished product could be moved in easily and swiftly, especially as new highways were created. Daughters and wives, and occasionally sons, of marginal farm families took up the needle and the loom to supplement the income of the homestead—a supplement which was generally greater than the total earnings of the farm.

This phenomenon—the rise of textile and apparel trades in societies moving from agriculture to industry—is not limited to the United States. It has repeated itself in every newly developing country of Asia and Africa, and for the same reason: easily taught cheap labor, low capital requirements, transportable material, and finished product. America's South and Southwest are our underdeveloped nations.

On the heels of light industry comes heavy industry. But because of its very weight, it moves more slowly. To move a steel mill is a far more expensive operation than to move fifty sewing machines or even to set up a new plant with large and costly looms. There is also the problem of shipping. As a result, heavy industry is likely to await the moment when there is a growing market for its products not too far from its plant.

In the 1960s, however, heavy industry making durable goods has been moving into the formerly agricultural areas. This development has been spurred by revolutions in production techniques. Instead of remaking an old plant in a settled area with high ground costs, high taxes, and a tight labor market, durable-goods makers have preferred to start fresh with new techniques in an area where space is cheap, labor is cheap, taxes are low, and where it is not necessary to teach old dogs any new tricks. This movement has been further spurred by "substantial defense contracts, particularly for scientific research and development . . . in the aerospace and electronics industries."

On the heels of light industry and heavy industry come trade and services. In microcosm, these newly developing areas repeat the pattern of the national macrocosm. The urbanization that follows industrialization demands stores, banks, insurance companies, keepers of books and makers of beauty, doctors and hospitals, nurses and clinics, bootblacks and barbers, police and firemen. As once-agricultural America moves through the industrial revolution, it plants the seeds of the service and white-collar revolutions.

While the country itself tends to become more homogeneous in its occupational composition, the labor force, too, tends to become more cosmopolitan. The reason is twofold: great migration within the United States; less migration into the United States. The latter fact is a result of statute. Since the 1920s, immigration into the United States has been severely restricted by law. Although that law has been changed because of its national quota system, the changes are not likely to increase total immigration. The complexion of the new immigrants may change but the total number will not rise meaningfully. The migration within the country is due, in no small measure, to the upheavals in the economy: the death of some industries, the removal of some factories, the decline in farming, the search for new opportunities in newly developing trades, the penetration of previously inaccessible areas by roads and highways, the burgeoning of the suburbs; it also reflects the everlasting restlessness of the American people. In 1963, the Office of Manpower, Automation and Training reported that the population of each state includes large numbers of people born and raised elsewhere in the country. "More than 25 percent of the Nation's population lives in a different state than the state in which they were born. In the state with the smallest percentage of in-migrants, 12 percent of the population has come from other states. The state with the largest percentage has had almost 70 percent of its population born in other states."

Here, then, is a profile of the new labor force—in being and still to be. From it will arise a new labor movement—like the present, as a child resembles the parent, but unlike it, too, as the child develops an independent personality to prepare it for its own life in its own time. The new mix in the labor force will give America a new mix in the labor movement.

CHAPTER 8

The New Labor Movement

Since the end of World War II, the American labor movement has not been keeping pace with changes in an economy that has undergone several revolutions. A labor force that was once manual, production-based, located in the North and Midwest, and containing few women, has become mental, service-based, moving to the South and West, and heavily female. The unions must move with the moving body of labor, or dwindle into insignificance. To catch up with the mobile army of wage earners is the great challenge before the trade unions.

In the twentieth century, the labor movement has three times been called upon to find itself and its place. It has done so twice: once at the turn of the century and again in the mid-1930s. It is now called upon to do so again.

At the turn of the century, American unions learned the art of organizing the skilled craftsmen. The unions composed a league of labor aristocrats, whose chosen form of organization was the craft local, generally limited to the skilled trades, with their "mysteries," limited apprenticeships, esprit de corps, and disdain for men with less skill. These craft unions sought to control the labor market to protect jobs, raise income, build securities—against employers, the unskilled, and jurisdictional intruders.

The great bases of these unions were in building and construction, transport, printing trades. Each of these vocations called for

finely honed artisans: ironmongers, carpenters, bricklayers, gla-
ziers, plasterers, lathers, painters, engineers, firemen, typesetters,
stone hands, pressmen, lithographers, engravers—each man an
aristocrat, joined in a fraternity of aristocracy.

The two other pillars of the trade unions were in the mines and
among the skilled craftsmen in manufacture. The miners were
bound together almost instinctively into a union—as they are in
all countries—not only by their peculiar skills but also by their
common dangers, work pits, and villages.

The foundations of the twentieth-century labor movement
were laid down as early as 1904. From then to 1937, the American
labor movement rested on railroads, construction, mining, and
printing. There were unions in the needle trades, shipping, to-
bacco, lumber, but they were less important and always leaned
heavily on their skilled sector for strength and survival.

Although the period from 1904 to 1937 was full of ups and
downs, it is not unfair to consider it in one piece. There is some
statistical evidence for this view. From 1904 to 1933, the trade-
union movement contained between 10 and 12 per cent of the
nonagricultural employees in America. The years 1934–1936 are a
transition to 1937, when the unions jumped to about 17 per cent
of the nonagricultural labor force. From 1938 on, the unions
moved to a new level, composing between 20 and 32 per cent of
the nonagricultural labor force. In short, a long view of American
labor shows it living on two plateaus: the first from 1904 to 1937,
the second from 1937 to the present.

Along the way there was a little plateau in the World War I
period, during which the unions represented between 16 and 19
per cent of the nonagricultural labor force. But this was a special
plateau created by special circumstances of the war. With labor
in short supply and the friendly Wilson in the White House, the
unions grew like a hothouse flower, doubling membership and
blossoming with 5 million adherents. But the artificial character
of this bloom became apparent with the first chill of the postwar
years. A recession and an open-shop campaign drove union membership down from 5 million in 1920 to 3.5 million in 1923. By

that year, membership was down to about 12 per cent of the non-agricultural labor force, right back into the pattern that prevailed from 1904 to 1937.

In the modern era, from 1937 to 1964, union membership has remained on a high plateau—never below 20 per cent of the non-agricultural labor force. There have been ups and downs, of course. Membership rose to 32.7 per cent of the nonagricultural force in 1953, thanks to the Korean War. It rose to 31.4 in 1957, thanks to a boom in capital goods. It has dipped 3 or 4 percentage points since, thanks to reasons we shall soon explore. But, by and large and viewed in the light of a century, the period starting with 1937 is a new era when contrasted with the years from 1904 to 1937.

Roughly, the two great plateaus run from 1900 to the mid-1930s and then from the mid-1930s to the present. They run historically from the turn of the century to Franklin Roosevelt and from Roosevelt to the present. The movement of 1900 was a product of the great divide in our national life—the critical, introspective, frictional last decade of the nineteenth century; the movement of 1937 was a product of the New Deal—the sociopolitical adjustment to the realities of the twentieth century.

From 1921 to 1937, the American unions were increasingly out of tune with their times. They had grown up in a craft period but they had to live in an industrial epoch. They were based on skilled artisans in a world increasingly filled with semiskilled operatives and unskilled laborers. They were solidly entrenched, even growing, in those sectors of the economy that resembled the past. But they had a weak foothold in the new economy, among the men on the assembly line.

By the mid-twenties the unions should have been thinking about ways to organize the man on the assembly line, the symbol of the new era. But organized labor was not ready for the undertaking, either spiritually or structurally. Most unions had no faith in the capacity of the semiskilled and the unskilled to build a union. The leaders of that time represented unions organized hor-

izontally to embrace the fraternity of a craft, rather than verti-
cally to encompass the brotherhood of a workplace.

It took the negative spur of a great depression and the positive
spur of the New Deal to get labor to rethink and restructure its
life. By 1933, the unions were reduced to 2.8 million members.
The AFL had hit bottom, back to where it was before World War
I. The base on which it built in 1904 was still the base in 1934
and, as that base became less significant, so did the movement.
Revival began with Roosevelt and recovery. As men returned to
work they returned to their unions. New shops were organized as
workers heard the government tell them, through the National
Recovery Act, that workers had the right to join unions of their
own choosing. The unions were rolling on.

But there was still an obstacle: the old habit of craft unionism.
The labor Establishment looked with disdain and distrust at the
idea of new unions built along vertical lines, challenging the craft
jurisdictions. Its leaders looked with disfavor on those of the
unions which got together in the Committee for Industrial Organization to organize the unorganized in the mass-production industries. The old order was changing but the old men were not.

The CIO went about its business with a series of organizing
committees—the Steel Workers Organizing Committee (SWOC),
the Textile Workers Organizing Committee (TWOC), and so on
through the basic industries of the nation—automobiles, rubber,
chemicals, shipping, electronics. Great drama surrounded these
organizing drives of the mid-1930s—sit-in strikes, massacres,
songs and psalms. A new day was at hand and the membership
figures proved it. In 1936, the trade unions counted 4.4 million
members; in 1937, that figure rose to 5.7 million; in 1938 to 6 million; in 1939 to 6.5 million; in 1940 to 7.2 million. And by that last
year, more than 20 per cent of the nonagricultural labor force was
unionized.

The expansion did not come exclusively or even mainly from
the new unions of the CIO. The idea of "industrial unionism" became contagious; the old AFL unions caught the bug. They

moved in heavily to organize factory workers in industrial unions under their own aegis. A labor movement that had appeared in 1933 to be bereft of membership, spiritually exhausted, politically bankrupt, and doomed to disappear made the necessary adjustments to revive itself. The unions caught up with the labor force. They also caught up with many other things, social legislation and political action among them. These will be discussed later. The prime point here is that, for the second time in this century, the unions showed the necessary flexibility to change their ways and establish a firm base in a new era. The change-over was not easy—it never is. There was some friction. But in the final analysis, the great readjustment was made.

In the 1960s and 1970s, the American trade unions face a parallel challenge. Can the unions organize the workers, many of them women, in service trades, in professional and technical occupations, living in the South and the West? These are relevant facts in answer to this question:

First, workers in the service trades and in the professions have been and are organizing into unions, most of them affiliated with the AFL-CIO. In other words, many of the workers in the new labor force are moving or have already moved into the mainstream of labor.

Second, professional workers have been organizing into associations that act like unions even though they disclaim union identity. They bargain, they strike, they sign contracts. They are unions in everything but name.

Third, the nature of work in service and the professions makes these workers highly susceptible to the union idea. These new ones may indeed turn out to be the most numerous, the most articulate, and the most political-minded sector of the American labor movement.

In other countries, workers of the brain have often set up separate federations of labor. The reasons varied. The regular unions lacked "class," in societies where "class" counted. The older manual unions lacked the language, the forms, and sometimes even the interest needed for organizing the white-collar and professional people. Finally, the existing federations often were mere echoes of political parties with ideologies which the professionals found either repugnant or irrelevant. But whatever the reason, there has been a tendency in some countries of Europe for the workers of head to separate themselves organizationally from the workers of hand.

It is not impossible that in America also unions of white-collar, service, and professional people will some day set up a separate federation. These elements in the labor force, especially the professionals and intellectuals, have been forming associations that tend to act more and more like unions. If they do not find the atmosphere of the AFL-CIO congenial, they may indeed form a separate federation or exist as separate national entities—associations, guilds, or unions.

There is reason to believe, however, that future and even some present organizations of these newer elements will get into the mainstream of labor, and most likely into the AFL-CIO. The reasons lie in the present character of the federation, in the nature of some of its affiliates, and in evolving trends among the new labor force.

The AFL-CIO of today, unlike the AFL of 1935 in its attitude toward industrial workers, has no inhibitions about the white-collar and professional workers. These new elements are welcome in the present house of labor. The AFL-CIO needs them, wants them, and seeks them. In these new elements, the federation understands, lies the immediate future of the labor movement. Articles on the evolving labor force appear regularly in *The Federationist* (the official publication of the AFL-CIO). The AFL-CIO has given moral and financial backing to those of its affiliates that are involved in organizing the newcomers.

One spur comes in part from the general loss of membership in the American unions. The movement slipped from 24.5 per cent of the civilian labor force in 1954 to 20.7 per cent in 1962. While the unions attribute this in part to adverse legislation—Taft-Hartley, Landrum-Griffin, and right-to-work laws in twenty states—the federation is also aware that its traditional base—production workers in manufacture, craftsmen in building and construction, railroaders, printers, and miners—is either shrinking absolutely or is not growing as rapidly as the economy. To play its role in the economy and the society, the movement must grow at least as rapidly as the work force, if not more so. And that calls for organization of the new arrivals in the labor force.

The unions are fully aware that the legal obstacles to organization of blue-collar workers are also obstacles in the organization of white-collar. For that reason, organized labor stresses a liberalization of labor-management law: repeal of section 14B of the Taft-Hartley Act in order to legalize the union shop everywhere in the country, softening of the Taft-Hartley and Landrum-Griffin laws to ease organizational restraints on unions. The labor movement is aware, too, that organization of workers—blue- or white-collar—in the South will require a change of political atmosphere and public attitude. But even after all this is done and the ambience is propitious for union membership growth, there will have to be special approaches, drives, and structures for the new types of workers.

The present AFL-CIO is likely to make the necessary transition more easily than the old AFL vis-à-vis the CIO because of developments over the last three decades in the American labor movement have widened the horizons of the federation. The old AFL —especially its most skilled craft unions—tended to be *exclusive* rather than *inclusive* in character. The new AFL-CIO, with its heavy ingredient of factory-based industrial workers, tends to be the opposite. The old AFL tended to think in terms of *craft;* the newer AFL-CIO tends to think in terms of *class.* This broader outlook makes it much easier for the federation to open the door to the white-collar worker.

The shift from the exclusive to the inclusive view of unionism is instructive for the future in that it shows how the ideology of the labor movement changes in response to its composition. The exclusive view of the old craft union was not the product of evil, narrow-minded leadership. The parochial approach is almost inherent in the nature of the craft union. The typical craftsman in

building and construction works in a delimited geographic
market within a reasonable radius of his home. His work is limited by the amount of building and construction in his area. To
maintain his status—a steady job and a good income—he must,
like any steel or automobile magnate, try to balance the supply
(the supply of labor) with the demand (the demand for labor)
in that vicinity. Hence, historically, these craftsmen have sought
to limit the supply of labor in the given craft in the area. This is
especially important in the building and construction trades
where a worker moves from job to job, from site to site, sometimes almost from day to day. He is heavily dependent on his union to find a job for him in the locale of its jurisdiction. Hence,
these unions ask for regulation of apprentices, insist upon high
standards for journeymen, and, until the practice was outlawed
by the Taft-Hartley Act, a closed shop, under which a worker
must have a union card before starting on a job. And when the
demand for labor fell, these unions added a *closed door* to the
closed shop, barring all new entrants into the union for lack of
jobs.

Factory-based unions find themselves in a different situation.
These workers do not as a rule produce for the local market in
the same way as do workers in building and construction. The
workers in mass production produce for a national market. Com-
modities made in New York sell in California and vice versa. Producers in Mississippi compete with producers in Massachusetts.
The organized worker in New England, if he wishes to protect
his job and his wages against Southern competition, *must* think
about unionization of the South. He wants the nonunion worker
to join the union, to protect those already organized against unfair competition. The factory worker thinks inclusively because
his basic protection lies in the establishment of basic standards
for all the workers in his industry.

The factory-based unions have rarely asked for a closed shop.
They settle for a "union-shop" or a "maintenance-of-membership"
clause. The union-shop clause does not insist that a worker be a
member of the union *before* going on the job; it stipulates that he

must join the union *after* a fixed period, such as thirty days. The maintenance-of-membership clause does not insist that all workers must become union members but does insist that those who are members at the time the contract is signed must maintain their membership for the duration of the contract. The factory-based unions differ from the craft unions in this respect because in the former, the organization is not confronted with a membership in constant movement from job to job and from place to place with the threat of unemployment between jobs, as is the case with the journeymen trades of the craft unions. A typical industrial union in mass production, once it signs a contract with an employer, is reasonably certain that the plant will remain in operation, supplying work to a given body of employees, for the life of the contract, and probably for many years thereafter. The work force may change in the plant; workers will come and go. But as each new worker comes in, he or she joins the union after thirty days, gets union wages, abides by union rules, pays union dues. The union, thereby, is able to maintain both the union and union standards by the inclusion of the new worker.

In unions that mix industrial and craft locals, it is common for the union to be inclusive for the less skilled crafts where workers are constantly pouring in and out of the union but to be exclusive with its more skilled craftsmen, for whom there are relatively fewer jobs and few of whom ever leave an existing job. The same union, in the former case, can afford to be generous, since there are new job openings all the time in good times and seasons; and, in the latter case, cannot afford to be so generous since the unemployed member may well have a hard time getting relocated once his job folds up. Hence, the former (less skilled with big turnover) is always ready to say welcome, and the latter (more skilled with little job turnover) is always inclined to say no place here.

The difference in attitude between the craft and industrial unions is instructive in understanding future developments, although it relates to the past. The difference emphasizes the fact that ideologies are a function of identities and that what you think depends on who you are. Applied to the future, this means that one of the keys to forecasting the character of the labor movement to be is the composition of future unions, not simply the vocalized ideas of present leadership. Moreover, the addition of the industrial ingredient to the old craft concept explains, in part, the likelihood that the present labor movement as a whole will embrace rather than reject new types of workers.

In the period 1961–1965, unions participated in 2,285 white-collar elections, won 56.5 per cent and added 31,370 members. The readiness of the AFL-CIO to organize the unorganized among the white-collar workers does not, in itself, provide an instrument for their organization. The AFL-CIO is a federation of existing national unions. It does not, in and of itself, have members paying direct dues to the federation. (There are "federal locals" composed of workers who do not seem to find any existing national union congenial or appropriate and who are affiliated directly with the AFL-CIO, but these are few and exceptional.) Hence, the organization of the white-collar workers must be done by the AFL-CIO through its affiliates.

One of the oldest of these affiliates is the retail clerks' union. When it was first chartered by the AFL in 1890, it was called the Retail Clerks International Protective Association. Its roots run all the way back to an attempt in 1865 to organize retail clerks in Cleveland, Ohio. The very name of the organization hints at its self-image. It was an "association," and not a "union," a choice that suggests its semipro view of itself. Even the adjective "protective" smacks of many other organizations of the time, put together by people of status, who were eager to "protect" their standing against the encroachment of new, oppressive forces. The response to the RCIPA was good from the first: membership rose from 3,000 in 1897 to 50,000 in 1904. But as the conditions of the trade changed and new, big employers had the means and the meanness to fight the union, membership fell to 15,000 by World War I and to 5,000 by 1933.

In the new era, beginning with 1936, the clerks began to make a comeback: in 1937, they had 23,000 members; by 1947 they had

149,000; by 1957 they had 324,000; and by 1964 they were beyond 400,000. By 1962, the clerks were admitted to the special
club of the top big ten in the AFL-CIO. Their president was
placed on the Executive Council of the AFL-CIO, a tribute to the
size and the significance of their union. In the period from 1954
to 1964, when the total membership of all unions slipped somewhat, the clerks increased their rolls from 223,000 to 400,000.
Within a decade, they just about doubled their membership.

In the 1930s, when the CIO was organized, it created a clerks'
affiliate of its own, the Retail, Wholesale, and Department Store
Employees. This began auspiciously. Between 1937 and 1947, its
membership rose from 40,000 to 117,000. And then it fell on hard
times because of nearly fatal internal differences. A number of locals left because of Communist influence; some others affiliated
with the teamsters; still others went independent. By 1950, the
national union had only 52,000 members. But the essential readiness of these workers in the service trades to organize reasserted
itself. By 1957, membership had risen to 130,000, and by 1962 to
140,000.

The total membership of the retail clerks and the retail, wholesale, and department-store union combined is between 500,000
and 600,000 members. To this number must be added members
of other unions that also organize in this area. A Department of
Labor estimate in the early 1960s showed nearly 850,000 union
members in "trade." The figure suggests two facts: first, that the
workers in "retail and wholesale" can be organized and have increasingly been organized; second, in view of the fact that there
are several million workers (perhaps 11 million) in this sector of
the economy and that there will be more, present union organization is just a beginning. The forecast is that unionization of employees in retailing and wholesaling will be one of the great areas
of expansion in American labor.

Another union whose composition is close to that of the retail
and wholesale unions is the Hotel and Restaurant Employees
and Bartenders. It operates in a growing service trade and includes both blue-collar and white-collar people. In 1935, it

counted 82,000 members. And since that time it has grown steadily, regardless of recessions, organizational rebuffs, or reactionary legislation. By 1962, it claimed 437,000 members.

Still another union in the service trades is the Building Service Employees' union. Although originally this union concentrated on porters, elevator operators, cleaners, and skilled maintenance people in both commercial and residential buildings, it has reached out to employees of hospitals, clinics, and other nonprofit institutions, who do more than just service the building. Its history is one of almost uninterrupted growth, no matter what was happening to the country or to the labor movement. In 1935, it had 27,500 members. In 1964, it showed almost 300,000.

Although the unions in these three areas—retail and wholesale trade, hotels and food, and building service—embrace both blue-collar and white-collar people, the percentage of professional people is relatively small. Three interesting examples of unions in the *professional* field are the Newspaper Guild, the Actors and Artists, and the American Federation of Teachers.

Early attempts by the AFL to organize newspapermen in the 1920s produced little more than the seedlings for unionism. In 1933, under the inspiration of the well-known columnist Heywood Broun, a guild was founded. It emphasized its separateness by the choice of this name and by the fact that it decided to be independent of the AFL. In 1936, after much struggling with its professional soul, the Guild affiliated with the AFL and then, significantly, with the CIO.

The Guild, like many of the professional unions, became deeply involved in a "left-right" fight between Communists and non-Communists and anti-Communists. Similar fights marked the history of the teachers and the unions in the performing arts. One explanation attributes this to the creative temperament of the professionals in these areas. They resent the disciplines of the job and tend to express discontent in militant revolt and by identification with rebel causes. A simpler explanation may lie in the fact that these are people who tend to get caught up in the intellectual struggles of the day. They are more susceptible to ideology than are manual workers and are apt to carry their commitments into their union meetings.

Up to 1941, the Guild was a battleground for ideologies fought out in an arena of about 13,000 members. When the Communists were finally decisively defeated, the Guild got down to the bread-and-butter business of building a union. By 1951, it had 22,000 members, and by 1962, more than 33,000.

Walter Galenson, who looks upon the Guild as "an important precedent in white collar unionism," also notes that it demonstrated that professionals could join unions without "loss of dignity and that unionization of newsmen would not hamper freedom of the press."

The Actors and Artists went through the typical evolution from independent professional association outside the mainstream to a union that ultimately was accepted by the AFL. It has shown steady growth, parallel with that of the Newspaper Guild. In 1935, it counted 4300 members; by 1945, 24,300; by 1955, 34,000; and by 1962, it boasted more than 50,000 members. The Actors and Artists is proof that the hourly wage is by no means the sole reason for workers to join unions. There are members of the Actors and Artists who earn thousands and tens of thousands of dollars a week, sometimes a day. Many of the dues payers are persons of world renown. They have fame and fortune, but they need, want, and join a union.

Teachers have traditionally been under a triple handicap in their attempts to organize. As professionals, many teachers felt that unions were beneath them. Second, as a rule the teacher is a government employee, and the right of government employees to unionize, or, more significantly, to strike, has always been shadowy. Finally, the teacher is in a *calling*, a dedicated soul pledged, by the nature of his work, to give rather than get.

Unions of teachers began locally before there was any national body or any affiliation with the AFL. The local bodies were generated spontaneously, in response to nothing but the teachers' own needs or aspirations or frustrations or insecurities, and appeared in New York, Butte, Gary, Scranton, and Washington,

D.C. The Chicago organization arose out of a dramatic series of events issuing from an order of the Board of Education prohibiting teacher membership in unions. It was the Chicago local that in 1916 issued the call for a national convention, out of which arose the American Federation of Teachers.

The struggle of the teachers to organize was long and fratricidal. When the great depression hit the country in 1929, the AFT had only 4,200 members. In subsequent years, this union, like others in the professions, was torn by the "left-right" fight. Despite this, by 1937, with the coming of the new era, it counted almost 23,000 members. And then its membership proceeded to climb. By 1947, it numbered 42,000; by 1957, 48,000; by 1962, 58,000. And then the Federation really began to move, as it won collective-bargaining elections in New York, Philadelphia, Boston, and Detroit.

When the AFT reached the 110,000 mark in 1965, however, it still included only 5 per cent of its potential of 2 million American teachers. The forecast is for a union of teachers in the United States that will be one of the greatest organizations not only in the American labor movement, but in the country as a whole. In part, its future will depend on its relations with the National Education Association, the largest of the teachers' professional organizations.

The teachers are not the only government employees who have been organizing. One of the most rapidly expanding unions in America is the representative of workers employed by state and local governments. In part, this is because (as we have seen) government employment has been growing most rapidly at the state and local level, but another cause is the growing popularity of the union idea among public employees, at all levels and almost everywhere in the country.

The American Federation of State, County and Municipal Employees got off to a late but quick start. It was, like the American Federation of Teachers, born out of a coming together of numerous local groups. Uniting them in one family was difficult because each had risen spontaneously in response to special local conditions. In the mid-1930s they totaled only 16,000 members. But within a decade they had risen to 76,000 members. By 1957, they counted 158,000 members, and by 1962, almost 220,000 members. By 1965, this union had passed the quarter-million mark.

Another reason for the growth of this union is that the growing political influence of unions in the community makes it easier for local government employees to organize. In many cities, the elected officials—thanks to union effectiveness in elections—are pledged to further formal collective bargaining through unions. Needless to add, this attitude on the part of the "boss," the elected public official, makes it much easier for the government employee to accept the union idea. If labor involvement in the political process grows in the near future (which we will discuss later), then the forecast for unionization of government employees is growth.

The state, county, and municipal employees' union is not the only one among public employees at the local level. One of the most powerful unions in America, which has for years included among its members an unusually high percentage of those in the craft, is that of the "firefighters"—the Uniformed Firemen's Association. They use the term to distinguish themselves from the firemen who used to fire engines on trains and also because they prefer to think of themselves as warriors who defend the hapless civilian. In 1935, the firefighters had 26,000 members; by 1962, they had more than 100,000. The membership grows as the number of firemen increases, because—without a union-shop clause, without a check-off, without the right to strike—they enroll close to 100 per cent of the firefighters in America. They do so because of the esprit de corps that exists among them. They instinctively know the meaning of cooperation, discipline, fraternity, and hence, in the baptism of fire, they are initiated into the religion of unionism.

The letter carriers are in a similar category, albeit their initiation ritual is not quite as severe. They know the value of a union that does the double duty of handling grievances and lobbying for postal legislation. Again, as with the firefighters, the uniform sets them apart as a status group and hastens their unionization.

The letter carriers moved toward organization at a very early time as a part of the Knights of Labor. In the 1880s the Post Office Department issued an order that exempted the letter carriers, against their expectations, from becoming beneficiaries of an eight-hour law for government employees that applied to "workmen, laborers or mechanics." The letter carriers were interpreted as being outside this protection: they were too good to get the eight-hour day. So they joined the Knights of Labor, which put up a vigorous and successful campaign to get Congress to include them.

Like other government unions, independent letter-carrier groups organized alongside the adherents of the Knights. Merging of these groups and affiliation with the AFL did not come until 1917, by which time they had a national union that reached practically every letter carrier in every city of the nation. Their union, like that of the firefighters, has grown as their numbers have increased. By 1962, there were more than 164,000 carriers paying dues to their union.

In examining the future of unionism in government and the professions, it is not sufficient to look only at those organizations that call themselves "unions" and are AFL affiliates. As brief glances at the past of existing professional and governmental unions reveal, they all have a tendency to start as professional societies outside the mainstream of labor.

At present there are several significant organizations that strongly resemble the present government professional unions before they became admittedly labor unions. One of the most influential and potentially the most meaningful is the National Education Association, with about 1,000,000 members. After resisting the union idea for many years, the NEA at its 1961 convention set out on a new tack. "The National Education Association," it stated, "believes that professional education associations should be accorded the right, through democratically elected representatives using appropriate professional channels, to participate in the determination of policies of common concern including salary and other conditions for professional service." This new policy, though phrased in professionalese, means "collective bargaining."

In practice, the NEA has gone beyond this polite assertion. It has called on teachers to refuse to sign contracts to work in areas and states where salary levels and working conditions have not met the NEA's "professional" standards. The NEA would of course deny that this is striking, although for decades the miners and other unions have simply stated that "no contract" means "no work." The NEA does not strike; it merely refuses to work.

The shift in NEA policy and behavior arises from two circumstances: the most obvious is the growing competition from the American Federation of Teachers, which between 1962 and 1965 rose from 58,000 to 110,000 members; the other, and in the long run the more important, reason is the mood of the teachers themselves—a mood of militancy about salaries, security, standards. In headlining a story about teachers in July 1965, *The Wall Street Journal* ran the following summaries: "MILITANT EDUCATORS—Collective Bargaining by Teachers Spreads, Bringing Contract Gains—Miami Schools Grant Record Pay Raise; Boycott Threats Used to Back Up Demands—Are Strikes Unprofessional?" In the body of the story, the *Journal* reported: "No longer content with negotiating such matters [pay scales and working conditions] on an individual basis, they are swiftly banding together and making strong organized efforts to back up their demands. It's estimated that some 25% of the nation's teachers this year had their contracts negotiated by teacher organizations, up from less than 5% only five years ago. Education authorities say that if this year is any indication the push to organize is sure to accelerate."

As the teachers begin to settle matters of salary and working conditions, they move into the areas of school policy—the traditional area of management prerogative. "Teachers are also making a major bid for a bigger role in policy," adds the *Journal*, "an area tackled so far by only the biggest and most influential labor unions. The Philadelphia school board recently agreed to a once-a-month professional consultation period with teacher groups in each school. Under the agreement, teachers are guaranteed an audience with their school principal to discuss such matters as the quality of teaching supplies, the library hours and how teachers are backed up by the principal in student discipline cases." In South Bend, Indiana, a four-day strike revolved around policy questions rather than salaries. One teacher was quoted as saying, "We feel we're more qualified than the school board to say what schools need because we teach there every school day." The strike was called off when the school board gave the teachers an audience for their ideas.

In reviewing this new mood of the teachers, *The New York Times* commented in 1964: "A resurgence of militancy among the nation's public school teachers marked the year of 1963. There was mounting evidence that teachers are no longer content to rule only the classrooms to which they are assigned. They want a hand in the assignment and a voice in the policy that controls their professional lives. They are not asking to run the schools, but they want their views heard and heeded."

Teacher militancy has come not as a result of loss in status but as a result of a gain. The teacher's salary, security, and standing have been rising and, as a result, he wants a voice and a vote in professional life worthy of his role in the society.

In a bulletin issued by the Office of Education of the U.S. Department of Health, Education, and Welfare, James P. Steffensen writes: "A more positive factor in teacher participation has been the change in the makeup of the public school teacher in the 1960's. Salaries and fringe benefits have improved. Education has received sufficient attention by the American public to elevate at least the degree of importance of teaching and probably its attractiveness as a career. Certainly the proportion of males is increasing so that they are now in the majority in the secondary schools. The public school teacher has also become better educated and more cognizant of the part that public education plays in shaping affairs far beyond the confines of his local school district—at State, national, and international levels. Perhaps it is this combination of greater sophistication plus the awareness of his importance and ability which has contributed most strongly to the increasing vitality of teacher groups at all levels."

NEA's president, Richard D. Batchelder, addressing the nation's school superintendents in Atlantic City on February 15, 1966, presented the association's new militant line: "The basic decision to secure and use written professional negotiation agreements," he said, "has been made in hundreds of thousands of minds. That decision will not be reversed."

This comment is instructive about teachers, about professional employees, and about the bases of trade unionism in all white-collar professions. Awareness of status among professionals can well be the great spur to unionization.

In an address before the National School for Teacher Salary Scheduling, entitled "A Philosophy, a Program and a Passion," T. M. Sinnet laid down a credo for teachers before an assembly of the National Education Association.

"The philosophical principle on which teachers will reject paternalism however benevolent is one as old as the nation itself— the principle of consent of the governed. Added to this is a principle not as old but as valid, that participation in the decision-making promotes a sense of responsibility and enhances the powers of the participants. These are basic principles of freedom and democracy, not of some strange cult of radicalism. I think this, in essence, should be our philosophy, our program and our passion in the difficult days ahead. It should form our basic credo, as we pursue the complex task of working with people in official positions who sincerely want to be our friends, most of whom, I have faith, want economic justice for teachers as fervently as do we."

In many ways, the teacher is symbolic of the new labor force. He is a white-collar professional in a service trade. He may very well become a bellwether for all those others in this expanding category.

In the professions, the old struggle between employee and employer takes on a new form. It is a struggle between professionals and bureaucrats. The former want freedom; the latter treat them as a mass. The former think of themselves as directors; the latter think of them as directed.

The relationship poses a problem for "professional persons in bureaucratic organizations"—the term used as the title of a study by David N. Solomon included in a Symposium on Preventive and Social Psychiatry. In this paper, the author describes the "class struggle" at the professional level:

"Our social life is to an increasing extent dominated by bureaucratic institutions. . . . By definition, professionals and bureaucracies are incompatible. . . . Consequently there is likely to be an uneasy tension between managerial authorities and professional specialists. The professional is driven or tempted to abandon his professional identity; but whether he does or not, he threatens to *usurp some of the power* of those who invited him into the house in the first place." (Italics mine—G.T.)

In the language of the economist rather than of the social psychiatrist, Jack Barbash made the same point in a lecture before the Wharton School of Finance and Commerce in 1960: "The largest factor working in favor of unionization (of the professional worker) is what might be called the socialization of the work situation. The individualistic bent which constitutes the hard core of the professional's values is having to give way to the realities of the industrial discipline. The realities are first the technological requirement of concentration of numbers of workers in one place. . . . The second reality stems from the first—that where you have large numbers of persons concentrated at one worksite you need to develop rules, regulations, measurements, standardizations, evaluations, procedures."

The "socialized work situation" among professionals becomes the matrix of organization—and ultimately of unionism, by whatever name it calls itself.

Because professionals are organizing into unions, because they are organizing into associations that increasingly act like unions, because they are being socialized and disciplined at the work site, and finally because it is easier for people with higher skills to be effective through organizations—for all these reasons, the forecast is the ultimate unionization of the professional employee in America.

An obstacle to the unionization of workers in service and white-collar jobs is often seen in the relatively great number of women in these pursuits. It is assumed that women are harder to organize into a union than men are. Surface statistical evidence seems to bear out this point. In 1962, there were 3.3 million women union members, representing one woman out of seven in the labor force, or about 14 per cent. Male union members were about one out of four, or 25 per cent. This contrast between the percentages of employed men and women who pay dues to unions appears to argue that females are not joiners.

A closer look, however, reveals that in the trades where unionism lags among women, unionism also lags among men. And vice versa, where unionism is strong among men, it is strong among women. In the needle trades, where unions are strong, the females in the unions outnumber the males by as much as four to one, simply because there are that many more women in the factories. On the other hand, in the service, white-collar, and professional trades that are just picking up momentum for large-scale organization, both men and women unionists are still a *small fraction of all those employed* in these occupations. But, since a very high percentage of all employed females is engaged in service and white-collar trades, it follows that the weakness of organization in general for these trades is reflected in an over-all statistic that shows relatively few unionized women in the labor force.

Should these trades, with their large female contingents, become organized, it may well be that the ratio of organized women in the labor force will move ahead more rapidly than the ratio of men. In short, the high percentage of women in unorganized trades lowers the percentage of union girls in the labor force.

This does not mean, therefore, that women cannot and do not organize. There are four unions where the female membership is more than 70 per cent of the total membership, with an aggregate count of 639,000 female dues payers. In twenty-two unions, women are a majority. Some of the unions with heavy female contingents are the International Ladies' Garment Workers' Union, the Amalgamated Clothing Workers of America, the International Brotherhood of Electrical Workers, the Hotel and Restaurant Employees Union, the Retail Clerks, the United Automobile Workers, and the Communications Workers. The sampling suggests that women can be organized in factories, stores, hotels, restaurants, telephone exchanges. The newly burgeoning unions in government and teaching, with their female battalions, suggest that no sector of the economy immunizes women against unionism.

Among women, however, and among school-age young men, there is a special factor that has proved and will prove to be an obstacle against unionization—namely, the growth of part-time employment. Part-time jobs have multiplied with the growth of the service and white-collar trades. They are filled mainly by women and youths. The holders of such jobs are among the very last to respond to the union message. The part-time job is not the worker's life: for many women, the home is the real center and the job is often pin money; among youth, the school is the real center and the job is often tuition or date money. The work site, for the part-timer, is a place to visit, not to live in. Very often, specific hours of work or location are far more important than wages or working conditions. If the job falls at the right hours or is located conveniently, the part-timer will take it, even if the hourly pay is poor and the working conditions uncomfortable. Because the part-timer is also a transient, he is not greatly concerned about retirement, medical benefits, holidays, vacations, grievance machinery, etc. Nor is he interested in the union as a way of raising status, as he often does not intend to stay with this kind of work as a career. For all these reasons, the union appeal to the part-timers is weak.

In union elections before the National or State Labor Relations Boards in the coming years, the unions are likely to ask for the exclusion of part-time workers from the bargaining unit, or from the election. In numerous situations, unions have found that while they could win an election among the full-time workers, they lose because of the ballots cast by the part-timers. In the great taxi election in New York City in 1965, the union's primary concern was the exclusion of the part-time hackies from the election. These part-timers worked a day, a weekend, a half-week, or a couple of hours each night; they were known to be negative about the union. They were more interested in the few dollars picked up by occasional hacking—a practice encouraged by the companies both to put pressure on the full-time cabbies and to load the vote against the union—than they were in raising earnings and establishing health, welfare, vacation, and retirement benefits for the lifetime driver. As a result of the union's demand that the election be limited to full-time drivers, the labor board offered a compromise that opened the voting booth to all those who put in three full days of work. The union won handsomely.

Because unions have difficulty in controlling the work situation with part-time workers, they will inevitably move along still another line once they achieve union contracts in the service trades. The tendency will be to limit the number of part-time workers. This forecast, however, is pure conjecture, for which there is little present evidence.

The coming pattern of union development will not be uniform for the country. Although the nation as a whole moves toward a more homogeneous mix for each part, there is and will be regional diversity. And this diversity in the economy of the regions will be reflected in the labor movement.

The number one regional problem for the American labor movement in the mid-twentieth century is the South. And the reasons are the same as those that caused President Franklin D. Roosevelt to proclaim the South America's number one economic problem. The South is proof positive that poverty per se does not produce unionism. If hunger, illiteracy, unemployment, illness, and exploitation made for strong unions, the whole South would be a union town. But quite the opposite is true. The South, with all its economic hardships, is the weakest large region in American unionism.

The reasons are well known. The rulers of the South—town fathers, constabulary, and employers—are anti-union. And in their dislike, they are not hesitant about taking the law into their own fists. In addition, they write local laws, such as state right-to-work laws outlawing the union shop and local ordinances outlawing union solicitation, to keep labor organizers from getting a foothold and to prevent union contracts from being truly effective. They use their financial institutions to harass union-minded workers and even liberal-minded employers. They pit Negro against white and vice versa and call upon the dominant white worker to vote down the union, the "red" tool of racial integration. They keep a ready pool of surplus labor to break strikes and a readier pool of surplus hoodlums to break the heads of union agitators.

Underlying these well-known facts about Southern antipathy to unionism—a generalization whose application varies from state to state and from county to county—is a more basic reality: the structure of Southern society. For here is a part of twentieth-century America based on a nineteenth-century economy and run by an eighteenth-century aristocracy. This at least was the situation until recently, and as changes have occurred, that significant sector of American civilization has been thrown into turmoil.

The rural economy of the South is a heritage of the last century. The standard of living for the lower classes was based on an agriculture impoverished and in decline. And for many Negroes, the standard was based on a plantation system in a state of exhaustion. The wage and work standards of an industrial society, as well as the rights of workers in such a system, were alien. Unionism appeared foreign.

The political structure of the South is an eighteenth-century heirloom. The plantation owner, with his peers, is the master of the realm. He once ruled the colony and he now rules the state. After slavery was abolished *de jure* it continued *de facto,* in the form of economic dependence and political disfranchisement. The sons of the old aristocracy became governors and senators, sharing political power at the lower ward levels with their henchmen of the courthouse gang. The alliance of the landed gentry with the backwoodsmen resembled the coalition of Bourbons and peasantry in the *ancien régime*.

The bloodless revolutions that have been moving across the United States since the turn of the century—for industrial democracy, political reform, civil rights—brushed past the South, touching it only lightly. And when these movements began to march south of the Mason-Dixon line, they came all at once, confronting the states of the old Confederacy at the same time with the challenges of industrialization, urbanization, and integration.

The civil rights revolution that struck the South on the centennial of the Emancipation Proclamation came at a time when the South was in transition, in a change-over from rural to urban society. This very change hastened the Negro upheaval. The decline of agriculture in the South dispossessed Negroes as well as whites from the soil. The whites drifted into factories and stores to find jobs. But where could the Negroes go? A people that had been denied many rights was now being denied the right to work. The one security provided by the old slavery and the new paternalistic system—a steady job—was being taken away. The injury of starvation was being added to the insult of slavery. The Negro revolt of the 1960s was as much economic as political, a fight for jobs as well as for rights.

The change in the Southern social system—from agricultural to industrial, from rural to urban, from nonunion to union, from politically conservative to liberal—will be a continuing process running over decades. But the ultimate outcome will affect the character of the trade-union movement as profoundly as the organization of the workers in services, white-collar trades, and professions. The impact of Negro liberation—a key item in the Southern change-over—will be felt in the unions in both North and South, adding a "new" Negro to the new labor movement.

CHAPTER 9

The New Negro

The American Negro is a worker: his future as a Negro depends on the rights he can win; his future as a worker depends on the job he can get. In pursuit of both, the Negro finds himself inextricably connected with the American labor movement.

"Negroes are almost entirely a working people," noted Dr. Martin Luther King in an address to the AFL-CIO convention in 1961. "There are pitifully few Negro millionaires and few Negro employers. Our needs are identical with labor's needs: decent wages, fair working conditions, livable housing, old age security, health and welfare measures, conditions in which families can grow, have education for their children and respect in the community. That is why Negroes support labor's demands and fight laws which curb labor. That is why the labor-hater and labor-baiter is virtually always a twin-headed creature spewing anti-Negro epithets from one mouth and anti-labor propaganda from the other mouth."

In the early 1960s, the American Negro was in the limelight of the dramatic struggle for rights. In 1964, the Congress of the United States passed a sweeping Civil Rights Act; in 1965, the Congress, at the historic urging of the President of the United States, passed a Voting Rights Act. Yet even as President Johnson was signing the bill, alert and sensitive civil rights leaders were talking less and less about the Negro as Negro and more and

179

more about the Negro as worker, whose problems in the future would be increasingly less *de jure* and increasingly more *de facto*.

"What good does it do to be able to eat at a lunch counter if you can't buy a hamburger?" asked Dr. Martin Luther King on August 4, 1965, in addressing an assembly of ministers. "What good is it to live in integrated housing if you can't afford to take your family on a vacation? Why be able to stay in hotels and restaurants if you don't have the money to take your wife out to dinner?"

As Negroes were finally winning on the legal front—the rights to vote, to public accommodations, to desegregated housing and integrated schooling, to an equal crack at jobs—they were opening a second front: the fight for the jobs, wages, vacations, the house at the seashore or in the mountains.

Simultaneously, far-sighted Negro leadership was proposing realistic politics to supplement dramatic protest. The sit-ins, march-ins, pray-ins, wade-ins had created a movement and awakened the nation's conscience. But by themselves, they could not get the great national action, legislative and executive, needed to convert newly won opportunities into realities. To obtain an economy with plenty of jobs, the labor-management legislation that would make the job meaningful in terms of pay and conditions, the education that would equip the Negro for better jobs, the livable lower-income housing—to get all this required political action.

Describing the Negro's *de jure* rise and *de facto* decline, Bayard Rustin wrote in 1964, in an article subtitled "The Future of the Civil Rights Movement," that "the very decade which has witnessed the decline of legal Jim Crow has also seen the rise of *de facto* segregation in our most fundamental socio-economic institutions. More Negroes are unemployed today than in 1954 and the unemployment gap between the races is wider. The median income of Negroes has dropped from 57 per cent to 54 per cent of that of whites. A higher percentage of Negro workers is now concentrated in jobs vulnerable to automation than was the case ten years ago. More Negroes attend *de facto* segregated schools today than when the Supreme Court handed down its famous decision; while school integration proceeds at a snail's pace in the South, the number of Northern schools with an excessive proportion of minority youth proliferates. And behind this is the continuing growth of racial slums, spreading over our central cities and trapping Negro youth in a milieu which, whatever its legal definition, sows an unimaginable demoralization. Again, legal niceties aside, a resident of a racial ghetto lives in segregated housing, and more Negroes fall into this category than ever before."

This is a description of the Negro as the low man on the economic totem pole, whose suffering derives less from his color than from his job, or lack of one. It is undoubtedly true that the problems of color and job are not separate, since the whole unfortunate history and conditioning of the Negro have served to place him at the grimy, unrewarding bottom of the economic pyramid. But now that he finds himself there, the civil rights movement as an action aimed at winning legal rights is not sufficient to resolve bread-and-butter problems.

"These are the facts of life," continued Rustin, "which generate frustration in the Negro community and challenge the civil rights movement. At issue, after all, is not *civil rights*, strictly speaking, but social and economic conditions. Last summer's riots were not race riots; they were outbursts of class aggression in a society where *class* and color definitions are converging disastrously."

The Negroes who in 1963 became involved in a civil rights movement began to learn in 1965 that they needed a socioeconomic movement to fill the empty vessels of legality with the nourishing milk of reality. In 1963, they marched on Washington. By 1964, they were marching to the polls. The first kind of march will undoubtedly continue in order to sound the tocsin. But the latter kind of march, though more prosaic, will also be more permanent in order to write the law.

The civil rights movement, concluded Rustin, "is now concerned not merely with removing the barriers to full opportunity but with achieving the fact of equality. From sit-ins and freedom rides we have gone into rent strikes, boycotts, community organization and political action. As a consequence of this natural evolution, the Negro today finds himself stymied by obstacles of far greater magnitude than the legal barriers he was attacking before: automation, urban decay, de facto school segregation. These are problems which, while conditioned by Jim Crow, do not vanish upon its demise. They are more deeply rooted in our socioeconomic orders; they are the result of the total society's failure to meet not only the Negro's needs, but human needs generally."

In describing this shift of emphasis, Rustin is moving the focus from the Negro revolution to the social revolution, from the problems of a black sector within our society to the total society. In some ways, the complexion of the Negro confuses the problem. What, indeed, if there were no Negroes in American society? About one-fifth of our people would still be ill-clothed, ill-housed, and ill-fed—but they would all be white. Maybe it would not be one-fifth; maybe it would be only one-sixth, because the past and present inhibiting of the Negro has been such as to retard his upward mobility even when there is upward opportunity. But take or give a fraction, poverty, illiteracy, disease, and insecurity would still be with us, oppressing white skins instead of black. (As it is, there are more whites than Negroes today who are their victims.)

Rustin's piece is titled "From Protest to Politics." He uses the term politics in a broad sense, to include actions outside simple voting. But, inevitably, the casting of the vote plays a central and dominant role because it is on Election Day that every man is king.

It is at this point, the casting of the vote, that the trade unions and the advancing Negro legions once more stand on common ground. They both want the same thing: a full-employment economy with plenty of good jobs and pay; protections against the hazards of illness, unemployment, old age, and death; better homes and schools. The war against poverty makes the Negro and the trade unionist natural allies.

The modern labor movement and the Negro are also bound by

their common interest in civil rights legislation. Ever since the movement for fair employment practice acts started, the trade unions have been in the forefront of that battle. When the FEPC fight finally came to the federal level, the AFL-CIO took the initiative in a difficult yet successful role in championing fair employment practices by law. The original drafts of the Civil Rights Act of 1964 did not contain any provision for fair employment practices—guarantees against discrimination in employment. The White House felt that such a clause was desirable but not possible and that to inject it in the proposed legislation might endanger the entire bill. In his appearance before Congress, however, President George Meany of the AFL-CIO strongly urged an FEPC section in the act. To get such a clause, the American labor movement, through its legislative department and its contacts in Congress and its rank-and-file action back home in the Congressional districts, began to turn on the heat. By the time the final act was readied for passage, the guarantee against discrimination in employment was in it. And the bill as amended by the AFL-CIO did pass.

Although Meany's stand came as a surprise to those who, having heard of discriminatory acts against Negroes by some local unions, had concluded that exclusion of Negroes was an official policy of the trade unions, those who knew the long-held position of the AFL-CIO on civil rights legislation and especially the part played in the past decade by George Meany, were surprised less by the strong stand of labor than by its success in making its policy public law.

Several years earlier, in 1957, when Congress was writing the Landrum-Griffin Act with its many restrictions against unions, the Southern contingent of the conservative coalition in Congress tried to arrange a peace pact with labor. If the unions would stop putting on pressure for civil rights legislation, a contingent of Southerners would, in return, withdraw support from the pending Landrum-Griffin. The nose count was close enough that such a deal might have made the difference. But labor turned it down.

The AFL-CIO stayed with civil rights and, incidentally, paid the price for its convictions. The Landrum-Griffin Act was passed and labor was hurt.

Again, in 1960, a civil rights act was passed, full of mouthings without teeth. Meany took the stand to flay those who had turned noble intentions into ignoble pretensions. "The Civil Rights Act of 1960 does not fulfill the hopes of the AFL-CIO for a truly meaningful bill. Once again, a small minority in the Congress has succeeded in thwarting the will of the vast majority of Americans who believe in, and wish to implement, the basic constitutional rights which properly belong to all Americans regardless of race or color or national origin. . . . With enactment of the Civil Rights Act of 1960, there must again be no moratorium. The AFL-CIO will be back again asking the 87th Congress to reinforce and to build on the foundation that has been laid so slowly and so weakly."

When Meany returned to the subsequent sessions of Congress he pleaded for strong legislation, not to throw stones at "others" but to clean up the house of labor. "The labor movement," he noted in his testimony before the House Judiciary Committee, "has not been the only advocate of civil rights legislation during the last decade; there have been the church groups and of course the Negro organizations themselves. But I think it is fair to say that we are the only ones, among the civil rights forces, which has openly called for legislation for the correction of shortcomings *in its own ranks*." Lest there be any mistake as to intent, Meany rubbed in his point before the Senate Committee with the blunt statement, "I want to state emphatically that we want unions covered by equal opportunity legislation."

The strong stand taken by the AFL-CIO on civil rights legislation is much more than the personal position of its president. Historically, the American Federation of Labor has always been for equal rights for Negroes, at a time when America did not even think about the kind of civil rights legislation we have come to know lately and at a time when prejudice against the Negro ran deep in a large sector of the labor movement. From a practical point of view, the old AFL argued that it was wise for a union to open its doors to Negroes if it did not wish to create an army of scabs outside the union and that it was also the morally right thing to do. The merger with the CIO strengthened the old AFL stand because the new unions came with heavy contingents of Negro members, and in recent years, the AFL-CIO has increasingly turned to legislation as a means of cleaning its own house, because the federation, with its limited powers, could not do the job. Since the Second World War, the wisdom of a Negro-labor alliance has become increasingly apparent as Negroes become an ever-rising percentage in the workplace and particularly as more and more of them are exercising the franchise.

The evolution of labor's position from a passive plea to a fighting stance is one of the most exciting, yet curiously unrecorded, chapters in the development of both labor and the Negro. The implications for the future affect the size of the unions, their effectiveness, their political power, their future leadership, and their social role.

In trying to integrate the Negro into the American labor movement, Samuel Gompers, the official and unofficial spokesman of the American Federation of Labor from the mid-1880s to the mid-1920s, was filled with moral fervor and practical frustration. He wanted to do the right thing but could not. So he did the next best thing: he made peace with the impossible. He preached and he prayed that the practice would some day catch up with the preaching. He bided his time, suffering segregation and discrimination among AFL affiliates, to "allow our agitation and time to work the desired changes."

In 1891, Gompers wrote: "The sentiment of organized labor of the country is decidedly in favor of maintaining and encouraging the recognition of the equality between colored and white laborers, so much so that at the last convention of a national union of machinists which is particularly located in the South and which prohibited colored machinists from becoming members, the Federation resolved to call for a convention of all machinists' unions for the purpose of forming a national union which shall recognize no color lines."

The war between Gompers and the machinists was won by both. The union changed its constitution to remove the "whites only" clause, but its locals in fact maintained an almost total closed-door policy against Negroes. Other unions followed the pattern: not in words but by deeds.

The victory of the AFL—and a victory it was—can only be appreciated against the background of the times. Some of the unions, the machinists among them, had a predominantly Southern membership. Other unions had had unfortunately bitter experiences with Negro workers. The former slaves who had been turned loose from slavery and from their old plantations had moved to industrial centers or, just as likely, had been shipped en masse into industrial centers by employers and scab-herders to break strikes. As a consequence, white workers came to associate "black" with "scab," and the unionists turned their fury against their black brethren as well as their white bosses. Still other unions, of artisans proud of their status, ran their locals like country clubs for "gentlemen only." And by that rule, they barred the Negro. For the AFL to have extorted even the verbal admission that it was not proper to write exclusion of Negroes into the constitution was a victory in those times.

In unions that were otherwise progressive and even radical, racial discrimination practices existed. The American Railway Union, for instance, was organized to combat the conservatism of the railway brotherhoods. Its Socialist leader, Eugene Victor Debs, led the ARU into militant and bloody struggle that was brought to an end only after the intervention of the federal troops. Yet in 1893, the ARU stipulated in its constitution that membership was open to "all railway employees born of white parents."

The verbal victory of the AFL, however, was short-lived. Reality won out over rhetoric. So common was the practice of excluding Negroes that enforcing the edict against writing such exclusion into the union constitution became pointless.

Exclusion in fact always outran exclusion by rule. Where Negroes were excluded by the constitution, the reason could be found in plain prejudice or in stupid status-seeking. In other cases Negroes were excluded because of the exclusive character of the craft union: an exclusiveness exercised against all "outsiders," regardless of race, creed, color, or national origin. After prejudice had given way to tolerance and social climbing to a more democratic air around the workplace, and even after a number of states had passed fair employment practices acts, exclusion from these craft unions continued, with Negroes as prominent victims.

The exclusionist policy of the craft unions, most common in the journeyman trades of building and construction, arises from the efforts of the local in a given area to balance labor supply with labor demand. The door to the trade, where that is admission to the union or entrance into apprenticeship, is kept closed or is opened with caution. The object is to protect the union member against unemployment or against the lower wages that come when many workers compete for few jobs. When the victim of exclusion is Irish, Italian, Jewish, Negro, Mexican, Puerto Rican —and all these have been victims—the act of exclusion looks like discrimination based on prejudice. In fact, it is exclusion based on self-interest.

The problem is complicated in these craft unions because work is steady and the wages good. A father therefore wants to pass his job on to his son—or perhaps his son-in-law—just as is done in corporations, law firms, and public office. And since most craft unions are disconcertingly democratic within the union, the leader of the local pays heed to the wishes of the member who, in the great American style, wants to "take care" of family and friends. As a result, the admissions policy of many such local craft unions is based on a system of patronage tainted with nepotism, a practice for which there is little defense beyond its universality.

The proud Knights of St. Crispin, the skilled fabricators of

shoes at the time of the Civil War, were not too proud to write a
"son only" clause into the constitution of their International
Grand Lodge in 1869. They were fighting to protect their jobs
against semiskilled workers armed with the newly invented Mc-
Kay stitcher. The Knights decreed: "No member of this order
shall teach, or aid in teaching, any part or parts of boot and shoe
making, unless the lodge shall give permission by a three-fourths
vote of those present and voting thereon, when such permission is
first asked; provided this article shall not be so construed as to
prevent a father teaching his own son." The clause turned out to
be a failure. If employers could not find skilled shoemakers where
the union had a grip on the trade, they went elsewhere to have
shoes made by semiskilled workers with new machines. But while
the Knights failed because shoes can be shipped easily, the identical tactic could be effective in building and construction because
a factory or highway or bridge cannot be made here and shipped
there. And as a result, less extreme forms of the tactic are common in certain craft unions, even though restrictions against outsiders are not written into constitutions.

To get anyone without a "contact" into some of these skilled
crafts is difficult. The "in" group tends to bring in "insiders," not
only members of the family but also friends, neighbors, and ethnic "neighbors."

The problem of the AFL has been double: to live up to a moral
imperative by getting Negroes into unions with an outright racial
bar; to carry out a socioeconomic imperative by getting Negroes
into exclusive crafts. The former has been easier than the latter
since it involves changing words and not changing jobs. But, in
both areas, the Federation has had a tough time because it is
nearly powerless to make policy for any affiliate.

The AFL-CIO has only two instruments: persuasion and expulsion. It has traditionally preferred the former, although it has
occasionally used the latter. It prefers persuasion because it believes that this is best for the labor movement as a whole (since
the strength that comes with unity is maintained) and best for
the Negro (since the Federation is in a position to use its moral,

organizational, financial, and personal influence to change the policy of the affiliate). It turns to expulsion only in extreme situations and has used this Draconic weapon only against unions found guilty of being controlled by gangsters or Communists.

George Meany attempted an explanation of the reason that some unions were expelled because they were run by "reds" or "racketeers" and others were not expelled when run by "racialists."

"Corruption—like communism—seizes the leadership of a union and works down to lower levels by perverting the union's democratic procedures. The rank-and-file members . . . don't know what's going on. . . . Expulsion was the only way to convince the membership of this domination by corrupt elements. . . . Discrimination is resisted at the top but perpetrated below. . . . Would we be better off to cast out these misguided members and remove them from the influence of the mainstream of the labor movement; meanwhile expelling in the same action the national leaders who deplore and fight discrimination? I think not. I think we can do more toward educating them if they're in the federation, with their own leaders getting broad AFL-CIO support toward the same end."

The process of education, however, is long and slow and hardly in tempo with the swiftly changing public attitude toward the Negro. If some locals in the AFL-CIO refused to open doors to the Negro, they might very well find themselves lagging behind a nation whose Supreme Court, whose President and Congress, and whose people were clamoring for integration as a moral right and as a social necessity. To help clean the house of labor, the AFL-CIO turned to the federal government.

The AFL-CIO found it easier to push for full civil rights legislation and for a firmer effort within its own ranks because of the internal alignment of forces since the merger of 1956. The CIO unions were strongly disposed toward civil rights almost from their beginning. The base of these unions was the factory, among semiskilled and unskilled workers, many of whom were Negroes. In these unions, organized in almost every case after 1935, there was absolutely no disposition to bar the Negro by writ. Nor was there any of the exclusionist attitude of the craft unions, since in the mass-production industries the union is less interested in controlling the job in the local market than in controlling work standards in the entire industry.

The AFL-CIO effort was further eased by the great decision of the U. S. Supreme Court in the school desegregation case. Integration became public policy, making it respectable to be moral. The educational efforts of the AFL-CIO were aided by the headlines in the daily papers. In the effort to integrate the Negro into the trade unions, the AFL-CIO moves along several lines. It works for legislation to outlaw discrimination in employment and in unions; it puts pressure on its affiliates through its civil rights committee; it tries to set an example through its actions and to set a tone through its statements; it involves local unions in local civil rights actions.

In an historic statement that has regrettably gone almost unnoted by the press and public, the president of the Plumbers' Union, Peter Schoemann, set the tone and direction for his local affiliates. His appeal reveals the anguish and final decision of a leader who is honestly torn between justifiable attitudes of his membership and the equally justifiable needs of the society. Schoemann wants to protect his plumbers; he also wants to help find a proper place for the Negro in American society. His statement which appeared in the *Journal* (April 1965) of the United Association of Journeymen and Apprentices of the Plumbing and Pipe Fitting Industry of the United States and Canada, is a classic in the resolution of complex problems with plain talk.

Schoemann begins by reading the riot act. There has been legislation. And if we do not behave, there will be more legislation. "So, Brothers, let's not blind ourselves to the signs of the times." Desegregation is part of the times. And what is more, adds Schoemann, many plumbers, who have moved with America, have "had an uneasy conscience about discrimination."

The United Association, asserts Schoemann, "has not tried to conceal or apologize for the system of preferring sons in the building trades. We have campaigned openly for the right of our programs to select apprentices in the same way that any private business might select employees, or that an elected public official selects his political appointees. This extends all the way to a pure patronage system for those local programs that desire it."

For those locals that wish to run a "patronage system" for their apprenticeship programs, however, Schoemann adds: "If you want to run a patronage system, then go ahead, but show us what patronage you are reserving for members of the minority groups." On the other hand, if a local wishes to run its program on a competitive merit basis, that, too, is okay. But, warns Schoemann, "we expect it to be followed to the letter. This means no point chiselling and no loophole hunting in favor of the member's son, the contractor's nephew, the mayor's brother-in-law, or anyone else."

Schoemann's call is an appeal against self-interest. In the short run, the old policy helps the member, makes friends for the union, and influences well-placed people. To deplete this reservoir of potential goodwill in order to admit outsiders, whether they be Negro or not, is to admit a "nobody" instead of a "somebody." Schoemann is asking members to dilute self-interest with public policy.

The AFL-CIO has found that its civil rights stand has in numerous instances worked against its short-run self-interest. The attempt to organize the South has undoubtedly been slowed by the fact that employers can point the finger at the Federation as an instrument of integration. In union representation elections, employers out to beat unions have used and continue to use the racist arguments common to Southern politicians. This has worked to hold back and weaken Southern unionism.

The AFL-CIO, however, holds to its course because it believes that full civil rights are morally correct and because, *in the long run,* it feels that integration of the Negro into the labor movement—even in those relatively few craft unions where an open admission policy would work against local self-interest—is ultimately best for the labor movement as a whole. Instead of creating an army of involuntary scabs, the long-run commitment of the labor movement to civil rights and Negro admission can raise an army of voluntary union men and women.

In the pursuit of this policy of admitting Negroes into every last corner of the labor movement, the AFL-CIO is of course aided by public policy and by public opinion. The labor movement feels, however, that the most realistic aid for full rights is full employment. When a plumbers' local, or any craft local, has plenty of jobs to hand out, the local and all its members can be generous. They can "take care" of all the relatives, and Negroes too. If, however, there are few jobs to distribute, then quite obviously the first to get the available jobs will be the old-timers, then the newcomers, and only then will the doors be opened to any new admissions to the union and finally, if at all, to any outsiders. So long as jobs are so tight that the admission of any new member becomes an either-or proposition—either Negro or white—integration will be needlessly difficult. But if there are enough jobs for all, tolerance becomes more tolerable. In a local union, as in a civilization, where men are richer in goods they find it easier to be rich in goodwill. A full-employment economy, with a job for everyone who wants work, is a *sine qua non* for a civilization seeking to increase acceptance of minority rights and to convert such rights into reality.

Finding full employment for the American Negro is a Herculean challenge. America must do more than put more Negroes on the payroll. If the job is not meaningful, in the long run it is bad for the Negro and for society. Within Negro ranks, there is growing awareness that if the Negro is to be free he must be independent; he must end his role as a dependent. Hence, Negroes should be given jobs that need doing and that should be done by qualified workers.

Finding meaningful jobs for Negroes makes the challenge more difficult. The economy has been moving away from the types of work traditionally handled by Negroes. And the Negro has not kept up with the change. Because the lower rungs of the economic ladder are being lopped off, more and more Negroes cannot even get one foot up for the long climb upward. To close the gap between the work market and the Negro's skills will require training. And with that training will have to go a whole family of changes: in housing, neighborhoods, family life, schooling, motivation. Many Negroes, caught in the web of past slavery and present poverty, will have to be trained to accept training.

For some Negroes, a prime step in their motivation toward self-elevation is involvement in the Negro revolution. Protest is an act of independence, a prelude to social maturity. It is an act of pride, a prelude to a new self-image. There is a political dimension, too, underlying motivation toward a new community, new family, and new self.

In 1963, more than one out of every ten Negroes in the labor force was unemployed—11 per cent, to be exact. Among white workers the unemployment rate was 5 per cent. This meant that there were 900,000 Negroes looking for work. These jobless constituted one out of four unemployed in the country, although non-whites represented only 11.7 per cent of the population. The Negro, then, is about one out of ten in the population, about one out of ten in the labor force, but about one out of four among the jobless.

Negro unemployment has been growing in comparison with that of white workers. "The disparity between non-white and white unemployment since 1955," states the U.S. Department of Labor *Manpower Report* in March 1964, "has been much broader than it was between 1947 and 1955."

The reason for this worsening relative position of the Negro is not rising prejudice but rising standards in the labor market. The traditional locus of much Negro employment was in the unskilled trades. "Unskilled occupations," continues the *Manpower Report*, "except private household work, had unemployment rates in 1963 above the national average of 5.7 per cent, ranging up to 12.1 per cent for non-farm laborers. This was in sharp contrast to skilled craftsmen whose unemployment averaged 4.8 per cent and professions with 1.9 per cent." Among these unskilled trades, unemployment was greater and longer. "Close to 3 out of 10 of the unemployed service workers, non-farm laborers, and operatives were jobless on the average for more than 15 weeks at any given time in 1963."

The forecast of the Negro unemployment rate is not good. It is even worse for young Negroes who face even greater competition in an even more crowded market. In 1963, the unemployment rate for all youths between 14 and 19 years of age was 15.6 per cent. Needless to add, the rate for Negro youth ran considerably higher—in fact close to twice that of white youth.

In some communities where the residents are Negro, unskilled, and with a high percentage of young people, real depression is under way. Whatever else may be happening in the country as a whole, in these dark spots there is a crisis as profound as that of 1929–1932.

Until American society finds ways to help the jobless Negro become a participant in the economy, an undertaking in which the Negro himself plays a self-imposed and perhaps dominant role, many of the *de jure* rights will not become *de facto*. In the struggle to reach this goal, the labor movement may be expected to play a significant part.

Of more immediate import to the labor movement are the Negroes who are employed and who represent almost 90 per cent of the Negro labor force. There were about 8 million nonwhite workers in the labor force as of 1963. There will be more in the future, since their proportion in the population has been constantly growing since the 1930s. Negroes have been moving from nonunion to union areas: from farm to city and from South to North. In the 1950s, about 1.5 million Negroes left the South for California and the Middle Atlantic, and East North Central states. The drain from the South has been so constant that by 1963 only 60 per cent of the Negroes in the United States lived in the South. The concentration of Negroes in cities is evidenced by the fact that, by 1960, 73 per cent of them lived in cities: a higher percentage than that of the whites. In other words, as of the 1960s, the Negro is more a city being than the white is, although the American Negro until World War I was a man of the soil.

The movement of Negro from land to city, from South to North, has brought him into unionized industries and into unions. The number of Negroes in American labor unions, though never officially counted, is constantly rising. And the forecast here is clear: as the population movement continues, as fair employment practices laws open the doors to more Negroes in hitherto inaccessible trades, and as law, precept, and pressure force craft unions to admit Negro apprentices to become journeymen, the absolute number and the percentage of Negroes in unions will continue to rise.

This movement will not be limited to service trades workers, operatives, and skilled factory people. The trend to white-collar and professional employment will carry the Negro with it. The *Manpower Report* for 1963 noted "a growth in the proportion of nonwhites in professional, operative, and clerical jobs and a concomitant decrease in the percentage employed as private household workers and as laborers." In part, this trend arises from the higher average educational level of Negroes. Between 1953 and 1963, the average number of years spent by Negroes in schools rose from 7.6 to 9.6, while the number of Negro high school graduates doubled.

In most respects, the forecast for the Negro worker is that he will travel the road of the white worker, although he will trail far behind: from farm to town, from field to factory, from blue collar to white collar, from little education to more education. In one respect, the Negroes reverse the white trend: while the population as a whole is shifting to the South, the Negro population is shifting out of the South—for understandable reasons. And in two respects, the Negro runs ahead of the white population: more women working (45 per cent of nonwhite women were in the labor force in 1963) and a greater rate of participation in the labor force (60 per cent for nonwhites). This higher participation rate is not due to Negro men (who participate at a lower rate than white males) but to the Negro women and to the large number of Negro youth who are not in school but out working or looking for work.

In their relationship with trade unions, Negroes will also travel the same road as their white brothers but will again trail behind. A rough estimate shows Negroes to be about the same percentage of the labor movement as of the work force. They hold positions at all levels from shop steward to national union president. As they gain experience and standing in the unions and as time makes more room at the top there will be more Negroes in top posts. In their trade-union attitudes, they may be expected to add a touch of the militant, especially in the 1970s and 1980s. Many of their union activists will be grown-up "children of the movement"—those teenagers and preteenagers who are veterans of Montgomery, Selma, and Americus. They will be a "causey" kind, with hardened purpose and skill in organization. Their ranks may very well be swollen by the Negro students of the 1960s who, still wed to their cause and their people a decade or two later, will follow their followers into the labor movement as an effective —perhaps the most effective—way for the Negro to taste the reality of his rights. Some of these may come into the labor movement through white-collar, professional, and government unions; others may simply throw in their lot with Negroes and the organization of Negroes wherever they may be. Such rising Negro leadership, working with white leadership, will also be strongly inclined toward the political uses of unionism. After all, for many Negroes, whatever their age, the late 1960s and the 1970s will be the first years of voting. They will want to use a right for which they fought so hard; they are apt to view balloting with all the enthusiasm of the novice.

The future role of the labor movement in the life of the Negro worker is a re-enactment of past social drama, played many times before with the same script and changing actors. When the nation was young, minorities were denied the right to vote for religious reasons. Workers were denied the right to vote, for property reasons. The latter fought for the right to vote, as does the Negro today, and did so with the help of their organizations of artisans and craftsmen: their early unions. Workers wanted their children to have good schooling, as the Negro does, and their unions entered politics vigorously for free and universal public education. Workers wanted job security, they wanted apprenticeship programs, they wanted vocational education for their children—and so they turned to their unions. In subsequent years, they turned to their unions for health care, for clinics, for hospitals, for vacations—for the realities of workers' rights. In their unions, leaders appeared who learned the arts and crafts of organization in labor's struggles. Many came out of the ranks of the workplace. Some came out of the colleges and the civil rights movement. And with each passing generation, new ethnic groups began their upward climb, from "nobody" to "somebody," from "slavery" to "freedom." To each new ethnic group, outsiders trying to get in, the wage system was looked upon as "wage slavery." And the struggle for "rights" on the job was termed the fight for "freedom." Each group drew strength from the unions and each group gave its share of leadership, new militancy, and inspiration to the unions. In a way, this is the story of America; it is also the story of its labor movement.

CHAPTER 10

Labor in Politics

American labor is entering an era of political unionism. To many, labor will appear in coming decades to be more a political party than a bargaining agent, although, in fact, bargaining will be as intense as ever and the unions are unlikely to organize a labor party. The enemies of labor will fear it too much and will try to limit or forbid union political action. The friends of labor will hope for too much and will turn to the movement for the kind of bold new ideas that unions are not likely to invent. Labor leaders will achieve some of the veneer of statesmen in order to pass muster in legislative halls as well as at bargaining tables, and the rank and file will learn increasingly to get out and vote and to do so for a reasonably consistent platform. The unions will find themselves in a "lib-lab" coalition with minorities and intellectuals, a massive political alliance built around a metropolitan core, whose ideology will penetrate the suburbs and the South. The specific gravity of the labor vote will increase as the one-man one-vote doctrine becomes a political fact. The end product will probably be a realignment of national parties with labor as the mass base for the party of liberalism.

This period of political unionism will be the third great period of the labor movement in twentieth-century America. As we have said earlier, the first, from the turn of the century to the New Deal, was dominated by the craft unions. In the second, from

FDR to LBJ, the industrial unions were added to the crafts. In the third period, from 1964 on, the old craft and industrial unions, joined with unionists out of new occupations and new geographical areas, will turn increasingly political.

Political unionism will not be the child of an edict, sprung full-panoplied out of the head of some laborite Zeus. Labor politics is the product of a long painful evolution that has taken place in spite of labor's natural bent. The instinct of the American unions has been to eschew politics for economic purposes. Such questions as minimum wages, maximum hours, unemployment insurance, and old-age pensions were matters to be settled over bargaining tables and written into contracts, not resolved in legislative halls and written into law. The unions did not want Uncle Sam invading their jurisdiction.

Under the tutelage of Gompers, the typical craft union in America worked out a rationale for this legislative negativism. First of all, it was argued, workers must learn to rely on their own strength rather than on government and politicians. What the government gave, the government could take away. What workers wrote into their own contracts in the blood of the picket lines, they would keep. Second, if government could write minimum wage laws, it could write maximum wage laws. To head off such economic dictatorship, it would be best to keep the government out of the wage area completely. Finally, if the government did pass a bit of favorable economic legislation, workers would still find this to be an empty promise forgotten by the enforcing agencies or frustrated by the conservative courts.

This negative attitude toward economic legislation stemmed from a fear of government, a fear which the unions shared with the rest of the nation. Labor too placed its faith in the rugged individualist and was suspicious of all "politicians." The way to get a job done was to do it yourself. If you can't do it yourself, get your neighbors to cooperate. If you must turn to those slimy politicians for help, go to the local people. But beware the leviathan, that monster in Washington.

This negativism was reinforced by the earliest experiences of the unions. Strikes were broken by local constabulary. Courts held unions to be conspiracies under the common law. Legislation outlawing homework was vetoed by administrative agencies. The Sherman Anti-Trust Act was transformed into an antilabor act by judges on the bench. A law ending child labor in factories was invalidated by the Supreme Court. Without ever using Marx's classic phrase, American unions had a firm belief that the government was "the executive committee of the ruling class."

Two major factional experiences of the AFL reinforced its rejection of the political path to liberation: the struggles against the Knights of Labor and against the Socialists. The Knights believed that the way out of industrial slavery was to put an end to the wage system by making it possible for every worker to own his own tools: by easy credit, by cooperatives, or by public ownership where necessary. The way to do this was by education and by politics. Against this escape from "wage slavery," the AFL urged workers to find a *modus vivendi* within the wage system, to fight for more and more in the contract. The way to do this was collective bargaining, backed up by strikes where necessary. In the struggle between Knights and Federation, viewpoints were driven to extremes. When the AFL issued victorious from the struggle, it turned its back on a solution of the "social question" through politics. This negativism was toughened in the long battle against the Socialists in the labor movement. Some Socialists, under Daniel De Leon, had broken away from the AFL to organize separate and dual unions which they hoped would someday form the labor government of the industrial commonwealth. The competition of the Socialist Trade and Labor Alliance gave the AFL occasion to blacken the Socialists as "splitters" and "scabs." The major Socialist faction that stayed within the AFL continued to threaten Gompers with its ideology and its votes at AFL conventions. The Socialists advocated a cooperative commonwealth and a series of social measures to pave the way for socialism. Both immediate and ultimate goals were to be won with the ballot. And to strengthen their influence, Socialists, in alliance with the non-Socialist miners, threw their strength against Gompers at

AFL conventions with enough force to remove him from the presidency for one term. Gompers retaliated by lifelong war against the Socialists, against their ultimate aims, against their immediate demands, and against their factional power in the federation. The heat generated in this conflict carried over into the 1920s, after the Socialists had lost influence and after Gompers had died, and caused the old craft-union leadership to reject both socialism and social legislation out of hand by force of habit.

Although by the 1920s the AFL old guard had accumulated a whole arsenal of words, clichés, and arguments against social legislation, their truest objection to it was not ideological but experiential. The old method had worked and was still working successfully, especially for the skilled-craft unions, who were winning "more." Their homespun philosophy was passing the pragmatic test: it worked.

Despite this political negativism, the seeds of an era of political unionism were spread widely in the Gompers years. These seeds could be found in the many exceptions the AFL made to its antipolitical posture. The Federation believed in political action to protect the right of the unions to carry on their business, free of tethers imposed by police, courts, and legislatures. And so the unions made their marriages of convenience with local politicians to neutralize or win over the constabulary or the bench. Gompers conducted a campaign in the first decade of the century to amend the anti-trust law to exempt unions from the act. The AFL also believed in social legislation to win by law what could not be won through contract: an end to prison labor, a halt to the importation of foreign labor under contract, democratization of the governmental machinery, etc. The AFL also believed in legislation to protect the "unorganizable": women, children, convicts, and others whose sad condition could not be improved through unionization; in legislation for public employees whose terms of work were set by law or administrative acts; and finally, in legislation at the state level for safety devices, for licensing of crafts, for building and construction codes, etc.

Against the background of the unions' wide political participation in all these areas, the refusal of the AFL to seek social legislation in those areas covered by contract appears in itself to be the exception. Indeed, it may well have been an exception that the unions shared with the American people: a common fear that Washington would extend its long arm into the economy.

It took the great depression of 1929 to shake both the unions and the country out of this puerile paralysis. By 1932, it was clear to the unions that the old way did not work. It was time for a change. Massive and mounting unemployment destroyed the premises for effective bargaining. The army of unemployed was an army of scabs. Unions could not bargain with employers who needed few, if any, employees. Wages fell; strikes failed; unions flopped. Capital was going bankrupt and so was labor. The traditional enemies labor and capital discovered that they needed each other, to feed each other and to fight with each other in a wholesome, hostile symbiosis. Yet neither alone nor both together could restore the climate required for their common existence: an economy of employment.

The federal government, under FDR, started America toward recovery. With Marx in its left hand and Keynes in its right, and a scared country behind it, the New Deal administration began to put America back to work. FDR added many new initialed entities to the lexicon of social action: WPA, PWA, CWA, NRA, AAA, FLSA, and TVA. His program also revived the AFL and gave birth to the CIO. He advanced a new program and simultaneously helped promote social forces to continue that program. And one such social force, with promise of great political potential, was the labor movement itself. In the great breakthrough following the formation of the CIO, millions of factory workers formed industrial unions, lifting organized labor to a new plateau. The American labor movement entered its second great period: the inclusion of the industrial worker into the family of labor.

The change was qualitative as well as quantitative: the new unionism accepted the federal government as a necessary, even desirable, instrument for economic action—the old AFL unions reluctantly, the new CIO unions enthusiastically. The new unions were the children of the New Deal, the "NRA babies," to use the labor tag. They were wise children who knew their father. By the early 1940s, the CIO had put together a permanent instrument for political action, the CIO–PAC (Political Action Committee). Although limited to a sector of American unionism, PAC fore-shadowed the future of the total movement.

During the earlier Roosevelt years, the less politically minded affiliates of the AFL were riding piggy-back on the New Deal. With only a few exceptions, their "action" consisted in passing a resolution of endorsement or making a contribution out of the union treasury to a friendly candidate, indulging the illusion that these normally meaningless motions were effective. After all, they could assure one another, if the man they endorsed won the election, his election must be due to their endorsement.

A second shock was required to shake the self-deluded out of their bureaucratic bliss. In 1947, Congress passed the Taft-Hart-ley Act. The unions denounced it as a "slave labor" act. President Truman vetoed the bill. But a conservative Congress, convinced that the unions had too much power at the bargaining table and at the ballot box, resolved to restrain labor's industrial and politi-cal arms and passed the law over the presidential veto. The un-ions learned a sad lesson: the President was not all-powerful, the unions were not as powerful as they thought, and the new power rested with a conservative coalition in control of Congress.

The conservative coalition that passed the Taft-Hartley Act so handily in 1947 had been building its strength for more than a decade. As far back as 1936, when FDR returned for a second term, the forces of the old regime, grouping around the GOP and the Southern Democrats, composed a bloc to check the rush of reform. Confronted with this challenge, Roosevelt decided to move against it in his own party, by using his power and prestige to defeat conservative Democrats in the primaries of 1938. This attempted house cleaning was one of FDR's signal and crucial failures. In that mid-term election, the conservative coalition came back stronger than ever; the Democratic delegation lost strength and most of the losses were in the Northern liberal wing of the party. In subsequent elections—even as labor was boasting of its successes in electing FDR—the coalition gained ground. Finally, in 1946, the take-over was complete: Roosevelt was dead, the country was war-weary, and the GOP won a clear majority in both houses. In the tick-tock of history, the pendulum had swung to the right.

While the nation was swinging to the right, the labor movement swung to the left. Under the goad of the Taft-Hartley Act, America's most conservative unions moved into the mainstream of liberal politics. Republican Senator Taft succeeded where Socialist agitator Eugene V. Debs had failed, in turning the craft unions leftward. For America's right wing, as in some Greek tragedy, fear produced what it feared the most.

In the winter of 1947, just a few weeks after passage of Taft-Hartley, the normally sedentary William Green, then president of the AFL, rose in political anger and called a conference of his affiliates in Washington, D.C., to establish a permanent political organization, the electoral arm of the AFL. It was christened Labor's League for Political Education (LLPE) and it sets its sights on the presidential and more especially on the congressional elections of 1948. A clue to the meaning of this extraordinary conference was the fact that, while Green presided, the moving spirit was the man who was then secretary of the AFL, a member of the plumbers' union and a spokesman for the traditionally conservative building trades, George Meany. Symbolically, the craft unions were parting with their past.

Although LLPE was intended to educate the rank and file in the why and how of politics, the first to benefit from its schooling was the labor leadership itself. LLPE became a school in politics where the union leaders were forcibly taught three great lessons: First, workers cannot be ordered to vote and to vote right; they must be educated to do so. Second, electoral machinery must be built in the neighborhoods where workers live, because they vote where they reside and not where they work. Third, labor cannot win elections by going it alone and must therefore learn the art of political coalition and compromise.

These basic lessons did not come easily to labor leaders. Their experience had led them to think otherwise. When a strike vote is taken at a union hall, the union leader can normally count on 100 per cent of the members to respect the strike call. But when a candidate is endorsed at a union meeting, the union leader cannot count on his membership to go along. In the shop where the member works, the union leader is an authority commanding power and even respect, but in the election precinct, the union leader is either nobody or just not there. Finally, when a union goes on strike, its few adherents can tie up a plant, an industry, or even a city. But when workers vote alone, they cannot win elections: they need allies.

Learning these lessons has sometimes been painful. In 1940, John L. Lewis, the great leader of the miners, turned his back on FDR to endorse the Republican Wendell Willkie. John L. called on his coal diggers to vote for the GOP. But, when the ballots were counted on election night, the mining towns had turned in heavy majorities for Roosevelt. Lewis could march his men out of the pits for the things they wanted but he could not march them to the polls for the thing he wanted. In 1950, the unions learned the same lesson in Ohio when they called upon their membership to defeat Senator Taft. The directive to the rank and file came down more as an edict than as an appeal, and Taft was elected easily. Union members once more proved that, although they might be persuaded to vote for a candidate, they could not be driven to the polls like cattle.

Through the 1940s and 1950s, the unions sharpened their political tools: education, organization, and coalition. They learned to unite their own and to unite with others. Adversity provided a grinding edge for further sharpening. In 1952, labor's candidate for President, Adlai Stevenson, was decisively defeated by General Eisenhower; in 1956, Stevenson was even more badly beaten. In 1959, Congress passed the Landrum-Griffin Act, imposing fur-

ther restrictions on unions. In twenty states, right-to-work laws
were passed, outlawing the union-shop clause from contracts.
Through the remainder of the 1950s labor had to learn to speak
for itself: there was no voice in the White House to carry the
message, no liberal majority in Congress to write the legislation.
Pushed out of the power structure, the unions learned to build
their own power.

The merger of AFL and CIO in the mid-1950s produced a
united political adjunct—the Committee for Political Education
(COPE). Although COPE operates at all political levels, its pre-
occupation has been the Congress of the United States. Located
in Washington, D.C., and closely informed by the legislative representatives of the unions, the COPE leadership understands only
too well the grip of the conservative coalition on Capitol Hill and
the country. For that reason, after each election, as headlines
focused on the name of the man who was elected President or the
name of the party with a majority in one house or the other, the
labor politicos carefully combed through the records of the men
elected to Congress, marking each name with an "L" for liberal or
a "C" for conservative or a "?" for the unknown. COPE kept score
on Congress, not by party but by program.

COPE's measure of the legislator is the record. This tabulation
of a man's political behavior is a listing of his votes on key issues
before the Congress, not merely those relatively few measures
that have to do with the rights of unions, such as Taft-Hartley or
Landrum-Griffin or right-to-work, but on a wide spectrum of issues. A typical voting record of 1950 covered ten issues: Taft-
Hartley, rules committee procedures, housing, social security, Korean military aid, Korean economic aid, Point Four, war mobilization speculators, war mobilization credits, excess profits tax. A
record for a nonwar year (1957) covered thirteen issues: civil
rights, education, wage-hour regulations, food and drug act,
TVA, atomic energy, public assistance, foreign aid, flood insurance, reciprocal trade, reclamation, unemployment compensation, states' rights. These issues become the bases for endorsement
of candidates; they also become ammunition for the campaigns.

The broad basis of labor's political judgments, as can be gathered from its published voting records, led Secretary of Labor Willard Wirtz to say that "labor's program, once, was 'more' for labor; it is now 'more' for people." President Lyndon Johnson went beyond his Secretary of Labor in appraising labor as a sociopolitical force. At the time the President signed the Older Americans Act, July 1965, he said:

"The legislative efforts of the AFL-CIO have done more good for more people than any other group in America. It doesn't just try to do something about wages and hours for its own people. No group in America works harder in the interests of everyone. It helps young and old and middle-aged. It's interested in education, in housing, in poverty programs, and does as much good for millions who have never belonged to a union as for its own members. This is my conception of an organization working in the public interest."

Even after this fulsome statement is politically discounted, there is enough validity in it to credit labor as one of the greatest bodies of citizens "working in the public interest." In the future, this will be even more true, because of the kind of issues in which the labor movement will be involved and because of the kind of people who will be coming into the labor movement.

The great issues around which labor's activities will revolve will be: (1) the relationship between government and the daily life of the unions, (2) a program for full employment, and (3) the war against poverty. Each of these will have special appeals for different unions. The war against poverty will have particular meaning for unions with low-income earners, whose members are situated on the slum side of the economy. Full employment will have poignant significance for unions in industries facing automation. Regulatory legislation and acts dealing with employer-employee relations or with internal union government will have universal interest. All three of these great issues will be with the nation, and hence with the unions, for decades to come.

The modern union is under constant legislative and administrative regulation. The law defines how a union shall be certified for collective-bargaining purposes, what it may or may not write into a contract, what an unfair labor practice is, which strikes are legal and which illegal, how far a boycott may or may not go. The law defines the rights of members, the responsibilities of officers, the legitimacy of union constitutions, the validity of union elections. The law demands reports on union finances and on the management of welfare funds. Boards and courts put new turns and twists on these laws with their daily interpretations.

As perennial as its interest in regulatory legislation will be labor's concern with full employment. The problem of the jobless threatens to continue under the push of rising population and automation. The solution will not be found at the bargaining table nor in any one magical law. Answers will be sought in many planks of a full-employment platform.

Labor's program for full employment is set forth in Chapter 5. The platform contains a mixture of collective bargaining and legislation. Through contracts, unions can raise wages to boost buying power, cut hours to spread work, and arrange to soften the blow of displacement by attrition, seniority, and added compensation for the jobless. But the contract cure is limited. Wages can be raised and hours cut only for those under contract—at present a clear minority of the work force. Protection through attrition is workable only in rich corporations with enough extra margin of capital and profit to carry the cost and even then is limited to the senior workers who come under the protective formula. For younger workers or for those in trades or plants operating with a narrow margin, attrition does not work.

"Given the increasing human cost factor of technological change and the increasingly linked nature of the economy," writes Daniel Bell, "it seems unlikely that any of these automation problems can be met by other than comprehensive action at the National Governmental level." In short, to maintain full employment, unions must look beyond the contract at the local level to President and Congress at the federal level.

The war against poverty is familiar terrain for some unions. George Meany once archly suggested that "poverty is caused by lack of money." He was relating the currently fashionable anti-poverty war to labor's ancient battle cry for more. He was simultaneously reminding his colleagues and the Congress that there are millions of union members—as well as the unorganized and unemployed—who know the stench of poverty first-hand. These are the dues payers in the slum side of the economy, working in trades where cruel competition yields low profits and lower wages. The unfortunate worker in these benighted trades is like a Dickens character, victimized by the accidents of birth, place, and time, unrewarded for his productive virtues.

Commenting on the inherent injustice of many such wage differentials in our economy. Secretary of Labor Wirtz noted:

"There is something strange in the fact that in the country among all nations in which we place largest emphasis on the individual, we still shape our programs on employment, manpower, wages, education and everything else on what the system demands, instead on what we have to offer.

"It doesn't make sense that the same kind of skill and effort is rewarded differently in different industries, just because the system dictates that. We've got to work towards that point at which throughout all industry in this country there will be some common standard which is based on the value and what's inside an individual instead of what the individual happens to add to the particular system."

To bring a measure of equity to the wage injustices of the system, labor turns to politics to supplement the traditional type of wage with a "social wage." For workers who cannot afford proper housing, unions seek laws to control rents, to erect subsidized housing, to have the government underwrite part or all of the rent, to extend low-interest mortgages. For workers who cannot afford medical care, unions seek free clinics and hospitals, prepaid medical insurance, low-cost or free nursing homes. For workers whose children cannot afford colleges, unions seek free tuition, loans, and scholarships. For mothers who must work, unions seek free day nurseries. And for families that cannot make ends meet even while working, unions seek relief and welfare programs. The

unions which are most keenly aware of the need for such a social
wage are those operating in the poor side of the economy, since
they know first-hand and too well the limitations of contract
gains. Such unions must carry their case beyond the employer,
who is limited in what he can yield, to American society, whose
affluence can afford to right the system's wrong.

To realize its program, labor needs sympathetic votes. It is a
labor maxim that the greatest potential for a liberal program in
America is the reservoir of normally uncast votes among the
lower-income groups of the nation. Hence, labor's program is to
ease voting regulations, to educate and goad low-income nonvoters into voting, to set up a machine to drag them to the polls if
necessary. The core of labor's strategy is to "get out the vote," on
the general assumption that a big vote is a good vote.

The single largest group of disfranchised are those who are self-
disfranchised. Only 50 to 60 per cent of the eligibles go to the
polls in America in an exciting presidential year, as compared
with 80 to 90 per cent for comparable campaigns in England, It-
aly, or Germany. In nonpresidential years, when interest slumps,
the vote slumps as well, falling to much less than half the eligibles. Of these nonvoters the greatest number are people who are
barred from the polls not by literacy tests or terrorism but by
apathy. And the greatest number of them are low-income people.

The labor politico has a rule of thumb for measuring habitual
voting participation in America: voting varies directly with
wealth, education, and the whiteness of the collar. COPE agitators
point to the study of a typical American city where in 1952 a "silk
stocking" district with 18,000 eligible voters turned out almost
twice as many votes as a labor district with 43,000 eligibles. Local
union leaders are shocked over and over again to discover that
loyal members who applaud the names of the endorsed candidates and even contribute funds for their election are not registered to vote.

To enfranchise the self-disfranchised, the unions must teach
new habits and undo old ones, converting apathy into action. The

chief means is education in the politics of economics, the dollar-and-cents rationale for voting. This approach comes naturally to unions; they tend to present politics as an extension of contract negotiations: a national election is collective bargaining on a grand scale; Election Day is a kind of pay day on which you write your own check.

While motivating the member to register and vote, the labor movement also seeks to remove the legal and mechanical obstacles to voting. Unions favor permanent registration to make it unnecessary for the voter to register every year or two; floating registrars who can sign up citizens in their homes, in their workplace, in shopping centers; abolition of literacy tests on the grounds that the English language is not the only medium for understanding the political score; minimal residence requirements for voters—an interest spurred by the knowledge that changes of residence are much more frequent among low-income families than among upper-income families; declaring Election Day a full holiday to make it easier for working people to vote. In short, the labor movement favors any and all changes in the registration and voting rules and regulations to encourage voting participation.

As a matter of history, voting regulations in America have been weighted conservatively in favor of the Establishment. In earliest America, the franchise was often limited to men of a chosen religious group and of property. It took time to break down the barriers of religion and wealth. It took more time to extend the franchise to Negroes and to women, the slaves of color and sex. As mass immigration brought millions of potential new voters to our shores, the dominant conservative elements, fearing the unwashed hordes in the cities, used the literacy test to disfranchise the newcomer. The literacy bar continued into the mid-twentieth century. Of the nineteen states that had literacy tests in 1965, half were Southern or border; the other half were states such as New York, which had been great ports of entry for immigrants. In New York State also, for many years there were two systems of registration, biased in favor of the rural conservative citizen. In

New York City, voters had to register annually and in person. In the small towns of rural New York, the voter was registered permanently and did not have to appear.

In 1965, COPE set up a special committee to map a long-range campaign for registration and voting reform. The basic document was a little-publicized report of a presidential commission appointed by John F. Kennedy to make recommendations for election law reform to maximize voting participation. Unfortunately, the report was scheduled to be made public at about the time of the Kennedy assassination. In 1965 COPE dusted it off and made it labor's bible for election reform. State affiliates of the AFL-CIO introduced legislation in their separate states and national coordination for the campaign was set up in Washington. In the decades ahead, this drive will become one of labor's key objectives.

As a result of the Voting Rights Act of 1964, the single greatest extension of the franchise in the decades after 1965 will probably take place in the South. The labor movement threw itself into the fight for this legislation, not simply to make the Fourteenth Amendment a reality a century after its passage but also to change the racial and ideologic complexion of Southern politics. In a sanguine memorandum to its political workers, COPE foresaw an era in which Southern politicians would reach out for the new Negro vote to compose winning coalitions. "Southern candidates," concludes COPE, "not only *can* be liberal but in many cases *must* to attract the new liberal coalition that the 1965 Voting Rights Act makes possible." The *St. Louis Post-Dispatch* had already commented. "The sound of hammering echoing across the South comes from politicians trying to build bridges into the Negro section of town."

Commenting on the newly emerging Southern politician, Joseph W. Sullivan wrote in *The Wall Street Journal:*

"Already there's been a rise in Southern support for the Johnson program. The 23 Southern votes cast for the President's Voting Rights Bill in the House in June, for example, more than tripled the faint show of Dixie support in 1960 for Congress's previous single-purpose strikes against barriers to Negro voting. Similarly, the 41 Dixie House votes in March for Federal aid to elementary and secondary schools nearly doubled the support total in 1961, the last time an effort at grade school assistance made it as far as the House floor. Medicare, moreover, might still be on the legislative shelf . . . were it not for the surprise help of such Southerners as Chairman Mills (D., Ark.) of the House Ways and Means Committee and Sens. Long (D., La.) and Smathers (D., Fla.)."

The liberal trend in Southern politics cannot, despite COPE optimism and some Congressional straws in the wind, be attributed solely to the rise in the Negro vote. The Southern Negro is still outnumbered. If Negroes step up their registration, so will whites, with the latter winning out: while there were 3,400,000 unregistered Negroes as of 1965, there were 8,100,000 unregistered whites. While the increased Negro vote gives predominance to the blacks in certain towns and counties and even Congressional districts, in most areas the strength of the new Negro vote can only be effective in a liberal coalition.

In the long run, this coalition depends upon the formation of a white bloc that is sufficiently tolerant of the new Negro to make a political alliance for economic aims. The base of such a white bloc will have to be found among the new unionists of the South in rising industrial and urban areas.

"Negroes generally are not forming all-black slates," said *The Wall Street Journal* in a report on Southern politics, "but have chosen to support some white as well as Negro candidates." The coalition idea has been taking hold. As part of the price of this coalition, Negroes will be asking for positions. At a church meeting in Camden, Alabama, this recent Negro folk song was heard:

> If you miss me in the white folks' kitchen
> And can't find me nowhere,
> Come on over to the courthouse,
> I'll be clerkin' over there.
>
> If you miss me on the paperwood truck
> And can't find me nowhere,

Come on over to Camden,
I'll be the mayor over there.

The development of a two-party system in the South will further tend to liberalize Southern Democrats. The GOP in the South appears in the latter 1960s to have set itself up as a right-wing opposition to the Democrats. A South Carolina Democrat, Senator Strom Thurmond, bolted to the GOP. Representative Watson of South Carolina did the same. Southern Republicans have worked out reasons for becoming champions of the past. They believe that "a decade of prodding from Washington on racial matters has soured white Southerners on all forms of Federal paternalism. . . . The average Southerner is well satisfied with his improving lot and doesn't see himself as poor. . . . The region's homogeneously Anglo-Saxon origins had made a lasting virtue of self-sufficiency, in contrast with the communal-type dependence of the Irish and European ethnic groups who've come to dominate the politics of many Northern areas." With this in mind, the GOP has reached out for the mantle of the Confederacy and conservatism in the South to create a real two-party system. At the same time, the GOP has been thinning conservatism out of Democratic ranks. Should this sort of separation run its course, the South may repeat the pattern of the North, dividing Republican from Democrat on a right-left basis.

A final factor liberalizing Southern politics will be application of the U.S. Supreme Court decision on apportionment of state legislatures. Following the one-man one-vote ruling, the Georgia House of Representatives in June 1965 seated seven Negroes, the first to be elected in this century.

The reapportionment decisions stemming from the court's action in *Baker v. Carr* in 1962 are expected by labor to have the profoundest effect upon the role of unions in politics in the North as well as the South. In the eyes of the AFL-CIO, the one-man one-vote ruling is a quiet revolution, a structural change portending a change in the direction of American society.

Since the turn of the century, state legislatures in the United

States have been conservative by design. They have been patterned to stifle the voice of the city. The motive for such distortion of the democratic process has been fear of the urban mob, with its bloc votes and its dirty machines. Apportionment became the great instrument for denying the vote to the city poor while ostensibly giving them the franchise: they had an equal right to vote but not the right to an equal vote. Malapportionment became the great dike by which the nineteenth-century mind held off the political waves of the twentieth century.

In the malapportioned legislatures, the labor vote was diluted. Most union members lived, and still live, in industrial and urban centers that have been under-represented in state legislatures. A legislative district with 100,000 urbanites might have no greater voice in the legislature than a district of 10,000 ruralites. In such a set-up, the typical industrial worker would have a vote worth about one-tenth that of his country cousin. Through the creation of many small rural districts, it has been possible for America's right wing to dominate state legislatures, even though, on Election Day, only a minority of the electorate voted to empower conservatism. In some states, as few as 10 per cent of the population have controlled state legislatures through systems of malapportionment that inflated the power of rural representatives.

Although the conflict over apportionment appears to be an urban-rural struggle, it is actually a war between centuries: between the do-little concept of an earlier America and a do-much desire of the present. Inflated rural strength is a cat's paw of conservatism. The dirt farmer does not represent himself in the state legislature: his spokesman is usually a small-town lawyer dependent on big-city banks and mortgage companies for his income. The rural legislator is the special soft touch for the "interest" lobbyist. In state after state, the dominant coalition has been that of silk stocking and cow county.

The distortions of democracy in the state legislature have been reflected in the federal House of Representatives. Since state legislatures draw the outlines of Congressional districts, they proceeded to do so to turn out a Congressional creature in the image of its maker. Unrepresentative state legislatures created an unrepresentative federal legislature. They proceeded without inhibition, since indeed there was no law to check their fanciful designs. Some districts were big in population, others were small; some districts were neat and clean, following quadrangular county lines, while others were nightmarish in their contortions. The guiding motive of the designers was simple: power. The faction running the state, often with a minority of the popular vote, tried to set up a similar artificial majority in the Congressional delegation, and generally succeeded.

The one-man one-vote concept is a democratic revolution because it means that every citizen, regardless of residence, will have about the same say in the state legislature, and hence ultimately in the House of Representatives. This means that the urban and industrial vote will not be debased and diluted and that the true weight of the labor vote will be felt at the polls.

The resistance to the one-man one-vote doctrine has been real and raw. No sooner had the Court made its ruling than a campaign was launched to reverse it by constitutional amendment and to remove from the bench the power to review apportionment in the future. In the U.S. Senate, Everett M. Dirksen of Illinois tried to tack a malapportionment rider on to a foreign-aid bill. Defeated in this shocking attempt to rewrite the Constitution by rider, Dirksen came back to the next Congress with a proposed constitutional amendment to allow states to apportion at least one house of a state legislature on factors other than population. Defeated again, he came back with a revised version. Parallel with these moves in Washington—all calculated to gain time for the once-entrenched conservative minorities in state legislature—resolutions were slipping through state legislatures, calling for a special national constitutional convention to undo the democratization of law-making bodies.

In a forthright assault on the one-man one-vote concept, columnist Raymond Moley reverts to the old fear of the city mob as the real reason for his opposition to majority rule: "Reapportionment, which will throw control of the legislatures to these city machines and unions, will mark a revival of the old order. For in many states the urban organizations, mostly Democratic, will dominate the state capitals. Through control of the legislatures, the urban legislative stooges will next redraw the Congressional districts and thus assure in the House of Representatives a majority capable of perpetuating what we have now." Unless this kind of majority rule is frustrated by "some constitutional means," he sees a future where "there may well be indeterminate domination of national affairs by the political and labor leaders in great cities."

While labor leadership appreciates the new strength coming to it from a democratization of the legislatures, it is not as sanguine as Moley that one man one-vote means a "lib-lab" majority per se. The unions are aware of the many conflicting minorities within the urban majority: ethnic, geographic, income, party, institutional. The city is no monolith: its politics are polycentric. More important, the greatest benefactor of reapportionment will not be the old central city but its outskirts and its suburbs. For that reason, COPE has written a great big question mark over suburban America, querying whether it is friend or foe.

The suburbs, rich in undecided voters, appear to be the coming battleground between Republicans and Democrats. "There are many Republicans in Pennsylvania—as in other states around the country—who suggest that the big battle for their party in the future must be fought in the suburbs," reported *U.S. News and World Report*. At the same time, COPE reports that "the long-range results of reapportionment will be to give more representation to the fast growing suburbs," and, it adds quizzically, "the political implications of the predominance of the suburbs are unsettled."

Suburban politics are likely to be decisive in the coming years for two reasons: first, because suburbs are growing so rapidly; second, because they are still swinging from right to left, from party to party. The population of suburbs of New York City, for instance, grew by 75 per cent between 1950 and 1960, while that of the city itself declined by 1.4 per cent during the same period;

the population of Chicago's suburbs went up 71.5 per cent while that of the city declined 1.6 per cent; the population of the suburbs of Minneapolis and St. Paul went up 115 per cent while that of the Twin Cities went down 4.4 per cent. All these suburbs, once considered fortresses of conservatism and the GOP, have moved into the doubtful column. In 1960, John F. Kennedy polled 47 per cent of the suburban vote in America. Lyndon B. Johnson in 1964 carried the major suburban areas by a margin of nearly 2,700,000 votes. In that year of catastrophe for the GOP, Republican representation from the twelve largest cities and their suburbs dropped from 52 per cent in 1952 (an Eisenhower year) to 30 per cent in 1964 (a Goldwater year). This shift of the suburbs from sure Republican to unsure is more than a response to the special appeals of Kennedy versus Nixon and Johnson versus Goldwater. The underlying reason is the changing character of the suburb. It is no longer chiefly inhabited by well-to-do commuters, their service retinues, and truck farmers; increasingly the suburb is the center for massive industry (space is cheaper than in the city), headquarters for national corporations, and a center for supermarts, commerce, publishing. Many suburbanites now are union members, who are paid well enough to afford a house across the city line, even while working in the city, or who now work, as more will work, in the suburb itself.

By 1963, the U.S. Department of Commerce reported that the number of blue-collar workers in the suburbs was greater than that of those in white collars: 9,081,336 blue to 8,844,801 white. Richard M. Scammon, at that time Director of the Census Bureau noted: "Away back, the suburbs consisted of the native wealthy families and the newcomers who were upper-middle-class white-collar people. But today, the suburb is less class and more mass. The idea that suburbia is one big picture window is just nonsense. The suburbs are more like the total population mix." As the better-paid white-collar workers, the professionals, and the government employees move toward unionism, they also tend to move toward liberal politics, adding further momentum to the leftward trend in suburbia.

In the longest run, however, what is likely to be decisive in shaping the political character of the American suburb is its urban nature. The suburb is part of the *urbs*, tied to its economy, linked to its highways, infected by its culture, sharing most of its nagging problems of water, air pollution, transportation, education, integration, industrial conflict, zoning, and housing. The suburbanite cannot tolerate the passive concept of laissez-faire government. The suburbs need dynamic programs to keep abreast of their own booms. Hence, the suburb is drawn toward a liberal coalition built around a platform for the metropolis.

Numerous among future active and articulate unionists living in the suburbs will be the members of labor's more literate affiliates: teachers and government and professional employees. They will bring special ingredients not only to the suburb (a fillip of liberalism) but also to the unions (a measure of political intellectualism). The government employees will contribute both interest and know-how: an interest in legislation regulating their bargaining and striking rights and their work and pay, and a know-how derived from their intimate contact with the ways of government. The educational background of these unionists, on the average greater than that of blue-collar workers, will provide labor a cadre with more capacity to grasp the total social scene and greater skill in carrying the labor message. If some of these white-collar unionists, such as the teachers, assume top leadership in the central labor bodies of their communities, they may well be expected to give labor politics a new scope and effectiveness.

Ironically enough, with all the growth and development of labor politics in the United States in the last three decades, interest in a labor party has declined. At the turn of the century and up to 1912, while the Socialist Party was growing, a mass party of labor, arising from the agitation of the Socialists and from the innate impulses of the organized worker, appeared inevitable. Although set back by World War I, when Socialists fell into disrepute because of their antiwar stand, the labor party idea revived brightly in 1924 when labor gave its endorsement to the Presidential candidacy of Senator Robert La Follette, who ran on the Progressive Party ticket. Through the late 1920s, agitation for a third party—socialist, labor, farmer-labor—continued. Then, in the mid-1930s, when some unions joined in a nonpartisan league to back FDR, it was hoped by some and believed by others that this league was the embryo of a new party. Since then, however, the trend has been in reverse: away from party and toward nonpartisan action.

The only third party in America with a labor base is the Liberal Party of New York State. It is the successor of the American Labor Party, organized in 1936 as a vehicle allowing traditional third-party voters in New York—Socialists, Communists, and others—to vote for FDR without doing so on the Democratic Party line, the line of hated Tammany Hall. After an internal fight with the Communists, the right wing of the ALP pulled out to form the Liberal Party in 1944. That year, it supported FDR for a fourth term and in every presidential election since has backed the Democratic candidate. In state elections for Governor or Senator, it has supported Democrats except on occasions when it did not see a real difference between the major party candidates (either because they were equally good or equally bad) and therefore ran its own candidate. In municipal elections, where the problem is more one of housekeeping than of national goals, the party has backed Republicans such as LaGuardia, Newbold Morris, and John Lindsay; Democrats such as Ferdinand Pecora and Robert F. Wagner; and its own Liberal Party independents. In short, the Liberal Party is really a pressure group applying special leverage by its line on the ballot.

The failure of the American unions, with their massive membership and wealth, to form a national party of labor constantly baffles the European observer and irritates the old-line third-party man in the United States. Both tend to attribute the failure to leaders suffering from spiritual gout and intellectual myopia or to an immature unionism that never severed its umbilical cord to the Establishment. In any event, the absence of a labor party is viewed as an evil attributable to bad leadership or backward membership.

Viewed in historic perspective, however, the failure of American labor to build a great party of its own appears to stem from (1) the nature of the economy, (2) the character of the working class, and (3) the structure of our political parties. Traditionally, the American radical advocate of a party of the working class held that the evolution of the economy would multiply and solidify the working class and compel it to form a massive party to transform the society. Experience since the 1930s, however, raises questions about the traditionalist evaluations of capitalism, the working class, and even parties.

The peculiar behavior of labor in American politics results from the facts that we live in a capitalist society that is not capitalist, that we have a working class that does not think of itself as a "class," and that we have political parties that are not "parties" in the classic European sense. This behavior is peculiar because it is nonimitative, autochthonous, and deeply rooted in our culture. To American labor, the behavior appears natural; but it appears unnatural to those who would instruct labor from the texts of pre-1939 Europe and who believe that the masses learn from the poignant phrase and not from the searing experience.

Our economy is not running on the Marxist schedule. The middle class is not disappearing; as an economic entity it is holding its own and as a sociopsychologic self-image it is growing almost disgustingly. The polarization of working class and capitalist class can only be proved by a semantic twist that defines poverty as "relative poverty" and wealth not as ownership but as "control." But defined in the light of common sense, the mounting poverty that was to drive the great mass to revolt against the handful who own the nation is not mounting at all. In short, the economic evolution that was to provide the sociopolitical dynamic for social revolution seems to be operating in reverse.

This has been the objective of the welfare state, which thus far has been attained, within limits. The failures have been in those areas where political power has been lacking to apply the welfare idea more fully. The combined economic and political impact has been the development of a system that is neither capi-

talist nor socialist, but a vacillating in-between that escapes classic radical categories because it was not envisioned in classic radical thought.

In fact, the inapplicability of the classic categories is presently
almost universal. The Soviet Union and China both claim to be
socialist (to the annoyance and discredit of Socialists) and find
themselves joined by the United Arab Republic. If these societies,
closed and orderly, defy classic definition, how much more elu-
sive is the character of the open and disorderly societies, such as
the United States, Great Britain, Sweden, and Mexico.

In the closed societies, the labor movements cannot make any
operational adjustments to their circumstances: they are told that
they are enjoying "socialism." They are prisoners of clichés and
commissars. In the open societies, especially where the welfare
state is a functioning factor, the political movements of labor tend
to adjust to reality, by modifying their definitions of socialism, by
seeking alliances with other classes, by seeking to establish a national party in place of a class party. This applies even to the
great socialist parties of England and Germany.

In America, where the labor movement was never deeply involved with Socialist tradition—despite the tremendous contributions of individual Socialist leaders, of Socialist critique, and of
Socialist legislation—the labor movement as a political force
moved easily into developing a program for the real society in
which it lives and which it seeks to change.

The reluctance of American labor to accept a socialist orientation has been viewed by some as a cultural lag. The assumption
was that as American labor became more educated and sophisticated, it would move toward a class party and toward socialism;
in other words, as American labor grew up it would look more
European. Actually, the reverse seems to be the case. European
socialists now look more American, de-emphasizing the class nature of their social-democratic parties and moving toward mixed
rather than purely nationalized economies.

Any attempt to measure the "backwardness" or "sophistication"
of American labor against, let us say, British labor, is rather a fu-

tile and meaningless exercise, like adding apple pies and York-shire puddings. The difference is more a matter of cultural taste than of level of development. The American workers, for instance, were the first in the world to have workingman's parties, back in the 1830s. Repeatedly, the American laborites reverted to class parties: Greenback, Labor, Populist, Socialist, Farmer-Labor, Communist. Ultimately, American workers—a majority of whom had never accepted any of these ideas—abandoned the concept of a national third party, not because of stupidity or sin but because such a party did not jibe with their concepts of their society or themselves. And because the class parties did not work.

The distinctive quality of American labor is its mobility, a trait common to our total culture: an upward economic mobility, a horizontal geographical mobility, and a diagonal ethnic mobility that is reflected in greater earnings and in movement into new neighborhoods. This mobility smudges, blurs, and sometimes even obliterates class lines.

To expect the average American worker, viewed not at a given moment but over three or more generations, to be class conscious is to expect him to substitute epigram for experience. And without class consciousness, there can be no lasting class parties. All this does not mean that there are no group or class conflicts in the United States. But where American labor has moved into politics, as an expression of its class aspirations, it has done so for specific programs rather than for class power. And, to accomplish this, labor has found it more productive to work within and through the established political patterns.

Our political parties are vastly different from the European. A European political party starts as an ideology; it spells out a program that flows from its philosophy; it sets up a membership organization to back this program; its membership is legally the party, naming its candidate usually by convention action. An American political party does not start as an ideology; it writes a program that reflects the fused aspirations of all the elements primarily wooed by the party; the political clubs are not legally the party; candidates are named in primaries in which people participate who have never been in or near a club or who do not even consider themselves members of the party.

The European party is generally the expression of a fairly definable economic, ethnic, or religious social grouping. The American party is generally the expression of a fusion and mixture of social groups. The European political party is a national entity: in America there is no legal national political party, since all parties operate under state law and enjoy title according to state regulations. A European political party usually can, by convention, deny renomination to a nonconformist member of the national legislative body; in the United States, a nonconformist can return to Congress indefinitely, if the people who vote in the primary in his district continue to support him.

Whether the American system is better or worse than the European is of less relevance than the cold facts that the U.S. method is here, is deeply rooted, and is the consequence of our social circumstances: geographic diversity, economic mobility, ethnic fractionalization.

The mechanical device that chiefly distinguishes the American system from the European is the primary. In the South, the struggle between liberals and reactionaries has been fought out until recently not through the organization of any liberal party but through the Democratic primary. In Wisconsin, La Follette battled the old-guard GOP through the primary. The primary is a mechanism that gives added flexibility to our highly flexible major parties. Farmers, labor, capital, Catholics, Baptists, Negroes, prohibitionists—these and many others have used the primary as a way of turning a national party, a program, or a local candidate in their direction.

For all these reasons, American unions are unlikely to move in the direction of a national third party of labor. A realignment of the major parties appears far more desirable—and even seems possible. Its desirability arises from the fact that an integrated governmental program requires a guiding intelligence, and such an "intelligence" is most fittingly a national party with a defined purpose and with internal cohesiveness. The possibility arises because our national party system has been moving in the direction of purpose and cohesion.

The big trend toward party realignment began with the New Deal. With FDR as standard bearer of social legislation, the Democratic Party by and large began to develop a New Deal complexion. The Republican Party, as opponent of FDR and New Deal, fixed upon itself the image of conservatism. This evolution of Democrats as New Deal and Republicans as the old order has continued for nearly a generation.

This process has not reached its ultimate and natural conclusion primarily because of the North-South division in the Democratic Party. This schism in the Congressional delegation of the Democrats has created a three-party system on Capitol Hill. There are the liberal Democrats, a reasonably cohesive formation, a large bloc but not a numerical majority; there are the Republicans who represent the hard core of conservatism (with about two dozen of them occasionally swinging to a liberal position); and, finally, there are the Southern Democrats, some of whom are liberal on economic matters but virtually all of whom are conservative on civil rights.

The grand legislative obstacle to the program of the labor and liberal forces is the greater ease with which Southern Democrats and Republicans can unite on an over-all program than the liberal Democrats can unite with their Southern party colleagues.

In the push for a liberal majority, labor's strategy will shift from North to South. In the North, the liberal-conservative contest is a matter generally settled in interparty struggle on Election Day. In the South, it is settled in intraparty struggle on Primary Day. The latter campaign is the more difficult of the two but will become the major focus of labor's drive. As the forces around the Democratic Party in the South are liberalized, a genuine realignment on the Hill will be inevitable.

The realignment of forces may include liberal Republicans. Their readiness to join with a Democratic Party that is solidly liberal in the North and sporadically liberal in the South is dependent on the direction taken by the GOP. So long as some urban and industrial Republicans feel that they can rescue their party for operation in the twentieth century, they are not likely to leave their party en masse and they certainly must, for reasons of inner party strategy, deny any intent to break away. But if the right wing of the GOP fastens an unbreakable grip on the party, modern Republicans will be forced into a liberal coalition in Congress—ultimately perhaps to be included in a national liberal party.

Although party realignment seems to be in the making, it is unlikely that the labor movement will make any conscious effort to hasten the development. The unions prefer not to be affiliated with any party. For principled and practical reasons, they find it wiser to back men on their records rather than parties on their name. But, as party realignment proceeds, labor's official policy of nonpartisanship will be more a fiction than a fact. Even during the 1950s and 1960s, union endorsements for Congress ran about 90 per cent for Democrats and 10 per cent for Republicans—not because labor preferred it but because it just turned out that way. Unions would prefer to have a wider choice of Republicans to whom they could throw their strength in order to prove to some Democratic politicians that there is an acceptable alternative. But, taken by and large, GOP legislators have a voting record that prohibits labor backing. Should party realignment produce two great national organizations, one liberal, one conservative, labor endorsement would become even more one-sided. Hence, even without formal affiliation with any one party, the unions would in effect be part of one, a continuing member of a grand alliance of liberalism in America.

Because labor will loom increasingly large in American politics, much will be expected of it—perhaps too much. Social reformers of many stripes will call upon the unions to produce answers to the many great queries of today and tomorrow. One such asks that labor solve the problems of "the arms race and the question of human survival" and also of "alienation" and the "dehumanization of the individual." Others ask that labor take the leadership in civil liberties, in the U.N., in medical care, in intergroup relations.

Whatever the virtues of the unions as a politically progressive force, however, it is questionable whether the labor movement has the omniscience to provide programmatic leadership in all areas. In economic matters—in devising a program for full employment—labor does have a special competence, derived from its experiences and interests. And even here, the unions are dependent upon specialists (usually economists within its own ranks or in the universities and government) for the detailed blueprints for achieving its generalized aims. But once the unions are removed from economic matters, they may be on grounds of deep and general concern but without any special expertise. In the areas of civil rights, civil liberties, world peace, and international relations, unions have a point of view behind which they can put their weight, but their elected leaders, who are chosen primarily for their competence in defending the economic standards and interests of their members, can hardly be expected to create or direct the strategy.

In a broad liberal coalition, labor will not have the first and last voice on all questions—nor should it. In a coalition, various groups will have their own programmatic priorities. Some will be primarily interested in the rights of Negroes and others with the rights of Puerto Ricans and Mexicans; some will be mainly concerned with civil liberties and others with quality integrated education; some with world peace and others with world freedom; some with urban renewal and others with societal rebirth; and some even with alienation and dehumanization. The very nature of a coalition is that it brings together all these and other elements into a working alliance to produce the political power to further these programs. With its great potential in manpower, money, and machinery, a politicalized labor movement can contribute much to electoral victory for such a united movement and can occasionally offer significant suggestions, ideas, and even programs. But for labor to assume that it alone has the answers would be presumptuous; and for others to relinquish decision-

making to the trade-union heads in every vital area of public policy would be a dangerous abdication of responsibility. In a "lib-
lab" coalition—no matter how great labor's influence may become
in the era of political unionism—the unions are only partners, not
sole owners.

Although, in this chapter, we have often spoken of the labor
vote, there really is no such thing. The phrase is a form of short-
hand to convey an idea quickly. The labor vote really amounts to
no more than the union's influence—moral, intellectual, psychological—among its members. The labor vote is not a monolith.
Within a union, there are many different people: some like the
union; some are neutral; some dislike it. The membership is divided. Also, every individual member is divided: he is a dues
payer to his union, but he is also a Catholic, Jew, or Protestant;
he is a Northerner, Southerner, Midwesterner; he is black or
white; he is a Democrat, Republican, communist, or fascist; he is
an apartment dweller or a home owner or even a landlord. The
individual unionist, like almost every American, is a plural individual. He is part of the labor vote to the extent that he listens to,
believes in, and acts on the union political message.

Because the labor vote is the product of cumulative education
and effort, the era of political unionism will come upon the nation
slowly. There will be no dramatic debut: the formal entrances
have already taken place with CIO-PAC in 1943, LLPE in 1947,
and COPE in 1955. There will be no great take-over of power:
formal victories have already been recorded with Truman in
1948, Kennedy in 1960, and Johnson in 1964. The real impact will
be in the changed political attitude of millions of individual
American workers: an interested and informed involvement in
national goals and a feeling of personal responsibility for decision-
making. This era of political unionism will mark a revolution and,
like so many other American revolutions, it will come piecemeal
and silently.

CHAPTER 11

Politics in Labor

In the coming decades, the labor movement will represent a significant power in the economy and politics of America. As a power it will be confronted with all the challenges inherent in power: institutionalization, corruption, self-indulgence, and internal struggles—palace intrigues or mass revolts—to decide who will wield that power. The axiom that "power corrupts and absolute power corrupts absolutely" applies to unions as well as to churches and states. Beyond the acceptance and solicitation of bribes and the misappropriation of treasury funds is corruption of the spirit: disregard of democratic procedures and individual rights, insensitivity to the real problems of the membership, dedication to self rather than the cause in short, the whole gamut of rot that comes to characterize any case-hardened bureaucracy ruling without inner compulsion or compassion. Unless unions find means and men to meet this inevitable challenge, the great power of labor can itself become an ultimate peril to the humane and democratic values of our civilization.

Talk about "union bosses" is rarely objective. The common discussion takes on the tone of adversary proceedings. Enemies of unions seize upon even the slightest sin of a union boss to characterize the labor movement as a societal cesspool. Friends of labor, faced with the same lapse, tend to deny the crime, to minimize its consequence, or to insist that the good or once-good labor leader picked up his bad habits from a naughty civilization. The truth of the matter is that labor leaders are, after all, only people, subject to the same weaknesses of flesh and spirit as the rest of mankind. They are neither subhuman nor superhuman, merely human.

Unfortunately for the labor leader and fortunately for his membership, society expects more from the union spokesman than from the businessman, because the former represents a constituency and talks about the difference between "right" and "wrong." In this respect, the union leader is under the same obligations as the man who leads a congregation or runs for office: more is demanded from those who would teach and lead in the paths of righteousness. Some meet this higher test; others do not; most do sometimes and do not at other times.

The time in which the union leader lives and works has much to do with his average behavior. Unions, like other social orders, go through stages—from militancy to indolence, from dedication to decay. They tend to follow the biblical pattern of ancient Israel, from King Saul to King David to King Solomon: from Saul the relentless warrior and empire builder, to David the sly political administrator, to Solomon the self-indulgent wastrel and sideline philosopher. The young union is likely to have the romantic, dare-devil, callow, awkward, self-confident, papa-damning attitude of all youth everywhere. The settled union is more likely to focus on the immediate, the attainable, the tangible, and the manageable, in the way of the middle-aged man. And the old, well-established union is apt to live on its past, on its accumulated money, members, and prestige, to rest on its laurels, in the ancient way of aged men.

In the American labor movement, the time is different for different leaders. Some affiliates are new and others old; some are dying and others are being born; some face few external challenges while others are hit with a daily crisis. Within national unions, there are different times: some locals are just being organized in unions more than a hundred years old, while others have lost all their members and have nothing but a treasury gathered in better times. For some leaders, the times are a personal equa-

tion: for one man, the hour is late and the day is done because he
has won a major contract for his men; for another, the hour is
early and the day is dawning because, though he has won much,
he has not yet even begun to do the big job of remaking the
world. The difference between the two men is not what they have
accomplished but what they would like to accomplish.

Because unions are so diverse and because their individual
leaders are even more so, any sweeping characterization of union
leadership is *ipso facto* wrong. Union leaders are as unlike one
another as are businessmen, politicians, and theologians. Hence,
agitational talk about the badness or goodness of union bosses is
without meaning.

Despite the vast personal and individualized differences, however, certain general propositions can be laid down about the
problems and prospects of union leadership. Each of the major
problems in the years to come will spring from some major success. What is success to a union leader?

Success consists in having a union, being its leader, putting it
on a lasting basis, and running the institution to meet your purposes—moral or immoral, social or antisocial, personal or public.
Each point in this short, short success story raises problems—especially purpose. Let us consider each.

A union leader is "somebody" because he represents an organization. Hence, he will seek to preserve that institution, and, usually, to extend its influence. This highly normal trait is, on the
face of it, a good thing: it is what makes a good father, a skillful
entrepreneur, an effective community organizer. It is what has
produced a labor movement with several hundred national affiliates and several thousand local unions. It is the sense of self-preservation expressed institutionally.

But self-preservation can also become self-destructive. For
many decades, local unions were involved in regular fratricidal
blood-lettings over the matter of jurisdiction: what union shall
represent the workers? Such wasteful bits of civil war, often conducted on the employer's terrain with the boss as the most injured
bystander, continue and will continue to plague the labor move-

ment. These jurisdictional disputes, commonly viewed as the product of self-seeking bureaucrats, are actually only the reverse of
the organization coin. Certain categories of workers look to their
union for job placement: if the union's jurisdiction is narrowed,
so is job opportunity. Different unions have differing contract
standards; hence, the entry of a second union into a field may de-
press working standards. In addition, there is the natural personal
ambition of the leader, who would like to extend his influence, for
noble purposes if he is noble and for others if he is not. The roots
of such jurisdictional rivalry go deep, as anyone who has ever
tried to tear them out has learned. They are the same roots that
nourish agency rivalry in the government or departmental rival-
ries on a campus, part of the costly overhead of a pluralist society
that resents centralization.

Keenly aware of the dangers inherent in jurisdictional wars, the
American labor movement in recent years has taken two major
steps toward eliminating internal frictions. The merger of the
AFL and the CIO was the great step, preceded by a no-raiding
pact to create the climate for it. Subsequently, the combined federation wrote an internal disputes act, consisting of a body of
rules and regulations and the establishment of machinery to enforce them. Although experience with the internal disputes procedure is still limited, the indications are that jurisdictional disputes are far less of a problem today than in the old AFL (before
1937), when crafts in the federation waged endless war against
one another, or in the days of the great split between AFL and
CIO.

The reduction of jurisdictional disputes, however, depends as
much on the nature of leadership as it does on peace-making machinery. The purely parochial leader or the totally self-righteous
leader is not likely to be interested in peace: the mediator is a
menace. The leader who takes a broader view, recognizing the
needs and interests of a rival group, is more likely to seek amity
and to invite an arbiter. Hence, the disposition of unions to become involved in jurisdictional disputes involves a political dimension: the goals and attitudes of the leadership of the union.

The great factor working against diminution of jurisdictional disputes in the future will be changes in the economy: new materials, new products, new methods of production. Consider the introduction of plastics, for instance. Many items that in the past were made of textiles, wood, rubber, metal, or ceramics are today made of plastics, in a process of premolding chemicals. In the past, a given item fell under the jurisdiction of a union in textiles, wood, etc. Today, the jurisdictional lines have become smudged or erased, making conflict inevitable.

Consider another example in the building trades. Once the construction of a wall in a building involved many skills: carpenter, painter, lather, plasterer, metal worker, bricklayer. Today, there are prefabricated walls, manufactured under factory conditions, transported in one piece or in a few easily assembled parts, and swung into place in a building.

Such changes in material, product, and method could mean an endless series of internal wars, even among well-intentioned unions eager to keep the peace. The central problem arises because union jurisdictions defined for one economy are being applied to a changed economy, where the old lines have lost their meaning. The best ultimate solution is a restructuring of unions, with mergers or common councils. Such redefinition of lines is logically desirable but rarely psychologically acceptable to the organization (or leadership) that is about to lose its institutional distinctiveness.

Again, the answer lies in the political area of inner union life, in the kind of leadership that must make the hard decision to surrender part or all of its sovereignty. Such decisions, involving restructuring, are particularly difficult in the American labor movement where there is no one great central power able to impose its will on reluctant affiliates.

Still another factor forcing a reconsideration of total union structure is the changing character of ownership, as more and more of the economy falls into the hands of the portfolio firm, the free-floating financing organization that buys up all kinds of enterprises, no matter how diverse. A gold-mining corporation merges with a brassiere maker and a kosher food factory. A copper company makes ladies' knitwear. Great retailing operations own or underwrite their varied suppliers. The new capitalists cannot be identified by their product: they are multiproduct, multistate, multiplant and—if they are unionized at all—multiunion.

In a struggle with labor, the finance capitalist in control of his portfolio firm is one; the unions are many. The owner can often afford to wage permanent war, since he can draw on part of his empire even while an effective union has tied up a subsidiary. In dealing with the new giants of finance ownership, union experience, in the long run, dictates union cooperation, perhaps even mergers. The tendency of these giants to gobble up the whole economy grows apace. In early America, great wealth came out of the ownership of land and out of trade and commerce. Then came banking and finance. Then big money moved into the extractive industries and basic manufacture and railroading. Then the nouveaux riches, in a partial alliance with old money, moved into retailing: mail order and national chains. Most recently, this wealth has moved into light industry. Curiously, this trend has been encouraged by the anti-trust laws that originally banned monopoly in any one field and later questioned vertical monopoly as well. The latest gimmick is to dodge the law by diversification, ownership in a wide variety of fields.

Organized labor has shown an awareness of the trend toward diversified ownership. Some instances are described in the Industrial Union Department publication of the AFL-CIO, *Agenda:*

"In the amusement or communications industry, the CBS purchase of the Yankees was hardly an anomaly. Rollins Radio owns Orkin Exterminating Co., the largest pest exterminator. Taft Broadcasting owns two bowling centers. Metromedia owns an ice show. On the reverse side, Mutual Broadcasting belongs to the parent Minnesota Mining and Manufacturing Corp.

"As for Minnesota Mining and Manufacturing (the 3 Ms), this company, founded originally to produce bonding materials for coated abrasives, now manufactures some 40 product lines turning out some 25,000 separate items . . . is sizeable enough to sustain a payroll of some 30,000 workers. In all, 18 unions are represented at 3M plants."

In 1961, several unions, the largest of them the Oil, Chemical and Atomic Workers, took steps in bargaining with 3M to establish a uniform national pension plan. *Agenda* reports that the "objective at 3M is uniformity of expiration dates and complete coordinated bargaining by 1967." In 1963, there were some twenty-four cases of coordinated bargaining reported by the IUD; by 1965, there were sixty. Labor is just beginning to shape its answer to the conglomerate corporation. Companies diversify and unions unify.

To carry through these programs, unions will have to surrender or combine sovereignties, a statesmanlike act reflecting political know-how in the face of pressures. Once more, the key ingredient is the caliber of leadership, its scope of vision and its readiness to break with past rituals.

In all these instances, the union leader must be someone who can see beyond his nose and feel beyond his skin. The natural bent of the natural leader is to take the short and narrow view: to speak for his people here and now, to be parochial rather than cosmopolitan, to concern himself with the here and not the hereafter. His members do not object; indeed, they insist that the leader be doing something for them "lately" against all comers. For the leader to ask his people to give up short-term advantage for long-term gain, or to surrender selfish benefit for the social weal, requires some vision, much courage, and immeasurable political skill.

Ironically, when the labor movement does take a stand in favor of the public interest at the cost of union gain, the heroic stance generally goes unnoted. The unions know that their sacrifice play will draw little or no applause. Within the past decade, there were two such situations in which labor accepted setbacks rather than compromise with principle. In both cases, the public noted the union "defeat" but left unnoted the public victory.

One case of such a labor setback was the passage of the Lan-

drum-Griffin Act in 1959, described in Chapter 10. Labor lobby-
ists knew that the bill could be defeated. But there was a price to
pay. The unions could have had the bill buried provided the labor movement called a halt to its legislative campaign for federal
civil rights legislation. A deal could have been worked with
Southern Congressmen who would have voted against the Landrum-Griffin bill or would have abstained from voting for it, if
the unions had promised to drop civil rights as a quid pro quo.

Here was a clear case of immediate narrow gain versus long-
term public interest. Defeat of Landrum-Griffin would have
served immediate union interests. The deal could have been
made quietly. There was little pressure on the unions from the
civil rights organizations on the outside to fight for rights legislation: in 1959 the Southern Christian Leadership Conference under Dr. Martin Luther King had not yet ignited the Negro explosion. In short, there was nothing to stop the AFL-CIO from putting in the "fix" to kill Landrum-Griffin—that is, nothing except
conviction about civil rights. The labor movement made its decision to continue the push for civil rights legislation and paid the
price in the form of punitive labor legislation.

The same kind of a choice between vested and public interest
was put before the unions in 1966 when the Senate was debating
repeal of Section 14B of the Taft-Hartley Act. For many years,
the unions had sought repeal of this section of the law, which allowed individual states to outlaw the union-shop clause by
state legislative action. The unions had thrown massive manpower and money into state campaigns to block such legislation.
By 1966, however, about twenty states had passed such laws. Although the unions had long yearned for federal repeal of 14B as the
swiftest way to knock out the state "right-to-work" laws, no serious effort was made in this direction until the 89th Congress came
in with a sweeping Democratic Party majority (294 to 141) and
with the first "liberal" majority in a generation.

The issue came to a head in 1966 when the House of Representatives passed a bill for repeal of 14B and the matter came before the Senate. In the upper house, there was also a majority for

repeal, but the matter never came to a vote. Majority will was frustrated by a filibuster led by Senator Everett M. Dirksen, the Republican minority leader. The necessary two-thirds vote to halt the filibuster was not there. Consequently, labor lost a bitter battle.

Labor could have won this victory. The president of the AFL-CIO was quite outspoken about how the trick could have been turned. The Dirksen filibuster could have been broken had the unions been ready to pay the price: to allow Dirksen to put through his constitutional amendment to reverse the one-man one-vote ruling of the Supreme Court by allowing states to apportion one house of their legislature on factors other than population. The labor movement refused to give up the principle of "one-man one-vote" in exchange for repeal of 14B.

Said Meany: "If you want to control a state legislature by having the rural areas outvote the urban areas, you don't need both houses; all you need is one. The issue of 'one-man one-vote' is more important to liberal forces than anything we could think of. . . . *I want the repeal of Section 14B, but before I would agree to a compromise that would nullify 'one-man one-vote' through the Dirksen Amendment, I would let 14B stay there forever!*"

The one-man one-vote principle is important to labor, of course. It is also important to all urban and suburban dwellers, to the minority groups, to the democratic principle of majority rule. Yet when the repeal of 14B failed, many expressed delight to see unions "kept in their place." There were virtually no voices praising labor for having sacrificed itself in order to preserve a greater democratic ideal.

The test of future trade-union leadership will be its ability to balance the immediate with the ultimate interests of the membership, to balance the well-being of the dues payers with the common good.

Where will the future trade-union leadership learn the needed insights into economy and society? Ordinarily, the broader view should be gathered from exposure to the intellectual friends of labor—economists, sociologists, industrial relations experts, political scientists, educators. Yet unfortunately there is a kind of built-in hostility between the intellectual and the practitioner. The former emphasizes the desirable; the latter the doable. The former eschews compromise; the latter makes it a way of life. The former is ready to scuttle a local union in the interests of the society; the latter must keep his local alive even if it embarrasses the bigger community. The former tends to fit people into designs; the latter tends to evolve designs out of people. This conflict is part of the age-old strife between critic and creator, between theoretician and doer, between political scientist and politician. In this instance the gap is widened by the simple fact that the two sides don't talk the same language: the theoretician learns his lingo in the university; the practicing labor leader generally learns his in the shop. Both tend to become specialists: the former in the jargon of his discipline; the latter in the argot of his craft. Out of this nondialogue arise mutual suspicion and contempt: the egghead looks down on the labor leader as an ignorant self-centered lout and the labor leader looks upon his professorial critic as a pretentious and uninformed, if not malevolent, bag of wind.

The gap between intellectual and practitioner is as unfortunate as it is common: the labor leader has much to learn from the academician and vice versa. The man of theory can be helpful to the union in pointing up the long-range implication of present policies; the union activist can be helpful to the theoretician in acquainting him with the thorny road of practical action.

In some unions there has been a traditional interplay between the manual and the mental. A classic example is to be found in the needle-trades unions where the dialogue began early, as far back as the turn of the century. These unions were formed by Jewish immigrants whose shops were peopled not just by peasant stock from the Old World but also by intellectuals—teachers, writers, professional student-type revolutionaries, who, for want of any other way to make a living, joined their fellow "greenhorns" at the sewing machine. In the shop, the soft-skinned intellectual learned to become a proletarian and the tough proletarian learned to talk like an intellectual. Out of the mix arose leaders who knew both the shop and the world. They respected both the man of mind and the man of muscle. Hence, in the decades that followed, they evolved a leadership that was heavy with college graduates who inhaled the smell of the shop and with shop people who breathed the heady atmosphere of the university.

The history of the needle trades repeated itself in the early days of the CIO, when radical youth with intellectual backgrounds threw themselves into the labor movement. Some went from classroom straight into class struggle, dropping their books and lifting picket signs. Others doffed their caps and gowns and donned overalls. In these unions, the mix of manual and mental repeated itself.

In the future, this kind of mix will again occur in some unions and in some parts of the country. The white-collar, professional, and governmental employee unions are likely to repeat this history. Out of the civil rights movements, militant students who ultimately turn to the unions as the most realistic way to reach their goals will furnish new cadres of proletarianized intellectuals.

In still other unions, the contact of union leadership with labor intellectuals will be formalized through employment of college graduates for specialized work: research, writing, editing, industrial engineering, education, legal work. In this relationship, the intellectual is most likely to be cast in the role of an agency head and only occasionally in the role of cabinet member, involved in basic policy making. The intellectual friend of labor who is not directly involved in the trade union as a staff member or elected leader can still play a vital role—especially as programer, critic, and unifier in a liberal political coalition.

As economists, intellectuals can shape broad programs. As students of intergroup relations, they can counsel toward ending prejudice. As educators, they can raise up new generations of inspired and instructed young people to play an energetic part in progressive social movements. As researchers and propagandists, they can enlighten the nation politically. As viewers of the total society, they can interpret labor to the civil rights movement and interpret the civil rights movement to labor. They can and should voice the needed criticisms of the many special-interest groups that make up the liberal coalition, a function they are able to perform from the vantage point of the disinterested yet dedicated scholar. They can serve as constructive critics—sorely needed in both the labor and civil rights movements. They can help put things in place and perspective.

A large number of liberal intellectuals do play this role. They can be found among labor educators, arbitrators, historians, sociologists, labor-relations teachers, political scientists, whose theoretical knowledge is backed by the experiences of hard reality. Some such intellectuals can also be found holding full-time posts in unions. But there still remains a large group of "labor friends" whose impact on unions is minimal, if not negative, because they are physically, rhetorically, and emotionally so far from the actual body of labor. Inside the unions or close to them, these people could be valuable; outside and far from them, they are almost valueless. To bridge the gap between the "myopic" leader of labor and the "far-sighted" friend of labor will probably require a conscious effort on both sides, in which both parties agree to be both teachers and taught.

Akin to the problem of the place of the union in the society is the question of the place of the leader in his union. A man who has built a union and run its affairs for many years tends to identify the institution with himself. One such local leader wrote a book entitled, *I, The Union*. This identification is a source of organizational strength: since a threat to the union is a threat to the man, he fights back as if his own skin were at stake. At the same time, this personalization of the union is a danger. The leader who views himself as the *sine qua non* of his union's very life can, in the name of organizational integrity, easily close all channels of internal dialogue.

The danger is real because unions, by their very nature, are easily affected by the virus of bureaucratic rule. Unions tend to be monosocial (like a parish church); to be combative (like an army); to be administrative (like a governmental agency); and to be market-oriented (like a business). Taken together, these traits form a strong natural bent in established unions toward the "one-party" system, resting in the hands of an administrative machinery. The point becomes more apparent when the nature of unions is compared with the nature of American society as a totality.

Unions are more homogeneous than the country as a whole. If the clash of varying forces is the dynamo of democratic competition, such clash is necessarily more limited within a one-class organization. The clash is even more limited in any one union in a single trade. And it is further limited in any one craft or local.

This is not necessarily a limitation imposed by existing office-holders. Nor is it a limitation that can be overcome easily by the writing of new union constitutions or the enactment of new laws. This limitation is existential, arising from the relatively homogeneous character of trade unions, typical of one-class or one-thought groups.

There have been doctrinal differences within trade unions, producing lengthy internal struggles. But such doctrinal differences are less likely to become the basis for a continuing internal battle than are class differences in a society, especially in an historical period when working people in general are not deeply divided on questions of political dogma. In the past, when trade unionists were diametrically apart on socialist-capitalist lines, on political action versus pure and simplism, there was a basis for more protracted internal discussion and competition than occurs in the present era when labor has shifted to a middle ground of mixed economy and limited politics.

Within trade unions, there are conflicts between different types of earners, involving skills, relative earnings, status. Where such differences exist, they are reflected in internal union politics.

The pluralism within a union generally arises around individuals and around trade problems. Such differences change character from year to year and hence afford no real basis for a continuing two-party or multiparty system.

Unions are also different from the society as a whole in that labor sees itself as an instrument of conflict. Hence, unions are subject to disciplines of a semimilitary nature. The democracy of unions, as of nations, has, in the past, been restricted by wars and cold wars.

Unions are also compelled to fashion their structure to meet the needs of an organization that is, when not at war, in a state of administrative siege. In the industrial area, the basic policy-making decisions of the union—contract and strike and settlement—occur relatively seldom. (And it should be noted that in these three basic policy acts there generally is a high degree of membership participation.) Beyond these, the basic work of the union is administrative and judicial in character, involving enforcement, interpretation, efficiency, honesty, diligence. Just as the administrative machinery of government is vastly different from the legislative branches, with the former involving a greater measure of authority, bureaucracy, permanency, practical know-how, so too the basic administrative character of the modern union carries with it a great measure of institutionalized controls, professionalized personnel, continuity in office.

Unions, like all other economic forces in our competitive economy, perform a market function. This market function, for each competing element in our total culture, is to stimulate demand, restrict supply, check competition—and thereby to get maximum return. This is true of the steel industry, of farmers, of doctors, of the electronics firms, of college professors, of lawyers, and of the unions.

This compelling factor in our economy—to interfere with the free flow of supply and demand—makes itself felt in every corner of our life and, of necessity, involves the labor movement, affecting its structure, its admittance practices, its jurisdictional claims, its dues, its apprenticeships.

For all these reasons, unions create forms of decision-making quite different from those prevailing in our formally constituted government. The union forms, with their heavy emphasis on discipline, administration, and bargaining, can be turned into models of bureaucratic government. Where the will to do so is present, the opportunity is at hand. The checks on the bureaucratization of unions come from three sources: first, the leadership itself, if it has sufficient insight to temper its passion for power with a love for democratic rights; second, the pressures of other leaders and of members; third, the regulatory influences of government.

Labor leadership would like to believe that, left to itself, it would guarantee the members' rights and maintain a viable system of decision-making by the members. Some sophisticated leaders, with a genuine commitment to the democratic ideal, have set examples of model self-restraint in the exercise of power. But the weight of evidence indicates that in unions—as in business, government, or the driving of a car—self-regulation is severely limited by the foibles and vanity of man. Few men of power encourage the powerless to challenge the establishment, wherever or whatever it may be. The few who do so are men of vast vision, deep belief, and endless self-confidence.

More traditional checks are to be found in the mood of the membership and in the ambition of other leaders. Normally, neither of these potential sources of opposition has been too bothersome to a leader whose union has moved steadily ahead in contract gains and whose service to the individual member is reasonably adequate. The opposition is meaningful when things go wrong: a poor contract, bad servicing. But even such opposition, in many cases, can be beaten down by threats of firing or by a simple denial of channels for the expression of open discontent.

The most serious denial of membership rights takes place in those unions that are unions in name only ("racket unions") or are real or once-real unions that have been taken over by the underworld. In these cases, the union is a form only. The leadership is self-appointed, sometimes without even the empty formality of a membership vote. The object of the union is to put the squeeze on employers merely to enrich the "owners" of the union. The strike becomes an instrument of extortion; the welfare funds become the personal property of the leaders; the contract is a "sweetheart agreement" to give the union heads an income, to give the employer relief from a real union, and to give the workers nothing.

While many such "racket unions" have been brought into being by employer encouragement, these racketeers really do not need outside prompting to open up a "union business." The top men in this field are gangsters who treat unions as just another source of income, along with juke boxes, gambling, prostitution, shipping, insurance, charities, and politics. The grip on some unions is just one tentacle of the giant octopus known as organized crime in America.

In such unions, it is idle to speak of membership revolt or even of effective opposition leadership. In too many instances, the union is merely a shell. In others, internal control is exercised through unmitigated terror. It is equally idle to expect the AFL-CIO to oust the leadership of such phantom unions, since many if not most of them exist outside the AFL-CIO. And even within the Federation, the only weapon against them is expulsion—often a license for untrammeled freebooting.

Where such denial of membership rights is patently imposed, then the intervention of government is virtually inevitable. Denial of rights on the inside invites governmental intervention from the outside. For the labor movement as a whole, governmental intervention is always a threat. Labor wants to run its own house. It would also like to clean it and let in the fresh air of membership rights. But, for better or worse, nobody in the AFL-CIO has the power to step into a national affiliate and tell it what to do or how to do it. If a national union wants to reorganize a local affiliate, it can do so. But if the national union itself has forgotten its commitment to the rights of its members, there is nothing to make it mend its ways, except the government.

What the future is for American labor on the front of government controls depends very largely on the behavior of the unions themselves. If leadership shows self-restraint, if membership is allowed its voice, and if administration is clean, governmental interference not only will be without justification but will in all likelihood be halted. But if union leadership goes dictatorial and corrupt, further regulation is inevitable.

In no small measure, the threat of federal intervention was responsible for the expulsion of the teamsters' union, together with other unions, from the AFL-CIO in 1957. Following hearings conducted by Senator McClellan that charged corruption and gangster control in several unions, Congress and probably the American people as well were ready for punitive anti-union legislation. To head off this threat, the leadership of the AFL-CIO had to move swiftly and dramatically.

Although imminent antilabor legislation was an effective external force in hastening a clean-up, there were internal pressures as well. Many unions were fearful that gangsterism, like communism, was an infectious disease that could spread like a cancer through the entire body of labor. These unions wanted surgery.

The instrument at hand was the AFL-CIO Ethical Practices Committee, established in 1955 as a result of the merger of the AFL and CIO. At that time a resolution on ethical practices warned that the "reputations of the vast majority are imperiled by the dishonest, corrupt, unethical practices of the few." The newly merged organization "accepted the responsibility for keeping its own house in order." To implement the intent, the first constitutional convention of the AFL-CIO created an Ethical Practices Committee. It was this committee, with this responsibility, that undertook the investigation of several unions charged with improper conduct.

Eight unions were investigated and charged with unethical behavior by the committee. They were the Allied Industrial Workers; the Laundry Workers' International Union; the Distillery, Rectifying and Wine Workers; the Bakery and Confectionary Workers; the United Textile Workers; the Waste Handlers Local 20467; the Can Workers Federal Local 22623; and the International Brotherhood of Teamsters, Chauffeurs, Warehousemen and Helpers. Some of these purged themselves by compliance with AFL-CIO directives; others were placed on probation; the two small federal locals were at the mercy of the Federation. The big problem was the IBT, the teamsters.

For the AFL-CIO the teamsters were not just another union. They were the largest, most powerful, and strategically most important union in the labor movement. They were growing rapidly and showed promise of greater growth. The teamsters were the jugular of the economy and to cut off the teamsters was like cutting one's own throat.

Their membership at the time of the expulsion from the AFL-CIO was 1,400,000—about one-tenth of the total membership of the Federation and far and away the largest of any affiliate. Their per capita dues were the great backlog of Federation finances.

More important than membership and dues was their role in the labor movement: other unions depended on the teamsters to win battles. If teamsters refused to handle "hot cargo" (products that were "on strike"), the employer could not function even if the strike of his own employees was ineffective. Teamsters could stop the inflow of supplies and the outflow of the finished product. "No other union has the power that we have. We touch every trade and industry," boasted Daniel Tobin, president of the Teamsters Union in the days before Beck and Hoffa. Einar Mohn, a key vice-president of the teamsters, simply noted that "it has become traditional and customary for labor unions in practically all industries to call upon the teamsters' local unions for assistance. This is not stated as a boast but just as an economic fact of life." This fact of life was familiar to many unions that had won battles against employers because the teamsters had refused to carry wares in or out.

The teamsters were a union of almost unlimited growth potential. Originally, they were a craft outfit of men who were literally teamsters: they handled teams of horses. The key men were the salesmen-drivers who would walk their nags down the street as they peddled and delivered milk, bread, ice, and coal. When horsepower drove out the horse, the driver-salesmen shifted to the gas-powered vehicle. They eschewed the company of the burly boys who drove the over-the-roads trucks from state to state and coast to coast: these were viewed as uncouth, thick-tongued, foul-mouthed slobs.

It was these over-the-road drivers, however, who were to revolutionize the teamsters' union. Because they roamed freely over large areas, they became the basis for area conferences, such as one on the West Coast under Dave Beck and another in the Central States under James R. Hoffa. When these once-despised long-trek men were organized they gave a new kind of power to a rising leadership in the teamsters, which thought less in terms of narrow geographical and craft (driver-salesmen) jurisdictions and more in terms of regional combines to control every man who managed any vehicle. With this power bloc, Beck succeeded Daniel Tobin in the presidency of the teamsters and James Hoffa succeeded Dave Beck. The over-the-road drivers became the key to control of the national union.

Once the teamsters broke the craft mold, they reached out in all directions. They began to organize the warehousemen to whom and from whom the teamsters carted supplies and finished products. Once the teamsters had the warehousemen, they began to organize the manufacturing employees who fed products to the warehousemen. In short, the teamsters undertook to organize not only all those who drove a vehicle on wheels but all those who made products that had to be carried on wheels. Any few inhibitions that existed for the teamsters while they were in the AFL-CIO were abandoned when they were expelled. In their 1961 constitution, they simply laid claim to "all workers, without limitation."

In 1957, when the fate of the teamsters as an AFL-CIO affiliate had to be determined, the IBT was in an interregnum: Dave Beck, who had taken over from long-time president Dan Tobin, was ruling very much on the sufferance of a relatively unknown newcomer, James Hoffa. Structurally, the union was in transition: what was once an exclusively craft union was well on the way to becoming one of the largest industrial unions in America. What once was a loose collection of highly autonomous locals was becoming an increasingly centralized union.

The teamsters' union was then, as it is now, a many-sided thing: a mix of pure-and-simple trade unionists, high-minded ideologists, gangsters, and self-seekers. It had the remains of an old leadership, described by Tobin as consisting of men who seemed "to have no other object in view except to enjoy themselves, have a good time, and stopped at nothing to bring about that condition." While Tobin railed against these good-time Charlies he was never able to clean them out. And to do so wasn't easy. When the Capone mob moved in on the milk-wagon drivers in the early 1930s, the courageous officers and members of the union fortified their headquarters and fought pitched battles with the underworld. The latter, using kidnappings, beatings, and machine guns won out. It would take more than letters and a famous "iron gate around his office" for Tobin to oust the gangsters. Confronted with the same problem, Hoffa viewed it philosophically: "You can't choose your associates. You associate with whomever you need to make you a winner."

Yet neither Hoffa nor the teamsters could be deemed in 1957 or now to be a gangster outfit, a brotherhood that had dropped the "brother" and held on to the "hood." For many years, a major force in the teamsters' union was the powerful Minneapolis affiliate headed by the Trotskyite Dunne brothers: its leaders were a group of militant, wily, and totally dedicated Irishmen who brought a total *Weltanschauung* to their work. It was one of these Trotskyites, Farrell Dobbs, who first recognized the power behind the over-the-road drivers, realized the potential for teamster organization of warehouses and production and taught Jimmy Hoffa the ABCs of class rather than craft unionism. Hoffa talks of Dobbs as "the architect and draftsman of our road operations." Although by 1957 the Dunne brothers had been ousted from the Minneapolis leadership (through the combined efforts of Daniel Tobin, pure muscle, and FDR—because of their party's opposition to World War II), and although Farrell Dobbs was no longer with the teamsters (having decided to become a full-time party functionary), the influence of radical ideology and erstwhile Trotskyite, Socialist, and Communist cadres continues in the IBT. This radical tradition makes the teamsters' union reasonably congenial to a number of proletarianized intellectuals, many of whom are among Hoffa's closest associates.

In the teamsters, too, are numerous locals—perhaps a majority—that are neither mobsters nor ideologues: just old-fashioned pure-and-simple unions. Some are happy in the IBT: "Leave us alone and we will leave you alone." Others are unhappy but stay: "We need one another."

Hoffa himself is many things. One can probably learn more about what makes him tick by reading Hobsbawm's *Social Bandits and Primitive Rebels* (where Hoffa is never mentioned) than by reading the McClellan hearings (where Hoffa is mentioned thousands of times). The latter records the lapses from virtue; the former explains why. Hoffa is a primitive, like a primitive painter who comes to his trade without formal training; he is a rebel, in that he identifies with the working stiff against the high hats; he is social, in that he has a hankering for social causes; he is a bandit, in the tradition of many would-be Robin Hoods. He has no private vices; they're all public—and these public vices he sees as virtues in the cause he serves at a good commission. In his power drive to take care of his people and himself he seizes the weapons at hand: muscle or mind, knuckleheads and eggheads. Hoffa's alliance, according to Ralph and Estelle James in their large-scale close-up portrait of Hoffa, includes "a strange collection of bedfellows, politicians and political fixers, gamblers, musclemen, Negro leaders, financiers, truckers, priests and bishops, racketeers, and of course trade unionists."

Such alliances are not unknown in other unions or in other organizations—corporations and political parties—that have to wage war in the American jungle. The big question before the AFL-CIO in 1957 was whether the IBT was exploiting corrupt influences or whether these influences had taken over the union. This decision had to be made on the facts developed at the McClellan hearings: they appeared to indict the IBT and its leadership. The teamsters had a chance to refute but preferred to deny the right of the AFL-CIO to probe or demand reform. Against this factual background and the mood of the time, the Federation moved to expel its largest and most powerful affiliate.

In subsequent years, the limited power of expulsion has become apparent. The good name of the AFL-CIO was protected somewhat; antilabor legislation was partially softened; the power of the teamsters to build an alliance within the Federation to take over or to split it was checked. But the IBT and Hoffa, as such, were not destroyed or even injured by the expulsion. From 1957 to 1965, the teamsters grew from 1,400,000 to 1,700,000 members. Hoffa's power was further centralized. Free of Federation fetters, the IBT gave itself unlimited jurisdiction. Using their grip on trucking and their foot in the door, the teamsters had a relatively easy "in" to organize not only production people but white-collar employees as well. In 1965, according to the Bureau of National Affairs, the teamsters were "the most active and most successful of the unions attempting to organize white-collar workers."

The only threat to Hoffa's power comes from the federal government through a concerted drive to "get" the teamster leader. For several years, he was in and out of the courts with mixed results. He has outwitted his opponents repeatedly, but it is doubtful that his luck is eternal. Upon his passing—for whatever reason—the clashing political forces within the teamsters' union will once more break out in a free-for-all. The inner wars of the IBT have, thus far, been subtle, like the maneuvers within the Kremlin: a subject for cognoscenti only.

The outcome in the teamsters, like the results in the labor movement as a whole, will depend on the political factors in the union. In this case, however, the outcome can be decisive for the entire labor movement. Should a post-Hoffa struggle result in control by the corrupt influences, the alienation of the teamsters from the main body of labor would continue to be a deterrent on the growth of unionism in America. Should the result be a change in the face of the teamsters to allow their return to the AFL-CIO, this political change may be a most decisive factor in the future expansion of the American labor movement.

Paralleling the problem of internal democracy in the unions is the problem of new leadership. Where old leaders have a firm grip and encourage no new leadership, what is the future? A delegate to one labor convention, faced with this dilemma, once cried out in gruesome optimism, "Where there is death, there is hope!" But even death is no answer, for too often the line of succession runs to men whose only claim to leadership lies in the fact that they were around and unnoticed.

In the labor movement, there are three paths to leadership for those worth their salt. Leaders are drawn, first, from among the men who helped build the union in its formative stage; second, from those who led an independent movement in a fight for new policies; third, from those raised under a conscious policy or tradition of encouraging, educating, and testing new generations of leadership.

The first path to leadership—involvement in the original struggle—is still open in large areas of American labor and will open up in other areas as the unions move into the South, into service, white-collar, and government employment, and the professions. In the established unions, there is far less opportunity for a new leadership baptized in fire.

The second path—the internal struggle for policy-making posts—is likely to be more wide open in the next thirty years than it has been in the past thirty. Until very recently the men who ran the big unions came from the age of the giants—even if some of the giants were just pigmies. These great figures rode high on the waves of their times. Whether they were men who achieved greatness or had greatness thrust upon them, they enjoyed reputations for having "built" the union, won advances, established treasuries and influence. Such men of repute are not easy to remove nor has there been much incentive for removing them. Other leaders within the organization had their jurisdictions and subempires. They and their members were pleased with the way things were going and had an identification with the top man during whose reign the progress took place. But today this relationship has changed. Some of the top men have died; others have retired; still others have become ineffective. Within the unions, new generations have arisen that knew not the hour of greatness nor its "giants." Once-acquiescent secondary leadership, eager to move up or responding to membership pressures for something new and better, becomes restless or ambitious.

Between 1960 and 1966, changes in top leadership have occurred in several major national unions in America, including steel, electronics, teachers, rubber, oil, chemical, building service, paper, state and county employees, machinists, garments. The list is likely to become longer in the future.

The fact that new leadership is arising does not mean that the future will produce better leadership. New men are generally younger, a dubious virtue, despite the assumption of our youth-oriented culture that what is new and fresh is inherently good. In too many cases, the new man is a less inspired, less knowledgeable, less seasoned echo of the old man. All that youth promises, on the average, is more energy, a raw life urge that takes on socially useful meaning only if it has socially useful direction.

The third path to leadership, conscious training of new leaders, therefore, is a decisive matter. In some unions, there are conscious programs of staff and officer training. The oldest and probably the best-known of these formal training programs is conducted by the International Ladies' Garment Workers' Union. In 1950, a full-time full-year training institute was established to recruit, train, and place young people for careers in the union. The program had a double objective: to begin training new people to replace the pioneers of 1909 and 1910 who were passing on, and to reach beyond the shop boundaries for personnel in an industry where about 80 per cent of the workers are female and not in a position to make full-time unionism a life's work. The institute drew its students from universities and liberal organizations as well as from the garment shops and other unions. This policy of conscious leadership recruitment and training also made it possible to pursue a deliberate program of encouraging Negroes and

Puerto Ricans, the newcomers to the garment industry, to prepare for full-time union posts.

In one form or another, this concept of an "institute" has continued for more than a decade and a half to train new blood. The curriculum seeks to turn out "craftsmen," proficient union organizers or representatives who know the minutiae of the shop; to orient the new generation on the socioeconomic traditions and purposes of the union; to equip the leader-to-be for effective work in the community, especially for political work.

The big shift in the institute from its earliest years has been a growing emphasis on "postgraduate" training: a continuation of classes and field work following the original institute. This approach allows the union officer to mix work and learning, to bring his shop experiences to the discussions. It also means that the union officer never leaves school. The institute, in the form of evening classes, weekend sessions, full week retreats, stays with the union officer throughout his union life.

The institute policy in the garment union has been accompanied by an "understudy" policy. Every top official, in charge of local, region, or department, as he approaches retirement, is obliged to name an understudy. The understudy is not necessarily a successor, but he is someone who can learn to carry responsibility as a second in command, fill in for emergencies, and be part of a reservoir of talent for top posts in the future.

The mixture of institute and understudy has produced startling phenomena in the garment union leadership. Its general executive board—the top governing body—gets younger every year. Almost one-half of the present board is composed of people who do not originally come from the shop. About a third of the board has college background. Most of the latter are law-school graduates.

When David Dubinsky, president of the ILGWU, voluntarily retired in 1966 while in full physical and mental health, he took the labor movement and the public by surprise. His initials, D.D., had become synonymous with ILGWU. He appeared to be the "indispensable" leader. He left in consonance with a policy: to prepare the older generation to step down and the younger generation to step up. This is a policy of conscious renewal and rejuvenation, a policy that is painful but possible.

In some unions, the only training is "on the job." In some unions, existing leadership holds on by denying to all comers the opportunity to learn the ropes of union officership. For that reason, the patterns of labor education are a crazy quilt of programs, reflecting the political varieties within the labor movement.

An increasingly popular center of leadership education is the university. Each year, thousands of unionists attend classes at American colleges, where they are exposed to training by union leaders and regular faculty members. The involvement of the schools of higher education in leadership training runs back to the first quarter of the century, when the School for Workers at the University of Wisconsin set up its summer schools. Since then, many universities—especially state-supported ones—have set up labor schools, supplementing on-campus sessions with extension divisions. A notable high-level experiment in exposing top union leadership to "big ideas" has been run by Brookings Institute; it is aimed at the presidents of great national unions.

Although these various educational efforts do have an impact on the development of leadership skills and outlook, most union officers do not form their attitudes or develop their techniques in formal courses. The basic "educator" still is the milieu out of which the union leader arises. This environment is in constant flux. As has been noted in previous chapters, the nature of the work force is changing; some trades and unions are dying while others are growing; within the unions, new problems arise in bargaining; within the community, unions play a greater role. These living circumstances shape union leadership.

In the coming years, there will be various milieus out of which new leaders will issue. Some will arise in well-established unions with minimum involvement in new organization and with little internal factional struggle. Others will come from unions in the making: new unions or newly vitalized unions, predominantly in white-collar, service, and government employment. Still others will be in older unions now confronted with new problems, either because of changes in industry or changes in rank and file or leadership.

The character of labor leadership as a whole will be determined by the mix rising out of these competing environments. Heterogeneity is inevitable. And the dominant mood of this heterogeneous movement will be determined by the outcome of many minor and major political struggles within the separate unions and within the federation.

If the 1970s become a replay of the 1930s, as a result of awakenings in newly organized trades, the South, and the suburbs, then a new burst of idealism may be expected in the movement as a whole. The 1950s and 1960s have been an era of consolidation; hence, an era of spiritual tempering. The coming decades will be an era of expansion; hence, an era of aspiration.

The image the unions project on the public, especially on younger people in pursuit of a cause, has much to do with the sort of new leadership that will be drawn to the labor movement. The days ahead can be a repetition of the industrial union upheaval, a spiritual as well as an organizational renaissance.

At its 1965 convention, the AFL-CIO changed about one-third of its top command, the officers of leading unions who sit on the Executive Council. This was but a straw in the wind. Behind this change were the more significant changes taking place in the national unions themselves. And behind these changes were the great motivating forces recounted in the earlier chapters of this book: a new labor force, a new unionism, a new Negro, a new liberal coalition in national politics.

The long-range forecast is for a new leadership more sensitive to public opinion and public law, more aware of its responsibilities to the movement as a whole, more political, and more sophisticated in handling the modern complex of unionism. This, in itself, does not mean that such leaders will not be tempted by power and pelf. Within each union and within each individual leader, the struggle to lift dedication to purpose above devotion to self will continue. Each new success—bigger membership, better contracts, stable relationships, fatter treasury—will become a challenge to preserve original ideals against aboriginal appetites.

To preserve its soul, the movement will require a sizable cadre of leaders who see the unions as a valuable and vital force in realizing the American dream: a society of free men lifting their material level and their individual rights. This cadre will form more readily as the movement conceptualizes its role—a task that the unions have so far left to the outsider. As the insiders begin to gain insight and outlook, they will move toward an articulated philosophy to give long-range direction to their instinctive reactions. In the rise of such a corps of doer-seers will rest the fate and future of American labor and. to some extent. of American civilization.

BIBLIOGRAPHY / INDEX

BIBLIOGRAPHY

Chapter 1

Since the early 1950s there has been a spate of books and magazine articles forecasting the organizational or moral doom of American trade unionism. A comprehensive review of the outstanding works in this genre appears in the *Harvard Business Review* (July–August 1964) by Albert A. Blum, "Labor at the Crossroads." The *Review* editors describe these as books that say "labor has not grown, that collective bargaining is obsolete, and that labor's leadership is old and unsupported." The key books are:

Paul Jacobs, *State of the Unions* (New York: Atheneum, 1963); B. J. Widick, *Labor Today* (Boston: Houghton Mifflin, 1964); Sidney Lens, *The Crisis of American Labor* (New York: A. S. Barnes and Co., 1961); Solomon Barkin, *The Decline of the Labor Movement* (Santa Barbara, Calif.: Center for the Study of Democratic Institutions, 1961); Paul Sultan, *The Disenchanted Unionist* (New York: Harper and Row, 1963).

Shorter pieces written in the same mood are:

George W. Brooks, "What Will Collective Bargaining Look Like in Twenty Years?" *The Next Twenty Years in Industrial Relations* (Cambridge, Mass.: Massachusetts Institute of Technology, 1957), pp. 3–21; Paul Jacobs, *Old Before Its Time: Collective Bargaining at 28* (Santa Barbara, Calif.: Center for the Study of Democratic Institutions, 1963); Daniel Bell, "The Capitalism of the Proletariat (A Theory of American Trade Unionism)," *The End of Ideology* (Glencoe, Ill.: The Free Press, 1960), Chapter 11, p. 208.

A symposium on the same subject is the November 1963 issue of *The Annals of the American Academy of Political and Social Science* devoted to "The Crisis in the American Trade Union Movement."

More current, but pessimistic, views of labor's future appear in *The Radical Papers* (Garden City, N.Y.: Doubleday, 1966), in the essays of Paul Jacobs and Harvey Swados.

In an optimistic tone are J. B. S. Hardman, "State of the Movement," *The House of Labor* (New York: Prentice Hall, 1951), Chapter 4; Irving Bernstein, "The Growth of American Unions, 1945–1960," *Labor History,* Spring 1961; Bernard Karsh and Solomon B. Levine, "The Coming Revolution in Labor Relations," *Mill and Factory,* December 1960.

Another approach is the symposium of the Center for the Study of Democratic Institutions based on an interview with industrialist spokesman J. Irwin Miller and labor leader Walter Reuther, entitled *The Corporation and the Union.*

Youth's disillusionment with the established unions is shown in essays in *The New Student Left* (Boston: Beacon Press, 1966), especially Daniel Schechter's "Why Does the Labor Movement Have Nothing to Say?"

The files of *New Politics* and *Dissent* contain a running debate extending over many years on the role of trade unions, especially in relationship to radical movements.

Chapter 2

Although this chapter is historical in character, it is above all an attempt to indicate the interrelationship of the labor movement with economic and political developments in the United States. For the period from the Civil War to the New Deal, Charles Beard's *The Rise of American Civilization* (New York: Macmillan, 1935), Vol. II, still remains a most readable and insightful work, especially Chapter XVIII on "The Second American Revolution," and Chapter XXI on "The Rise of the National Labor Movement." A companion piece —shorter, lighter, and more heavily labor-oriented—is Mary Beard's *A Short History of the American Labor Movement* (New York: Macmillan, 1924). A useful supplement is Louis Hacker, *The Triumph of American Capitalism* (New York: Simon and Schuster, 1940), especially Chapters XX and XXVI.

For a multifaceted examination of "The Watershed of the Nineties," Henry Steele Commager offers a chapter under that name in *The American Mind* (New Haven: Yale University Press, 1952). For an interpretation of the Eisenhower era, Eric F. Goldman offers a provocative book-length essay in his *The Crucial Decade* (New York: Knopf, 1956).

The classic John R. Commons and Associates *History of Labor in the U.S.* (New York: Macmillan, 1951), 4 volumes, is still the fountainhead of information on the origins and history of the labor movement. That basic work has been expanded and reinterpreted by the voluminous researches of Philip Taft in his two-volume *The AFL in the Time of Gompers* (New York: Harper and Row, 1957), and *Organized Labor in American History* (New York: Harper and Row, 1964).

Useful one-volume works are Foster Rhea Dulles, *Labor in America,* second revised edition (New York: Thomas Y. Crowell, 1960); Joseph G. Rayback, *A History of American Labor* (New York: Macmillan, 1959); Henry Pelling, *American Labor* (Chicago: University of Chicago Press, 1960).

The political side of labor's involvement in the pre-New Deal years is presented in Nathan Fine, *Labor and Farmer Parties in the U.S., 1828–1928* (New York: Rand School of Social Science, 1928). A leftist evaluation of American labor is Philip S. Foner, *History of the Labor Movement in the U.S.* (New York: International Publishers, 1955), 2 volumes.

A handy small book of readings is Leon Litwack, *The American Labor Movement* (Englewood Cliffs, N.J.: Prentice-Hall, 1964).

For a neatly organized, comprehensive, and sophisticated listing of writings see Maurice F. Neufeld, *A Representative Bibliography of American Labor History* (Ithaca, N.Y.: Cornell University Press, 1964).

Chapter 3

The search for a "field theory" about the trade-union movement has been under way for many years. Perhaps because the labor movement is many different things at many differing times, the focus of the various theories shifts over the years. In recent decades, the "institutional-historical" approach to unions has been displaced by theories of what unions *ought* to be and by econometric studies of union impact on manpower, wages, profits, productivity, and prices.

Certain key documents, however, provide background for the over-all theory presented in this book. Implicit in Commons' four-volume history (op. cit.) is a theory of the trade-union movement presented and defended vigorously in Robert Ozanne's essay, "The Labor History and Theory of John R. Commons," *Labor, Management and Social Policy* (Madison, Wis.: University of Wisconsin Press, 1963). A classic statement of the Wisconsin school is that hardy perennial, Selig Perlman's *A Theory of the Labor Movement* (New York: Macmillan, 1928). Other views are:

Frank Tannenbaum, *A Philosophy of Labor* (New York: Knopf, 1952); Daniel Bell, "The Capitalism of the Proletariat (A Theory of American Trade Unionism)," *The End of Ideology* (Glencoe, Ill.: The Free Press, 1960), Chapter 11, p. 208; Philip Taft, "Labor History and the Labor Movement," *Labor History*, Vol. 7, No. 1, pp. 70ff.; Paul Meadow, "Culture Theory and Industrial Analysis," *The Annals of the American Academy of Political and Social Science*, 1951; E. Wight Bakke, Clark Kerr, Charles W. Anrod, eds., *Union Management and the Public* (New York: Harcourt, Brace and World, 1964), especially pp. 29–65; Gus Tyler, *A New Philosophy for Labor*, An Occasional Paper of the Center for the Study of Democratic Institutions, 1959; also the essay by J. B. S. Hardman referred to in Chapter 1.

Chapter 4

Automation has been so widely, diversely, and heatedly discussed in the last half-decade that almost any bibliography is bound to be either inadequate or lopsided. Nevertheless, a key volume to reading in the area is *Economic and Social Implications of Automation*, an annotated bibliography (Lansing, Mich.: Labor and Industrial Relations Center of Michigan State University, 1961).

To bring some order out of the intellectual chaos encircling automation, the President of the United States appointed a National Commission on Technology, Automation and Economic Progress, whose 1966 report, *Technology and the American Economy*, is available from the U.S. Government Printing Office, Washington, D.C. A simplified version was issued by the Industrial Union Department of the AFL-CIO as a reprint from its publication *Agenda*, February 1966. A sophisticated evaluation of the report is Robert Lekachman's "The Automation Report," *Commentary*, May 1966.

The changing job picture flowing from automation is authoritatively discussed in six essays published by the U.S. Government Printing Office, 1965, under the title *Manpower Implications of Automation*. These are papers presented to the 1964 Conference of 21-Nation Organization for Economic Cooperation and Development (OECD).

Valuable primary material is to be found in the *Economic Report of the President* together with the *Annual Report of the Council of Economic Advisers* (U.S. Government Printing Office) for the years 1964 and 1965.

Other valuable insights may be found in: Eli Ginzberg, ed., *Technology and Social Change* (New York: Columbia University Press, 1964, especially Solomon Fabricant, "Productivity and Economic Growth," pp. 108–136; "What Automation Means to America," a symposium, *Automation*, Vol. II, No. 4, containing pieces by Barry Goldwater, Ewan Clague, George Meany, James Hoffa, John L. Lewis, Hubert H. Humphrey, Seymour Wolfbein; *The Challenge of Automation*, papers delivered at the National Conference on Automation (Washington, D.C.: Public Affairs Press, 1955); *The Computer and Society* (a special section in *The New York Times* of Sunday, April 24, 1966) with essays by Michael Harrington, Charles E. Killingsworth, Stanley Lebergott, et al.

Chapter 5

The trade-union program for full employment—the unions' answer to automation—is most authoritatively expressed in the various documents of the AFL-CIO and its very articulate affiliate, the Industrial Union Department. These position papers and resolutions are a primary source readily available to the student or the teacher, since many of them are reprinted for wide consumption. Though popularly written, they contain tables, charts, and statistics, usually drawn from governmental sources. The raw material is gathered by the professional staff of the labor movement, its Research Department. The papers are carried regularly in *The American Federationist*, Washington, D.C., often in a special section entitled *Labor's Economic Review*.

A few key pieces from *The American Federationist* over recent years are: "The National Economy," "Tax Policy and the Budget," "Trade Technology and Resources," "Wages and Hours," Policy Resolutions of the AFL-CIO Convention, Proceedings of the Miami Beach Convention, December 1961; "The Rebirth of the Cities," "Union Funds Create Homes," "Modern Monopolies and the Public Interest," "Fringe Benefits," April 1962; "The Long Trend to Shorter Hours," August 1962; "America's Unmet Public Service Needs," "Moonlighting—Its Cause and Effect," September 1962; "The Unequal

Sharing of U.S. Wealth," "Creating Jobs Through Shorter Hours," November 1962; "The New Trade Act: Tool to Expand Markets," "The Positive Role of Fiscal Policy," January 1963; "Fair Taxes and Full Employment," February 1963; "The Cause, Effect and Cure of Poverty," March 1963; "TVA, the Controversial Success," April 1963; "The Pattern of U.S. Export Trade," May 1963; "Jobless Pay and the Longterm Unemployed," July 1963; "America's Need: Social Services and Jobs," August 1963; "Wage Gains Under Bargaining," September 1963; "The Shorter Work Week Trend," November 1963 and July 1965; "The Holiday Gains of Union Families," December 1964; "Union Labor Costs," December 1965; "The National Economy," Policy Resolution of the AFL-CIO Convention, Proceedings of the San Francisco Convention, December 1965. Also, *Agenda for Tomorrow*, Report to the Industrial Union Department, AFL-CIO, 1965, especially pp. 6–41; and *Shorter Hours*, publication No. 135 of the AFL-CIO, July 1964.

The general theme of the labor movement is carried through by Leon Keyserling, former Chairman of the Council of Economic Advisers, in several booklets printed by the Conference on Economic Progress, Washington, D.C. Some of these are *Progress or Poverty*, December 1964; *The Role of Wages in a Great Society*, February 1966; *Two Top-Priority Programs to Reduce Unemployment*, December 1963.

For a more academic presentation of the Keynesian approach, see *The New Economics*, edited by Seymour Harris (New York: Knopf, 1950), especially the essay by D. B. Copland, "Public Policy—the Doctrine of Full Employment." For a highly provocative, different, though not always contrary view, there is the landmark work of John Kenneth Galbraith, *The Affluent Society* (Boston: Houghton Mifflin, 1958).

Chapter 6

To keep abreast of union contract clauses arising from job displacement or job changes caused by automation requires constant compilation and digest of ever-new bargaining arrangements. The examples used in this chapter are, of necessity, fugitive in character. They are clues as to the many challenges and responses brought on by technological change. At best, these citations are illustrative rather than conclusive.

In selecting cases, the work of John McNiff, Research Director of the International Brotherhood of Pulp, Sulphite and Paper Mill Workers, AFL-CIO (Fort Edward, New York), entitled *Automation: Economic Implication and Impact Upon Collective Bargaining,* 1964, was extremely helpful. The book was published by the union. Its voluminous pages are replete with cases that the author has slotted into a design.

Three publications of the U.S. Department of Labor bear on the subject and add items of current significance: *Management Rights and Union-Management Cooperation* (Bulletin No. 1425–5); *Supplemental Unemployment Benefit Plans and Wage-Employment Guarantees* (Bulletin No. 1425–3); *Severance Pay and Layoff Benefit Plans* (Bulletin No. 1425–2). These were published in 1965 and 1966.

For the professional who wants to keep abreast of future changes there is the Contract Clause Finder of the Bureau of National Affairs, Washington, D.C., with a running file on relevant sections of new agreements.

A book of case studies on *Managerial Freedom and Job Security* (New York: Harper and Row, 1964) by Morris Stone examines clauses and arbitration awards. Especially relevant is Chapter 8 on "Attrition and Automation."

Neil Chamberlain, *Source Book on Labor* (New York: McGraw-Hill, 1958) contains a compilation of writings on "Union Security and Management Rights," pp. 547–613. The same volume also explores the related subject of "Productivity and Wage Determination," pp. 710–37 and pp. 782–830. The position of the United Auto Workers on the same matter is advanced vigorously by Kermit Mead in a lengthy mimeographed statement, "How the UAW Looks at Work Standards."

Other labor statements on union response to automation are Joseph A. Beirne, *New Horizons for American Labor* (Washington: Public Affairs Press, 1962), Chapter III, "Facing Up to the Problem of Automation," and an article in *American Federationist*, "Protecting Jobs Through Attrition Clauses," June 1965.

Chapter 7

Since changes in the labor force are continuous, the best sources are the primary reports issuing from the Bureau of Labor Statistics and other governmental agencies. A staple in this field is the *Manpower Report of the President,* an annual publication of the U.S. Government Printing Office. A companion publication is the *Occupational Outlook Handbook* of the U.S. Department of Labor, whose 1963 and 1964 issues supplied raw material for this chapter.

Four recent selections from *The Monthly Labor Review,* a publication of the BLS, were also used. These are Stella Manor, "Geographic Changes in U.S. Employment from 1950 to 1960," January 1963; "Special Labor Force Report," for March 1963 and May 1963; Max Rutzick and Sol Swerdloff, "The Occupational Structure of U.S. Employment, 1940–1960," March 1962. Also *Population and Labor Force Projections for the U.S., 1960–1975,* BLS, Bulletin No. 1242.

A digest of a Senate Committee hearing was edited by Garth L. Mangum under the title *The Manpower Revolution* (Garden City, N.Y.: Doubleday, 1965).

Three non-governmental sources, with varying emphasis and approach, are Stanley Lebergott, *Manpower in Economic Growth* (New York: McGraw-Hill, 1964); Victor R. Fuchs, *The Growing Importance of the Service Industries* (New York: National Bureau of Economic Research, Columbia University Press, 1965); Neil Chamberlain, op. cit., pp. 1–9.

The American Federationist, October 1963 ran a typically popularized piece, "The Erosion of Jobs and Skills."

See also "Exit Stopwatch, Enter Standard Data," June 1962.

Chapter 8

Although discussion of labor's future in America inevitably involves figures about growth or decline of union membership, there are few hard or sharp facts on how many dues payers there are in the separate unions or in the movement as a whole. All methods for gathering figures on this subject have, thus far, been faulty.

One method is to count union membership on the basis of percapita dues to the AFL-CIO. This figure is faulty because most unions do not pay the Federation for full membership, since the affiliate wants to save on its dues. Another method is to send a questionnaire to the individual national unions. In many cases, the national union does not really know its exact membership, especially where there is no auditing of books in the locals by the national body. Convention reports are not much more accurate; a report may inflate or deflate figures, depending on the internal situation in the union. Many unions present no detailed breakdown.

Equally frustrating is any effort to determine how many white-collar and professional workers are organized. Unions do not generally report their membership on the basis of a craft breakdown. Thus, for instance, the electrical unions have sizable numbers of professionals—engineers, researchers, examiners, supervisors. Yet because of the over-all character of the union, these are generally thrown into the blue-collar category. On the other hand, many members of the government employee unions are blue-collar, though they are generally viewed as white-collar.

Figures on union membership are even more unreliable when broken down by states or cities.

Finally, there is no accurate count on how many workers are covered by union contracts but are not actually members of the union.

Some idea as to how far apart "experts" can be is indicated in the piece by Irving Bernstein cited in the bibliography for Chapter 1.

Classic works on union membership are Leo Wolman, *The Growth of the American Trade Unions, 1880–1923* (National Bureau of Economic Research, 1924), and *Ebb and Flow of Trade Unionism* (National Bureau of Economic Research, 1936).

More current studies are Leo Troy, *Trade Union Membership, 1897–1962* (New York: National Bureau of Economic Research, 1964); "Membership of American Trade Unions," *Monthly Labor Review,* November 1962.

Everett M. Kaslow, "White Collar Unionism in the U.S.," was used in its draft form as a chapter in a book on the subject covering seven countries. Other discussions of white-collar and professional organization are:

C. Wright Mills, "White Collar Unionism," *Labor and Nation,* May 1949; Albert Blum, "Prospects for Organization of White Collar Workers," *Report Card,* September 1964, State School of Industrial and Labor Relations; Jack Barbash, "Unionizing the Professional

Worker," paper to Wharton School of Finance and Commerce, University of Pennsylvania, Labor Relations Council Conference, November 1960; Jack Barbash, "Union Philosophy and the Professional," *The American Teacher,* December 1957; Israel Kugler, "Professors, Physicians and Unionism," American Federation of Teachers leaflet; David Hamilton, "Will the College Teachers Organize?" *I.U.D. Digest,* Spring 1962; *Teachers Negotiate with Their School Boards* (Washington, D.C.: U.S. Department of Health, Education and Welfare, Office of Education, 1964). The last of these contains an adequate bibliography on the subject of teaching unions at the back of the booklet.

Two useful volumes on the history of a service and a government employees' union are: Leo Kramer, *Labor's Paradox* (New York: John Wiley and Sons, 1962), the story of the American Federation of State, County and Municipal Employees, AFL-CIO; Michael Harrington, *The Retail Clerks* (New York: John Wiley and Sons, 1962).

Chapter 9

The changing condition of the Negro and the South is reflected in the shifting emphasis and content of the literature on the subject. This is especially so as the discussion relates to the Negro worker and his relationship with trade unions and politics.

The following readings are listed chronologically to reflect the changing scene and the up-dated attitudes of the commentators:

Sterling D. Spero and Abram L. Harris, *The Black Worker: The Negro and the Labor Movement* (New York: Columbia University Press, 1931); Herbert R. Northrup, *Organized Labor and the Negro* (New York: Hayes and Brothers, 1944); Robert C. Weaver, *Negro Labor: A National Problem* (New York: Harcourt, Brace, 1946); Norman Ross, "The Struggle for the Negro-Labor Alliance," *Political Affairs,* June 1949; William Green, *American Federationist,* July 1945, May 1952; Rupert B. Vance and Nicholas J. Denerath, *The Urban South* (Chapel Hill, N.C.: University of North Carolina Press, 1954); Eli Ginsberg, *The Negro Potential* (New York: Columbia University Press, 1956); James Q. Wilson, *Negro Politics* (Glencoe, Ill.: The Free Press, 1960); Ray Marshall, "Some Factors Influencing the Growth of Union in the South," *Proceedings of the Thirteenth Annual Meeting of the Industrial Relations Research Association,* December 1960. *Madison: The Association* (Madison, Wis., 1961); Leon E. Lunden, "Anti-Discrimination Provisions in Major Contracts, 1961," *Monthly Labor Review*, Vol. 85, No. 6, June 1962; Marion Hayes, "A Century of Change: Negroes in the U. S. Economy, 1860–1960," *Monthly Labor Review*, Vol. 85, No. 12, December 1962; Gunnar Myrdal and others, *An American Dilemma: The Negro Problem and Modern Democracy* (New York: Harper and Row, 1962); "Union Program for Eliminating Discrimination," *Monthly Labor Review*, Vol. 86, No. 1, January 1963, pp. 58–59; George Meany, "Equal Rights Here and Now," *American Federationist*, Vol. 70, No. 8, August 1963, p. 8; Abe Raskin, "Civil Rights: The Law and the Union," *Reporter*, September 10, 1964, pp. 23–29; William Brink and Louis Harris, *The Negro Revolution in America* (New York: Simon and Schuster, 1964); Bayard Rustin, "From Protest to Politics," *Commentary*, February 1965; Peter Schoemann, "How About It," *United Association Journal*, Washington, D.C., April 1965; Herbert R. Northrup and Richard L. Rowan, eds., *The Negro and Employment Opportunity* (Ann Arbor, Mich.: University of Michigan Graduate School of Business Administration, 1965); Walter C. Davis, "Equal Employment Opportunity," *American Federationist*, June 1965; Ray Marshall, *The Negro and Organized Labor* (New York: John Wiley and Sons, 1965); "The South on the Rise—Success Story," *U.S. News and World Report*, August 22, 1966, p. 54; Whitney M. Young, Jr., "The Negro's Economic Future," *The New York Times* (a special section entitled "The Computer and Society"), April 24, 1966, Section 11, pp. 12–14; Herman D. Bloch, "Negroes and Organized Labor," *Journal of Human Relations*, Vol. 10, No. 4.

Chapter 10

There is no up-to-date book on the history of labor in politics. In the many books listed in Chapter 2 on the history of the American labor movement, there are individual chapters on politics. In addition, there is the book by Nathan Fine, op. cit., that runs up to 1928 and emphasizes third parties rather than labor political action per se. A limited book for a limited period is Marc Karson, *American Labor Unions and Politics, 1900–1918* (Boston: Beacon Press, 1965).

Because of the present author's roles as Director of the Political Department of the International Ladies' Garment Workers' Union, as a member of the Operating Committee of the Committee on Political

Education, and as a Vice-Chairman of the Trade Union Council of the Liberal Party, he has been called upon to write dozens of short pieces for the *American Federationist, New Politics, New Leader, New Republic, Progressive.* Specific references are omitted, since the essence of these pieces is condensed and synthesized in the chapter of this book. The section in the chapter on prospects for a third party carries several pages which originally appeared in *New Politics* and are reprinted herein with their permission. A chapter in *Politics USA* (Garden City, N.Y.: Doubleday, 1960), entitled "The Labor Vote," by the author, does contain additional material. Also another study by the author, "Court Versus Legislature," *Law and Contemporary Problems,* Duke University School of Law, Summer 1962, pp. 390–407, deals at greater length than does this chapter with the meaning of reapportionment.

The House of Labor, edited by Neufeld and Hardman, op. cit., has a good running summary by Henry David on "One Hundred Years of Labor in Politics," and Joseph D. Keenan, "The AFL-LLPE," and Jack Kroll, "CIO-PAC." *The Source Book on Labor* (Chamberlain, op. cit.) has supplementary material on union politics, pp. 284–322.

For the current impact of reapportionment see Gordon E. Baker, *The Reapportionment Revolution* (New York: Random House, 1966).

Chapter 11

On types and problems of union leadership, see Chamberlain, *Source Book on Labor* (op. cit.), pp. 178–238; Jack Barbash, *Labor's Grass Roots* (New York: Harper and Row, 1961).

On the knotty problems of jurisdiction and efforts to deal with them, see *The AFL-CIO Internal Disputes Plan, 1962–1963,* containing the texts of Federation policy, reports on findings, and awards. This volume is published by the AFL-CIO, Washington, D.C.

For a discussion of the relations between labor and intellectuals, see Gus Tyler, "The Legacy of Jewish Labor," *Midstream,* Vol. XI, No. 1, 1965. Also Maurice Neufeld's chapter in *The House of Labor* on unions as viewed by the progressive intelligentsia.

On the sensitive and controversial question of union democracy and membership rights, the following:

Alice Cook, *Union Democracy: Practice and Ideal,* Cornell Studies in Industrial and Labor Relations, Vol. XI, 1963; Burton Hall, "Law

Democracy and the Unions," *New Politics,* Vol. III, No. 4; Mitchell Sviridoff, "Labor's Public Responsibility in Internal Affairs," chapter in *Labor's Public Responsibility* (Madison, Wis.; National Institute of Labor Education, 1960), pp. 58–71; Clyde Simmons, "The Public Responsibility of Unions in Internal Affairs," chapter in *Labor's Public Responsibility,* pp. 72–89; Seymour Martin Lipset, "The Law and Trade Union Democracy," *Virginia Law Review,* Vol. 47, No. 1, 1961; Joel Seidman, *Democracy in the Labor Movement* (Ithaca, N.Y.: N.Y. State School of Industrial and Labor Relations, Cornell University, 1958); Clark Kerr, *Unions and Union Leaders of Their Own Choosing* (New York: Fund for the Republic, 1957); Jack Stieber, Walter E. Oberer, and Michael Harrington, *Democracy and Public Review* (Santa Barbara, Calif.: Center for the Study of Democratic Institutions, 1960); William Herberg, "Bureaucracy and Democracy in Labor Unions," *The Antioch Review,* September 1943; L. A. Reynolds, "Discussion of Democracy in Trade Unions," *American Economic Review,* 1946; Philip Taft, "Democracy in Trade Unions," *American Economic Review,* 1946; Sylvester Petro, *Personal Freedom and Labor Policy* (New York: N.Y. University Institute of Economic Affairs, 1958).

On the special problem of the teamsters' union: Sam Romer, *The International Brotherhood of Teamsters* (New York: John Wiley and Sons, 1962); Ralph and Estelle James, *Hoffa and The Teamsters* (Princeton, N.J.: D. Van Nostrand, 1965); Clark R. Mollenhoff, *Tentacles of Power* (Cleveland, Ohio: World, 1965); and the authorized biography by Jim Clay, *Hoffa! Ten Angels Swearing* (Beaverdam, Va.: Beaverdam Books, Inc., 1965).

INDEX